D0805902

ASCENT TO ORBIT

A Scientific Autobiography

ASCENT

H.R.H. Prince Claus of the Netherlands presenting the Eighth Marconi International Fellowship Award to Dr. Arthur C. Clarke

Dr. Arthur C. Clarke following the Marconi Award presentation ceremonies and Professor Yash Pal, 6th Marconi Award recipient and keynote speaker for the presentation

Dr. Arthur C. Clarke and Gioia Marconi Braga during presentation festivities for the Eighth Marconi International Fellowship Award in The Hague, 1982

H.R.H. Prince Claus of the Netherlands signing the Marconi Fellowship presentation book and Gioia Marconi Braga, Chairperson of the Fellowship

Published in honor of the
Marconi International Fellowship

TO ORBIT

A Scientific Autobiography

The Technical Writings of
Arthur C. Clarke

A Wiley-Interscience Publication

John Wiley & Sons   New York · Chichester · Brisbane · Toronto · Singapore

BOOKS BY

ARTHUR C. CLARKE

Non-Fiction

Ascent to Orbit: A Scientific Autobiography
Boy Beneath the Sea
The Challenge of the Sea
The Challenge of the Spaceship
The Coast of Coral
The Exploration of the Moon
The Exploration of Space
The First Five Fathoms
Going Into Space
Indian Ocean Adventure
Indian Ocean Treasure
Interplanetary Flight
The Making of a Moon
Profiles of the Future
The Promise of Space
The Reefs of Taprobane
Report on Planet Three
The Treasure of the Great Reef
The View From Serendip
Voice Across the Sea
Voices From the Sky
1984: Spring
With the Editors of "LIFE"
  Man and Space
With the Astronauts
  First on the Moon
With Robert Silverberg
  Into Space
With Chesley Bonestell
  Beyond Jupiter
With Simon Welfare and John Fairley
  Arthur C. Clarke's Mysterious World
  Arthur C. Clarke's World of Strange Powers

Fiction

Across the Sea of Stars
Against the Fall of Night
Childhood's End
The City and the Stars
The Deep Range
Dolphin Island
Earthlight
Expedition to Earth
A Fall of Moondust
The Fountains of Paradise
From the Oceans, From the Stars
Glide Path
Imperial Earth
Islands in the Sky
The Lion of Comarre
The Lost Worlds of 2001
The Nine Billion Names of God
The Other Side of the Sky
Prelude to Mars
Prelude to Space
Reach For Tomorrow
Rendezvous with Rama
The Sands of Mars
The Sentinel
Tales from the "White Hart"
Tales of Ten Worlds
The Wind from the Sun
2001: A Space Odyssey
2010: Odyssey Two

Copyright © 1984 by Arthur C. Clarke.

Published by John Wiley & Sons, Inc.

All rights reserved. Published simultaneously in Canada.

Reproduction or translation of any part of this work beyond that permitted by
Section 107 or 108 of the 1976 United States Copyright Act without the
permission of the copyright owner is unlawful. Requests for permission or
further information should be addressed to the Permissions Department,
John Wiley & Sons, Inc.

Library of Congress Cataloging in Publication Data

Clarke, Arthur Charles, 1917–
   Ascent to orbit.

   "Published in honor of the Marconi International
Fellowship."
   Includes index.
   1. Astronautics—Addresses, essays, lectures.
I. Title.
TL794.5.C528   1984   629.4   83-26039
ISBN 0-471-87910-X

Printed in the United States of America

10 9 8 7 6 5 4 3 2 1

Foreword

In 1945 Arthur C. Clarke, in his now famous *Wireless World* article, launched, at least in a figurative sense, the era of satellite communications. Others, such as John Pierce, Eric Burgess and Harold Rosen, certainly played key pioneering roles in the years that followed, but Arthur Clarke is now recognized worldwide as the father of satellite communications for his pivotal role in making global satellite communications a reality for billions of people on the planet earth. Each year more and more people bestow that recognition in referring to the geosynchronous orbit, where these satellites operate, as the "Clarke Orbit."

If Arthur Clarke is the father of communications satellites, then surely he must also be the grandfather of INTELSAT or, more formally, the International Telecommunications Satellite Organization. On August 20, 1964 INTELSAT was born—a blend of high space science, global communications technology and international political cooperation. And it worked. In April 1965 "Early Bird" translated theory into fact by becoming the world's first international commercial satellite. That satellite began to knit the world together through telephone, through telegraph and, for the first time, through live transoceanic television broadcasting. The INTELSAT System, born so modestly, now works full-time, 24 hours a day, with 2,000 times more capacity, to unite some 170 different countries, territories and jurisdictions. During this year some two billion people—almost half the world's population—will witness some part of the Olympic Games "live via INTELSAT satellites." During 1984 INTELSAT will also probably relay more than a billion telephone calls around our ever-smaller planet.

It is thus with great pleasure that INTELSAT, on its twentieth anniversary, can in a small way give tribute to the father of satellite communications and to its own grandfather—Arthur C. Clarke.

Richard R. Colino

Director General
INTELSAT

February 6, 1984

Contents

ASCENT TO ORBIT

A Scientific Autobiography

I | *The Marconi International Fellowship*

The Marconi International Fellowship

*A program to recognize creative work
in communication science or
technology and its benefit to humanity*

The Fellowship was first announced in 1974 to mark the centennial of Guglielmo Marconi's birth, April 25, 1874. It commemorates his contributions to scientific invention, engineering and technology, and his profound commitment to their use for the betterment of the human condition rather than for its exploitation or devastation. The Fellowship's goal is to recognize and inspire scientific achievements by living men and women whose lives are characterized by a similar dedication.

The individual to whom the Marconi Fellowship is granted will have made a significant contribution to the advancement of the technology of communications through discoveries, inventions or innovations in the physical or information sciences or engineering.

THE FELLOWSHIP COMMISSION

The Council of the Marconi International Fellowship invites the recipient to develop creative work that will add to the science of communications and its technological application to the improvement of human life.

$35,000 GRANT

The Marconi International Fellowship is to be awarded once a year and is accompanied by a grant of $35,000. Marconi Fellowship recipients also receive replicas of an original sculpture, created by the contemporary artist Otello Guarducci.

CRITERIA GOVERNING THE MARCONI FELLOWSHIP

The Marconi International Fellowship invites nomination of individuals whose work in the fields of communication science and technology exemplifies the technical creativity and concern for human welfare of Guglielmo Marconi.

The Marconi Council wishes the Fellowship to be an anticipatory more than a retrospective award. The Fellowship Selection Committee will give special attention to the identification of emerging fields of communications science and technology that are likely to be in the forefront of future applications for the benefit of society.

The criteria that guide the selection of each year's recipient are:

1. The importance of the nominee's contributions to communications science or technology.

2. The present and future value to society of these contributions; and

3. The degree to which the nominee's work exemplifies commitment to the betterment of the human condition.

ADMINISTRATION OF THE FELLOWSHIP

Polytechnic Institute of New York, recognizing the need to commission innovative work of the highest quality in this domain, has undertaken the administration of the Marconi International Fellowship.

A distinguished Marconi Council, chaired by Gioia Marconi Braga, daughter of Guglielmo Marconi, governs the Fellowship and reviews it annually to ensure that it fulfills the ideals of the Marconi program. A Selection Committee reviews and rates all nominations for presentation to the Council.

Dr. George Bugliarello serves as Secretary to the Marconi Council and oversees the administration of the Fellowship in the New York City offices of Polytechnic Institute of New York.

FELLOWSHIP RECIPIENTS

Dr. James R. Killian, Jr. 1975
Massachusetts Institute of Technology, USA

To honor a lifetime of public service in science and engineering. In association with LORD BRIGGS OF LEWES, Oxford University, England. To commission a study of the social implications of radio in the development of the science and art of broadcasting.

Presented by the Honorable Nelson A. Rockefeller, Vice President of the United States of America, at the eleventh annual banquet of the National Academy of Engineering, Washington, D.C.

Professor Hiroshi Inose 1976
University of Tokyo, Japan

To recognize exceptional creative achievements in the application of digital technologies.

Presented by HRH Prince Philip, Duke of Edinburgh, at The Royal Society of Arts, London.

Professor Arthur L. Schawlow 1977
Stanford University, USA

Cited for his research in the fields of optical and microwave spectroscopy, nuclear quadrupole resonance, superconductivity and lasers.

Presented by HM King Carl Gustaf XVI of Sweden at Ulriksdal Palace, Stockholm.

Professor E. Colin Cherry 1978
Imperial College, England

To honor notable contributions to the field of communications, both in the scientific/technological sense and in terms of human perception.

Presented by HIH Prince Hitachi at the Japan Academy, Tokyo.

Dr. John R. Pierce 1979
California Institute of Technology, USA

To recognize outstanding advances in space and satellite technologies relevant to improving world communications.

Presented by the Honorable Alessandro Pertini, President of the Republic of Italy at the Palazzo Delta Civilita Del Lavoro, Rome.

Professor Yash Pal   1980
Space Applications Centre
Indian Space Research Organization, India

To recognize wise and humane leadership in applying modern communications technology to meet the needs of isolated rural villagers in India.

Presented by His Excellency Sir Zelman Cowen, Governor General of Australia, at the Sydney Opera House.

Dr. Seymour Papert   1981
Massachusetts Institute of Technology, USA

Cited for imaginative use of advanced microcomputer technology to aid the cognitive and affective intellectual development of children.

Presented by His Excellency Saraiva Guerreiro, Minister of Foreign Affairs, acting on behalf of the President of Brazil, at Itamarati Palace, Brasilia.

Dr. Arthur C. Clarke   1982
University of Moratuwa, Sri Lanka

Cited for first specifying in detail the potentialities and technical requirements for the use of geostationary satellites for global communications; for other innovations in communications and remote sensing from space throughout a lifetime of promoting the benevolent use of advanced space technology.

Presented by HRH Prince Claus of the Netherlands at De Ridderzaal, The Hague.

Professor Francesco Carassa   1983
Politecnico di Milano

Cited for his leadership in radio frequency engineering including both land and microwave satellite communications.

Presented by his Excellency the Right Honorable Edward Schreyer, Governor General of Canada at Government House, Ottawa.

Professor Eric Albert Ash   1984
University College, London

Cited for his leadership in electronic technology including acoustic wave devices and fiber communications.

MARCONI INTERNATIONAL FELLOWSHIP COUNCIL

Mrs. Gioia Marconi Braga, *Chairperson*

Dr. George Bugliarello, *Secretary*
Polytechnic Institute of New York

Mr. Charles F. Adams
Raytheon Company

Avv. Giovanni Agnelli
Fiat S.p.A.

Mrs. Vincent Astor
The Vincent Astor Foundation

Dr. William O. Baker
Bell Telephone Laboratories

Ing. Cesare Benigni
Telespazio

Dr. Lewis M. Branscomb
*International Business
Machines Corporation*

Dr. Antonio Cacciavillani
Selenia

Sir John Clark
The Plessey Company, Ltd.

Dott. Alfredo Diana
*Federazione Nazionale dei
Cavalieri del Lavoro*

Ing. Domenico Faro
Italtel

Dr. John S. Foster, Jr.
T.R.W., Inc.

Mr. Robert W. Galvin
Motorola Inc.

J.A.L. Hooke, Esq.
*Amalgamated Wireless
Australasia Ltd.*

Dr. Anton Christian Jacobaeus
LM Ericsson

Mr. Belton K. Johnson
*American Telephone and
Telegraph*

Dr. Augustus Kinzel
*National Academy of
Engineering*

Ing. Carlo Enrico Martinato
Italcable

Dr. Martin Meyerson
University of Pennsylvania

Mrs. Henry B. Middleton
Helen Hay Whitney Foundation

Dr. Lloyd N. Morrisett
The Markle Foundation

Lord Nelson of Stafford
*The General Electric
Company Ltd.*

Dr. A.E. Pannenborg
*N.V. Philips'
Gloeilampenfabrieken*

Mr. Daniel L. Ritchie
*Westinghouse Broadcasting
and Cable, Inc.*

Dr. Walter Orr Roberts
*University Corporation for
Atmospheric Research*

Mr. Thomas B. Ross
RCA

Mr. Robert W. Sarnoff

Mr. Harry E. Smith
CBS Inc.

Mr. Sidney Topol
Scientific-Atlanta, Inc.

Mr. Donald J. Yockey
*Rockwell International
Corporation*

SPONSORSHIP OF THE PROGRAM

The Marconi International Fellowship is sponsored by corporations and organizations concerned with furthering advances in communications.

* Amalgamated Wireless Australasia, Ltd.
* American Telephone & Telegraph and affiliated companies:
  Western Electric
  Bell Telephone Laboratories
  CBS Inc.
* LM Ericsson
* Federazione Nazionale dei Cavalieri del Lavoro
* Fiat S.p.A.
* General Electric Company
* The General Electric Company, Ltd. and affiliated companies:
  * The Marconi Company, Ltd.
  * Canadian Marconi Company
  * Marconi Italiana, S.p.A.
  * Marconi South Africa, Ltd.
  * Norsk Marconi A/S
* General Telephone & Electronics Corporation
* International Business Machines Corporation
  International Telephone and Telegraph Corporation
  Italcable
  Italtel
  Motorola, Inc.
* N.V. Philips' Gloeilampenfabrieken
  The Plessey Company, Ltd.
* RCA
* Raytheon Company
  Rockwell International Corporation
* Selenia
* Sony Corporation
  Telespazio
  T.R.W., Inc.
* Westinghouse Broadcasting and Cable, Inc.

*Founding Sponsors

1 | *In the Hall of the Knights*

Although most of my writing—both fiction and non-fiction—over the past fifty years has been intended for the general public, during the period 1936–1950 I produced a considerable amount of work of a much more specialised nature. Virtually none of this has been reprinted since its first appearance in technical journals, and indeed I had never considered collecting it in one volume until the Marconi International Fellowship gave me both the incentive and the opportunity to do so. It is therefore with great pleasure that I express my thanks to the Award's Founder and Chairperson, Mrs. Gioia Marconi Braga, as well as to the Fellowship Council, for the honor they have accorded me. I hope that this volume will be a permanent record of my appreciation, and would like to open it with the address I made at the Hague in the Ridderzaal (Hall of the Knights) on June 11, 1982, when receiving the 8th Marconi Fellowship Award. The ceremony and its associated functions were superbly arranged by N.V. Philips Gloeilampenfabrieken's Vice Chairperson Dr. A.E. Pannenborg and his staff, and the actual presentation was made by H.R.H. Prince Claus of the Netherlands:

Your Royal Highness, Mrs. Marconi Braga, my kind hosts from Philips, distinguished guests—

My great pleasure in receiving this Award is at least doubled by the knowledge that it has already been won by two very good friends, who deserved it far more than I do.

Dr. John Pierce was the first engineer-scientist to publish a detailed technical analysis of communications satellites. Even more important, he was the driving force behind the pioneering *practical* demonstrations with

ECHO and TELSTAR. He and Dr. Harold Rosen—who played a similar role with the first geostationary comsats—are the true fathers of satellite communications. That title has sometimes been given to me, but honesty compels me to disclaim it. I am not the father of comsats—merely the *God*father. . . .

The other friend, whom I'm delighted to see here today, is my northern neighbor Dr. Yash Pal. I've known Dr. Pal since the early days of the Indian SITE project, which he directed so brilliantly after the untimely death of its founder, Dr. Vikram Sarabhai—whose work he is still continuing as Secretary-General of UNISPACE. By a happy chance, I was in Ahmedabad when Dr. Pal received notification of *his* Marconi award, and was wondering how best to utilize it. Yash, I'd like to resume that discussion, just as soon as convenient. . . .

I am not indulging in false modesty—a concept which all my friends would reject with hysterical laughter—when I say that *my* contribution to satellite communications was largely a matter of luck. I happened to be in the right place, at the right time. In the winter of 1944–45, World War II was obviously coming to an end, and one could think once more about the future. Dr. Wernher von Braun—another good friend, whom I miss badly—had demonstrated that big rockets were practical, to the grave detriment of London as target, and the Hague as launchpad. The time was ripe to think about reviving the British Interplanetary Society, which has been in suspended animation since 1939.

But how could one possibly raise money for such a fantastic enterprise as space travel? Prewar estimates by the BIS had suggested that a lunar expedition might cost the truly astronomical sum of *one million dollars*, and it was ridiculous to imagine that governments would spend such awesome amounts on purely scientific projects. We would have to find money ourselves; was there any way in which rockets could earn an honest living?

Rocket mail had been suggested, but that seemed a rather limited application, and it might take some time to overcome the poor advance publicity generated by the V2. . . .

I was pondering these matters in my spare time as an RAF radar officer, while helping to run the Ground Controlled Approach (GCA) system invented by Dr. Luis W. Alvarez and his Radiation Lab team. This operated at the then fantastically high frequency of 10 Gigahertz, producing beams a fraction of a degree wide. I can recall, with some embarrassment, using the dear old Mark I to fire single pulses at the rising Moon, and waiting for the echo three seconds later. (Obviously, the available power would have been orders of magnitude too low.)

So communications and astronautics were inextricably entangled in my mind, with results that now seem inevitable. If I had not proposed the idea of geostationary relays in my *Wireless World* letter of February 1945, and developed it in more detail the following October, half a dozen other people would have quickly done so. I suspect that my early disclosure may have advanced the cause of space communications by approximately fifteen minutes.

Or perhaps twenty. My efforts to promote and publicise the idea may have been much more important than conceiving it. In 1952 *The Exploration of Space* introduced communications satellites to several hundred thousand people—including John Pierce, whom I first met in May of that year, and did my best to turn into a space cadet. (He was already one in secret, but as Director of Electronics Research at Bell Labs, he had to conceal such unfortunate aberrations.) When he published his influential "Orbital Radio Relays" in May 1955, he had never even seen my own paper of a decade earlier; but of course he had no need of it—the mere suggestion was enough to an engineer of John's calibre.

From today's vantage point, it's amusing to note that "Orbital Radio Relays" was published in *Jet Propulsion*, the Journal of the American Rocket Society. Not long afterwards, the ARS became the American Institute of Aeronautics and Astronautics; but in 1955 there was not the slightest mention of space flight in the society's Byelaws. Even the word "rocket" was avoided as too Buck Rogerish; only "jet propulsion" was respectable. . . .

In complete contrast, the British Interplanetary Society was *only* interested in space travel, and would have been quite happy to abandon rockets as soon as someone got round to inventing antigravity. I am not claiming that one viewpoint is superior to the other. The world needs uninhibited thinkers not afraid of far-out speculation; it also needs hardheaded, conservative engineers who can make their dreams come true. They complement each other, and progress is impossible without both. If there had been government—and dare I say industrial?—research establishments in the Stone Age, by now we would have had absolutely superb flint tools. But no one would have invented steel.

Let me end by sharing with you a discovery I've just been delighted to make, by pure luck—or serendipity, to use the now over-popular word derived from the ancient name for Sri Lanka. It links the pioneering days of European astronautics with the great man whose memory we have now gathered to honour.

Back in 1939, the British Interplanetary Society was always alert for publicity, and for several weeks we waged verbal war against sceptics in the dignified pages of the BBC's *The Listener*—until the editor finally declared that "this correspondence is now closed." I had completely forgotten that the controversy was triggered by a radio talk, "Myself and Life," by Dr. W.E. Barnes, then Bishop of Birmingham. It contains words as relevant today as when they were spoken forty-three years ago:

> It cannot be true that the earth is the only planet on which life exists. . . . On other planets of other stars there must be consciousness; on them there must be beings with minds . . . some far more developed than our own . . . wireless messages from such remote conscious beings must be possible. The only time I met Marconi he told me of his search for such messages. So far we have failed to find them. [*The Listener*, February 9, 1939]

Yes, we have failed. But one day we will succeed. And then Marconi's last and greatest dream will have been fulfilled.

II | *First Flights*

2 | *Amazing Story . . .*

I first became addicted to the pleasures of scientific controversy at the ripe age of seventeen, in the pages of the magazine which did so much to shape my youth— *Amazing Stories*. Almost half a century later, I can still recall how it started.

Some of *Amazing*'s more naive authors, in their quest for superlatives, referred to spaceships travelling at "the square of the velocity of light"; presumably they felt that, since the velocity of light was already enormous, its *square* would be still more impressive.

I was indeed impressed—but only for a moment. As soon as I tried to work out what the phrase actually meant, I ran into a problem. My thought processes ran something like this:

"The velocity of light is 186,000 miles a second—so the spaceship must be traveling 186,000 times faster than light! My goodness!" (Or possibly "Blimey!")

Then I did a double take. . . .

"But if I use the metric system, it's 300,000 kilometres a second. So the ship must be traveling *300,000* times as fast as light! Something's wrong somewhere—both figures can't be correct!"

It did not take long to spot the fallacy, and I composed a letter which filled a whole page of the February 1935 *Amazing Stories*. Except for contributions to my school magazine, this was probably my first appearance in print, and was presented under the heading "An interesting letter from an English Reader."

I had clearly never anticipated a career as a professional writer, for the opening was hardly calculated to endear me to any editor:

I don't think yours is the best magazine on the market, but in some respects it is better than the others. You have the best Editorials, the best Discussions and the best printing. And judging by the manner your readers still rave over Dr Smith and Mr Campbell, you have published some of the best stories. Only you don't do that so often nowadays. . . .

After various other digressions, I got to the point:

Several of your writers have been using the term 'the square of the velocity of light.' I would like to point out that such a term is more or less meaningless. Velocity is length divided by time. Therefore the square of a velocity is a length squared (or an area) divided by a time squared. I don't know what it is, but it's certainly not a velocity.

I thought this made the matter perfectly clear—but I had underestimated the obtuseness of *Amazing*'s editor, T. O'Connor Sloane. Although Dr. Sloane was then in his 84th (!) year, age hardly seems sufficient to account for all his deficiencies as the editor of a science-fiction magazine. To quote from that invaluable compendium, *The Science Fiction Encyclopedia**: "he sported a long white beard and exhibited an appropriately Rip Van Winkle-like approach to the job . . . he actually lost John W Campbell's first story, and returned Clifford D Simak's first submission after four year's silence, remarking that it was 'a bit dated.' " And in one of his editorials, he was tactless enough to assert that man would never achieve space travel.

Though he was kind enough to say, "We wish we had more such letters," he entirely missed the point of my criticism, merely replying, "As the velocity of light is a definite quantity there is no reason why it cannot be squared." He might have added that if you also multiply it by mass, you get energy, as Einstein had proved.

By this time, I had already discovered, through an encounter with David Lasser's 1931 book *The Conquest of Space*,[†] that rocket flight away from the earth was not pure fantasy, but an idea which some engineers and scientists took quite seriously. Soon afterwards, as an example in a mathematics textbook, I came across the fundamental equation of rocket propulsion, often referred to as Tsiolkovski's equation:

$$V = v \log_e M/m$$

where V is the final velocity of the rocket, v the velocity of the exhaust gases, M the initial mass, and m the

---

*Edited by Peter Nicholls (Doubleday/Dolphin, USA). Also published in UK by Granada, under the title *The Encyclopedia of Science Fiction*.

[†]Lasser's book undoubtedly changed my life, and in November 1982 (51 years later!) I had the great pleasure of thanking him personally, when we met at the TRW plant in Los Angeles. He is now working on another book.

final mass. So if *M/m* (sometimes referred to as the mass-ratio) could be made large enough, a rocket could travel faster than its exhaust—a fact which seemed counterintuitive. I can still recall the surprise of my applied mathematics professor at King's College—the distinguished cosmologist Professor G.C. McVittie—when I pointed this out to him as late as 1948. (And *my* surprise at his surprise . . .)

In January 1938 the magazine *Astounding Stories* tried to blind its readers with science by publishing an article on the theory of rocket propulsion—unfortunately by an author who seemed blissfully unaware of the basic facts. This provoked me to righteous indignation, and gave me the opportunity to display a little calculus. Although the second integral of the rocket equation is of no practical use to human or E.T., I wanted to see what it looked like; and here it is in the May 1938 issue of *Astounding*, eight years before my first story appeared there. . . .

We'll expect a reply from Leo Vernon. As for fuels—how about atomic H, not H_2?

Dear Mr. Campbell :

The folk who have the misfortune to work with me will confirm the statement that it took me at least two days to cool down after seeing Mr. Vernon's first differential equation, in "Rocket Flight", and for a week I was shouting things about "kv" in my sleep.

I make no claims to mathematical ability—my maths master always said I'd be a darn good chemist. I wouldn't know a Zeta function if I saw one, and my favourite cuss-words are "Reimann-Christoffel Tensor". But I do know a bit more than my two-times table, and I also happen to have spent some little time playing with the equations of rocket flight.

Run back to your marbles, you Brass Tackers, or you may get hurt. This is where men are going to fight.

I'll keep Mr. Vernon's symbols to prevent confusion, though I'd prefer to kick out X and k. Greek looks better, too, but it's hard on the printer. I insist, however, on using "g" for the acceleration of gravity, and not for the gravitational constant which is usually written G.

Force = Mass x Acceleration.

Now the force exerted by the rocket blast is equal to Xk, and the mass of the rocket at time t is (M-kt).

Therefore,

$$Xk = (M-kt)dv/dt.$$

where dv/dt is the acceleration.

Now, Mr. Vernon, where in the names of the perishing planets did you get your term "kv" from? Do I see the hideous shade of Karl van Campen looming before us again! Heaven forbid!

The solution to this equation is :—

(1) $v = X \log m/(m-kt)$

which you will find in any mathematical exposition of the subject worthy of the name. It is the most important equation in astronautics. Mr. Vernon's result, to make myself brutally clear, is balony.

From a second integration we obtain :—

(2) $s = Xt + X(M-kt)/k\log(m-kt)/m)$

These results ignore gravity. To allow for it, subtract gt from (1) and $\frac{1}{2}gt^2$ from (2), if you're not going very far from the Earth. Please handle these equations very carefully, Mr. Printer—they're fragile things. Mr. Vernon's second equation could be read in half a dozen different ways, each worse than the one before. How right he is when he says that his results differ considerably from those obtained by other writers on the subject !

Equation (1) is the most important. If you rewrite it as

$$\frac{v}{x} = \frac{m}{m-kt}$$

you can see at a glance (or at any rate two) that for a rocket to travel as fast as its exhaust it must burn "e" times its final or dead weight of fuel. And *not* an amount equal to its final weight, as Mr. Vernon so blithely states. Poor Willy Ley spent a whole column in the March 1937 A. S. explaining this supremely, this vitally important fact. And now along comes Mr. Vernon—— But words fail me. Excuse me for a moment while I take another bite out of the table.

Will all readers who were deluded enough to believe Mr. Vernon please reread Willy Ley's article "Dawn of Conquest of Space"? It will save me from wasting some more room.

Mr. Vernon's remarks on exhaust velocities show how little he is in touch with the practical side of rocketry. The highest possible value of X with known fuels is about 3 m.p.s. or 5 km.p.s. It is very unlikely that stable fuels will be discovered with very much higher exhaust velocities. So Mr. Vernon's tables, which start with values of 50 Km.p.s., are of no use whatsoever, even ignoring the not unimportant fact that their theoretical basis is as wet as a lump of calcium chloride in a turkish bath.

Rocket researchers such as the Technical Committee of the British Interplanetary Society are designing space ships using known exhaust velocities and aren't waiting for fabulous fuels to come along. They may—but for numerous reasons anything much better than oxy-hydrogen mixture is rather improbable. This means that we are designing ships on the "step" principle which enables very high load ratios—say 50 times as much fuel as dead load—to be reached. I would like to reiterate Ley's remarks that the only remaining problems are purely practical and financial ones, and there is no need to expostulate the enormous exhaust velocities that Mr. Vernon dreams of.

As an honest, fair minded editor, Mr. Campbell (subtle, aren't we?) you ought to give this letter as much prominence as Mr. Vernon's article. It's nearly as long, anyway. My only fear is that Willy Ley has beaten me to it and is already heading for Massachusetts with a suspicious bulge in his hip pocket and murder in his heart.

There are a lot of other things I'd like to say if I had the time and you had the space, but I think I have dealt with the most important matters. I'm really very sorry to be so rude to Mr. Vernon, who I'm quite sure is a nice enough fellow, but I can't resist the clarion call of duty. On which note, I will gracefully return to my usual semi-comatose condition until the next issue of A. S. comes over here——Arthur C. Clarke, Hon, Treasurer, B.I.S., 21, Norfolk Square, Paddington, London, W. 2, England.

[Published in *Astounding Science-Fiction*, May 1938]

3 | *An Elementary Mathematical Approach to Astronautics*

My mathematical education did not proceed much further while I was at Huish's Grammar School, Taunton, because in 1936, at the age of nineteen, I left for London and a career as a civil servant in H.M. Exchequer and Audit Department. However, this gentlemanly occupation gave me ample time to pursue my real interests—writing science fiction and designing spaceships with my fellow amateur astronauts in the newly formed British Interplanetary Society.

The grandly titled "Technical Director" of the BIS was an eccentric near-genius named John Happian Edwards, who earned a living designing and manufacturing radio tubes, or "valves," as we British called those basic tools of the Paleoelectronic Age. He had an extraordinary grasp of the principles of space travel, but some of his solutions to its problems were, to say the least, uninhibited. I may be doing his memory an injustice, but I think he once suggested the use of trained ants to operate small space-probes. Well, if the microchip hadn't come along in time. . . .

Edwards and I coauthored a number of papers for the prewar *BIS Journal*, one of which follows. I can still recall that I carefully chose the phrase "for which I am indebted to Mr Edwards" as a code message to mean "if there are any mistakes, don't blame me."

Certainly Jack Edwards' interesting (and I think novel) little table would have to be revised in the light of today's astronomical knowledge. But the changes would be minor—and it is indeed awe-inspiring to realise that our space-probes have not only surveyed *every one* of the bodies listed in it, but have already travelled far beyond its confines.

AN ELEMENTARY MATHEMATICAL APPROACH TO ASTRONAUTICS.

The fundamental equation of rocket flight, as derived from the ordinary $P = Mf$ law is

$$(M-wt)\, dV/dt = vw$$

where M is the original mass of the rocket, w is the rate of combustion of fuel, v is the exhaust velocity, V is the final velocity and t is the time.

Integration between the limits $t = o$ and $t = t$ gives :-

$$V = v \log M/(M-wt).$$

Since $M-wt$ is the mass of the rocket at time t, we may write this equation $V = v \log R$, where R is the ratio between the original mass of the rocket and the final mass after combustion. If all the fuel is burnt, R will equal the load ratio.

In the case of a rocket leaving a planet and requiring merely the escape velocity E, we have

$$E = v \log R$$

and we can thus calculate the load ratio required for any given exhaust velocity. For instance, taking the theoretical exhaust velocity of oxy-hydrogen mixture as 5 Km./sec. and the escape velocity from the earth as 11 Km./sec., the necessary R is found to be about 9.5.

For actual voyages the same formula can be used but V becomes more complicated, since the planets are moving in different orbits and their orbital velocities must be considered besides the velocities of escape from them. After the initial acceleration, a spaceship travels in some type of astronomical orbit, either an ellipse, a parabola or a hyperbola. The path requiring minimum power is the ellipse touching the orbits of the two planets, and this curve would normally be used if the time factor were not considered.

To obtain the velocities needed on a voyage between two planets, take the energy of release from the body of origin and add the energy of transfer from the planet's orbit to the voyage orbit (i.e., half the square on the difference in velocity). The velocity corresponding to this total energy is V for the start of the voyage. If the start is made from a satellite, add the energy of release from its orbit to the other two energies. Since the release velocity from an orbit is $\sqrt{2}$ times the orbital velocity, the extra energy in the case of a satellite is proportional to $(\sqrt{2} - 1)^2$ times the orbital energy.

The same treatment is used at the destination and the resulting velocities are added arithmetically. For a return journey V is doubled. This of course ignores errors due to air resistance and also an error due to the fact that on larger bodies the acceleration has to be reduced to avoid damage to vessel or crew. These corrections are rather indefinite and their values would depend largely on the skill and practice of the pilot. A small margin for errors in calculation should also be allowed.

The table, for which I am indebted to Mr. Edwards, shows values of V in Km./sec. for a one way trip between the more important bodies in the Solar System, excluding the outer planets. Deimos and Yapetus are shown as possible fueling stations, but as fuel materials could hardly be found " in situ " on such small bodies, they cannot be considered for the first voyage. The figures for Saturn would have to be increased in practice to avoid the rings. It will be seen that Saturn is about at the limit for jet-propelled vessels, as the present designs would just about allow landing but not taking off again.

In practice the planetary orbits are elliptical, and the planets travel fastest when nearest the sun. Consequently corrections in

[Published in the *Journal of the British Interplanetary Society*, January 1939, pp. 26–8]

	Mercury	Ven.	Ear	Moo.	Dei.	Mar.	Cal.	Gan.	Eur	Io	Jup.	Yap.	Tit.	Rhe.	Mi.
Venus	19.7	Ven.													
Earth	23.9	22.2	Ear												
Moon	18.3	14.3	13.6	Moo.											
Deimos	22.3	16.3	14.4	6.5	Dei.										
Mars	23.6	17.9	17.3	9.4	6.0	Mar.									
Callisto	26.6	23.1	21.0	15.8	11.5	13.4	Cal.								
Ganymede	27.2	23.8	21.8	16.6	12.4	14.4	5.6	Gan.							
Europa	27.6	24.3	22.4	17.2	13.0	15.0	6.8	5.5	Eur						
Io	28.7	25.4	23.6	18.4	14.4	16.3	9.3	8.2	5.8	Io					
Jupiter	78	75	74	69	65	67	67	69	70	72	Jup.				
Yapetus	25.6	21.6	20.8	16.2	12.4	13.9	6.4	7.5	8.3	9.8	60	Yap.			
Titan	26.4	22.4	21.6	17.0	13.3	14.8	8.0	9.2	10.0	11.5	62	3.6	Tit.		
Rhea	26.8	22.8	22.2	17.5	13.8	15.3	8.9	10.1	10.8	12.4	63	5.3	6.2	Rhe.	
Mimas	27.8	23.9	23.4	18.6	15.1	16.6	10.5	11.7	12.4	14.0	64	7.7	8.2	6.5	Mi.
Saturn	55	52	51	47	43	45	40	41	42	43	94	38	40	42	43

velocity and direction are needed according to the configurations at the time of the voyage. Moreover, the planes of the orbits do not exactly correspond. The allowance for this is best made by taking the distances of the points of arrival and departure north or south of the mean plane and dividing the difference by the time which is expected to be taken. A corresponding N.—S. velocity component can then be given to the vessel.

Although the path of the ship has so far been taken as the co-tangent ellipse, this is only approximately the case. It is true for the central portion of the voyage, though even here it may be necessary to allow for the perturbations of the nearer planets. At the beginning and end of the journey the path is actually that of a satellite round the respective primary, perturbed by the sun.

The main orbit is first determined to give the correct appointment, ignoring the attractions of the planets involved. The relative velocities at start and finish thus obtained are used as the velocities of approach from infinity for the calculation of the circumplanetary orbits at the beginning and end of the voyage. Since the main field does not leave off when the destination field commences, there will be a small error produced by considering them separately. This error is small enough to be ignored except when the destination planet is in the Saturnian or Jovian systems, or for voyages between Moon and Earth.

Voyages between satellites of the same system can be treated in a precisely similar manner to the above. Voyages between a planet or satellite and a satellite of another system are more complicated. In the immediate vicinity of the satellite an orbit must be calculated about the satellite ; at moderate distances an orbit must be caculated about the primary, and at long distances an orbit must be calculated about the sun. The corrections for perturbations may become extremely involved. This is particularly true of the Earth—Moon system, owing to the large size and mass of the moon as compared with the earth. Consequently in this case no satisfactory approximate algebraic solutions can be used and it is necessary to arithmetically integrate the orbit.

III | Waves and Circuits

4 | *More Television Waveforms*

By a strange irony of fate, the outbreak of war gave me both the opportunity and the incentive to further my mathematical studies. And at this point I will make a confession that has never yet appeared in print, although it concerns what was probably the single most decisive act of my entire life.

As a civil servant (then evacuated to North Wales, auditing the accounts of the Ministry of Food) I was still in a reserved occupation in 1941, and not liable to be called up for any of the armed forces. But that state of affairs could obviously not be expected to last; sooner or later, I would have to go. I determined to go where *I* wanted to—not where the random processes of the draft decided.

My interest in astronomy dictated my choice; I would learn celestial navigation and make myself useful to the Royal Air Force. So I bought books on the subject by Francis Chichester (later famous as a single-handed round-the-world sailor) and studied them avidly. Then, *without telling my superiors*, I went to the nearest recruiting office and volunteered for the RAF.

Forty years later, there's nothing the Civil Service Commissioners can do about it. I can plead the Statute of Limitations—or, as last resort, take refuge in Sri Lanka's benign extradition laws.

My call-up papers arrived a few weeks later—and, as it turned out, I had acted in the nick of time. Soon after I had started my basic training, I was summoned to the C.O.'s office and gravely informed that the Royal Army Medical Corps was looking for me as a deserter. I could honestly swear that I'd never received any notification from the AMC, and that was the last I heard of the matter. But even now, my blood runs cold when I think of the narrowness of my escape.

As an Aircraftsman II (Under Training) I had another stoke of luck. One day we were lined up on parade and inspected by the senior Warrant Officer, who selected me, of all people, to be his Batman. As life on the farm had bred in me a complete indifference to tidiness and even to general hygiene, the W.O.'s choice has always struck me as somewhat astonishing; perhaps I merely looked less moronic than the rest of the recruits.

In any event, my far-from-onerous duties consisted of polishing boots and brass and keeping the W.O.'s quarters neat, which I managed to do with remarkable speed. While my unfortunate colleagues peeled potatoes in the cookhouse, carried sacks of coal or scoured latrines, I used my ample spare time to struggle with differential equations. When he discovered what I was doing, my kindly *padrone* let me use his quarters as a study while he was bawling out squads on the parade ground. I have long since forgotten his name, but I recall his thoughtfulness with gratitude.

And then I had yet another bit of luck, though it didn't seem like it at the time. Instead of being posted to a flight school where I would learn celestial navigation, I was selected for training on something called RDF. This, we were told, stood for "Radio Direction Finding." It wasn't exactly what I wanted, but it certainly sounded a lot better than the Medical Corps.

It was, in fact, Radar—though both the word and the technology were still secret at the time. First as a trainee, then as an instructor (finally with the exalted rank of Corporal), I spent the next couple of years in the bleak and windswept—yet to me wildly exciting—world of Number 9 Radio School, Yatesbury, on the Wiltshire Downs not many miles from Stonehenge.

Number 9 Radio School had a good library, and I spent much of my off-duty time reading such improving literature as the *Bell System Technical Journal* and textbooks on electrical circuit theory (and the science-fiction magazines, though they were no longer easy to get, there now being more important cargoes contending for space on the North Atlantic). I became fascinated by the extraordinary tricks one could perform with electronics, and the strange, evanescent figures that could be made to dance on the face of the cathode-ray tube. A particular revelation was the discovery of Fourier's Theorem, one of the most beautiful and useful in the whole of physics. How incredible it was that *any* waveform, no matter how unprepossessing and irregular, could be built up by adding together a sufficient number of perfectly smooth sine and cosine waves, all harmonics of each other, according to simple mathematical laws!

Even a vertically rising and falling square wave could be synthesised from enough sine curves, of increasing frequency and dwindling amplitude, according to the aesthetically satisfying function:

$$\sin\theta + \tfrac{1}{3}\sin 3\theta = \tfrac{1}{5}\sin 5\theta \ldots + 1/n \sin n\theta \ldots$$

Of course, it would take an infinite number of them to do the job perfectly, but it was surprising how good an approximation one could get after a mere handful of terms. I used to amuse myself adding the first few harmonics together and plotting the result on graph paper. Yes, Fourier was right.

Many of the basic circuits in radar were designed to produce deliberate distortions in the waveforms passing through them—turning square waves into spikes or triangles, and so on. The results could be understood easily enough in terms of charging and discharging capacitors in the CR (capacity-resistance) circuits involved, but another way of looking at the matter was to analyse the behaviour of the Fourier components. Even if these were purely mathematical fictions and had no physical reality, it would be interesting to trace the behaviour of such an assembly of waves as it passed through a CR circuit. Each harmonic would have its amplitude and phase affected in a different way, depending on its frequency; and the final result should match that predicted by elementary circuit theory.

It was an amusing mathematical exercise, and the result was an impressive display of equations which I submitted, via official channels, to the magazine *Electronic Engineering*. In 1942 it was probably hard to find material which would not upset Security, but no one could claim that Fourier's Theorem was classified, so the article was duly published. Of course, there was no mention of its real context; but then the technology (and much of the hardware) of radar had been wholly derived from television, so the title was perfectly accurate.

More Television Waveforms
By ARTHUR C. CLARKE

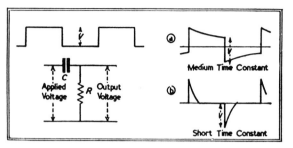

Fig. 1 (left)

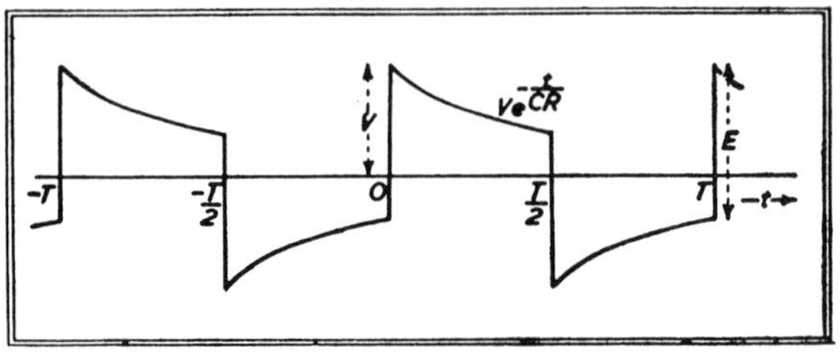

Fig. 2 (above)

MR. LOCKHART'S article on "Television Waveforms" in the June, 1942 issue of *Electronic Engineering*, dealt exhaustively with the subject of rectilinear waves, *e.g.*, sawteeth and rectangular waveforms. An additional important variety is the "peaked" or exponential wave such as that obtained when a rectangular voltage is passed through a resistance-capacity coupling.

When the time-constant of the coupling is long (*i.e.*, the C.R. product is great compared with the period of the applied wave) the output voltage is sensibly unaltered. If on the other hand the time constant of the circuit is small, distortion occurs as in Fig. 1 (a) and (b). The resulting waves have steep vertical fronts followed by exponential slopes due to the charge and discharge of the condenser. There is no d.c. component and the waves are always of equal area above and below the datum line, though they are perfectly symmetrical only when produced by square waves.

Since these "differentiated" waves have important applications their harmonic analysis is of interest, and it can be obtained without undue difficulty when certain mathematical artifices are employed. In this paper, only the results of peaking square waves will be directly considered, though as will be shown the treatment can be extended to any type of wave.

Consider a peaked wave (Fig. 2) of period T, varying between the limits $+V$ and $-V$. Assume that the origin ($t = O$) is as shown. Then from the well known discharge law of the condenser the wave can be defined by:

$$v = f(t) = Ve^{-\frac{t}{CR}} \quad \text{from } t = O \text{ to } t = \frac{T}{2}$$

$$v = f(t) = -Ve^{-\frac{t}{CR}} \quad \text{from } t = \frac{T}{2} \text{ to } t = T$$

Inspection of the wave reveals the relation $f(t) = -f(T/2 + t)$, hence the function is "odd-harmonic" (*see* for example Eagle's "Fourier's Theorem"). The absence of even harmonics is in any case revealed by the symmetry of the wave. The Fourier series may therefore be written :—

$$v = f(t) = a_1 \cos \omega t + a_3 \cos 3\omega t + a_5 \cos 5\omega t \ldots$$
$$+ b_1 \sin \omega t + b_3 \sin 3\omega t + b_5 \sin 5\omega t \quad \ldots \quad (1)$$

and the coefficients are given by the expressions

$$a_n = \frac{4}{T}\int_0^{\frac{T}{2}} f(t)\cos n\omega t.dt = \frac{4}{T}\int_0^{\frac{T}{2}} Ve^{\frac{t}{CR}}\cos n\omega t.dt$$

$$b_n = \frac{4}{T}\int_0^{\frac{T}{2}} f(t)\sin n\omega t.dt = \frac{4}{T}\int_0^{\frac{T}{2}} Ve^{-\frac{t}{CR}}\sin n\omega t.dt \Bigg\} \quad \ldots \quad (2)$$

These expressions can both be directly integrated, but it is more convenient to combine them by multiplying b_n by j and adding it to a_n.

$$a_n + jb_n =$$

$$\frac{4}{T}\int_0^{\frac{T}{2}} Ve^{-\frac{t}{CR}}(\cos n\omega t + j\sin n\omega t)\,dt \quad (3)$$

$$= \frac{4V}{T}\int_0^{\frac{T}{2}} e^{-t/k}\,e^{jn\omega t}\,dt \quad (4)$$
$$(\text{putting } CR = k)$$

$$= \frac{4V}{T(jn\omega - (1/k))}\left[e^{(jn\omega - \frac{1}{k})t}\right]_0^{\frac{T}{2}} \quad (5)$$

$$= \frac{4Vk}{T(jn\omega k - 1)}\left[e^{(jn\omega - \frac{1}{k})\frac{T}{2}} - 1\right] \quad (6)$$

Now $\omega = 2\pi f = 2\pi/T$ $\therefore$ $T = 2\pi/\omega$

$$a_n + jb_n = \frac{2V\omega k}{\pi(jn\omega k - 1)}\left[e^{jn\pi}.e^{-\pi/\omega k} - 1\right] \quad (7)$$

By Euler's well known theorem,

$e^{jn\pi} = -1$ when n is odd

$\therefore a_n + jb_n$

$$= \frac{2V\omega k}{\pi(jn\omega k - 1)}\left[-e^{-\pi/\omega k} - 1\right] \quad \ldots \quad (8)$$

Removing complex quantities from the denominator by multiplying by $(jn\omega k + 1)$

$$a_n + jb_n = \frac{2V\omega k(jn\omega k + 1)}{\pi(n^2\omega^2 k^2 + 1)}\left[e^{-\pi/\omega k} + 1\right] \quad \ldots \quad (9)$$

Equating real and unreal parts

$$a_n = \frac{2V\omega k}{\pi(n^2\omega^2 k^2 + 1)}\left[e^{-\pi/\omega k} + 1\right]$$

$$b_n = \frac{2Vn\omega^2 k^2}{\pi(n^2\omega^2 k^2 + 1)}\left[e^{-\pi/\omega k} + 1\right] \Bigg\} \quad (10)$$

Referring to Fig. 2 it will be seen that

$$V\left[e^{-\pi/\omega k} + 1\right] = V\left[1 + e^{-T/2CR}\right]$$
$$= E$$

the change in voltage, or the peak-to-peak voltage of the original square wave. Thus the series may be written :—

[Published in *Electronic Engineering*, November 1947, pp. 245–7]

$$v = f(t) = \frac{2E}{\pi} \sum_{n=1}^{n=\infty} \frac{\omega k}{n^2\omega^2 k^2 + 1} \cos n\omega t +$$

$$\frac{2E}{\pi} \sum_{n=1}^{n=\infty} \frac{n\omega^2 k^2}{n^2\omega^2 k^2 + 1} \sin n\omega t \quad \dots \quad \dots \quad (11)$$

for *odd* values of *n*.

These terms may be combined to give a single sine series of the form

$$v = \sum_{n=1}^{n=\infty} A_n \sin (n\omega t + \phi_n) \quad (12)$$

where A_n is the amplitude of the *n*th harmonic and ϕ_n is its phase angle. In this case :—

$$A_n = \sqrt{a_n^2 + b_n^2} \text{ and } \phi_n = \tan^{-1} \frac{a_n}{b_n} \quad (13)$$

Hence

$$A_n = \frac{2E}{\pi} \sqrt{\frac{\omega^2 k^2}{(n^2\omega^2 k^2 + 1)^2} + \frac{n^2\omega^4 k^4}{(n^2\omega^2 k^2 + 1)^2}}$$

$$= \frac{2E}{\pi} \sqrt{\frac{\omega^2 k^2 (n^2\omega^2 k^2 + 1)}{(n^2\omega^2 k^2 + 1)^2}}$$

$$= \frac{2E}{\pi} \frac{\omega k}{\sqrt{n^2\omega^2 k^2 + 1}} \quad \dots \quad (14)$$

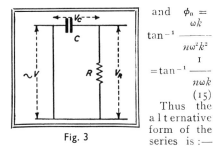

Fig. 3

and $\phi_n = \tan^{-1} \frac{\omega k}{n\omega^2 k^2}$

$= \tan^{-1} \frac{1}{n\omega k}$ (15)

Thus the alternative form of the series is :—

$$v = \frac{2E}{\pi} \sum_{n=1}^{n=\infty} \frac{\omega k}{\sqrt{n^2\omega^2 k^2 + 1}}$$

$$\sin (n\omega t + \tan^{-1} \frac{1}{n\omega k}) \quad \dots \quad (16)$$

for odd values of *n*.

The physical meaning of this series can best be considered from a slightly different point of view. The exponential wave under consideration was obtained by passing a square wave through an R.C. coupling. As is well known a square wave with the origin chosen at the centre of a positive-going front (*see* II, table I, *Electronic Engineering*, June, 1942) may be expressed in the series :

$$v = \frac{2E}{\pi} (\sin \omega t + \frac{1}{3} \sin 3\omega t \cdots$$

$$+ \frac{1}{n} \sin n\omega t) \quad \dots \quad (17)$$

$$= \frac{2E}{\pi} \sum_{n=1}^{n=\infty} \frac{1}{n} \sin n\omega t \quad (18)$$

when *n* is odd.

If such a wave is passed through an R.C. coupling each harmonic component will be individually affected in phase and amplitude, according to the values of *R, C* and *n*ω.

From elementary a.c. theory (*see* Fig 3) if a sine wave $v = V \sin \omega t$ is applied to an R.C. coupling the output v_r across the resistance is advanced in phase by an angle ϕ and reduced in amplitude by the factor

$$\frac{R}{\sqrt{R^2 + (1/\omega C)^2}} \text{ or } \frac{R\omega C}{\sqrt{R^2\omega^2 C^2 + 1}}$$

$$\therefore v_r = V \frac{R\omega C}{\sqrt{R^2\omega^2 C^2 + 1}} \sin (\omega t + \phi) \quad (19)$$

Now $\phi = \tan^{-1} \frac{1}{\omega CR}$ and putting

$CR = k$

$$v_r = V \frac{\omega k}{\sqrt{k^2\omega^2 + 1}} \sin (\omega t + \tan^{-1} 1/\omega k) \quad (20)$$

Operation on the expression for a square wave (equation 18) by the above factor gives the result :

$$v_r = \frac{2E}{\pi} \sum_{n=1}^{n=\infty} \frac{\omega k}{\sqrt{n^2 k^2 \omega^2 + 1}}$$

$$\sin (n\omega t) + \tan^{-1} \frac{1}{n\omega k})$$

which is the equation already derived from harmonic analysis (16).

This is represented graphically in Fig. 4. a, b, c, d, e, f is a square wave of which the first two harmonics **A** and **B** are shown, together with their resultant C. When this wave is passed through an RC circuit of time constant .1 of a complete period, the exponential wave D is produced. The curves $A_1 B_1$ show the effect of the coupling on the original components A, B. The higher harmonic B is less affected both in amplitude and phase. The resultant of A_1 and B_1 is the wave C_1 which no longer possesses the symmetry of C and is tending towards the exponen-

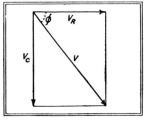

Vector diagram for Fig. 3

tial form D. When a sufficient number of harmonics are combined the resultant is indistinguishable from D.

From this demonstration it follows that the harmonic content of any wave after passage through a circuit giving phase and amplitude variation may be determined without actual Fourier analysis such as that in equations 1-16.

If the series for the original wave be known, it is only necessary to operate upon it term by term by a factor expressing the characteristics of the circuit, such as was done in equation 20, and the resulting series will be that which would be obtained if the full analysis were performed. Table I in the June *Electronic Engineering* can thus be extended to deal with almost all the non-rectilinear waveforms likely to be encountered in practice.

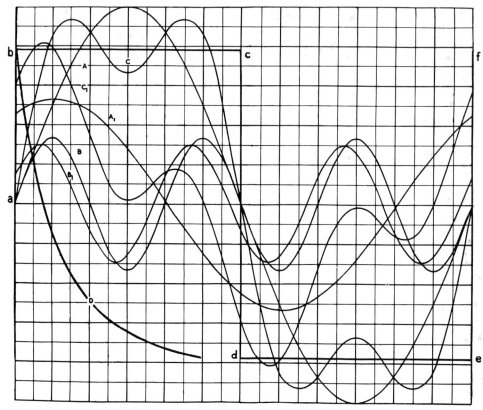

Fig. 4. Exponential Waveform resulting from Square Wave harmonics

5 | *You're on the Glide Path— I Think*

I suspect that *More Television Waveforms*, trivial though it was, helped me to obtain my commission; it was not, after all, the sort of thing the average RAF corporal would be expected to produce in his spare time. In any event, soon afterwards I changed my rank and number, left Yatesbury, and became technical officer on a microwave (3 Gigahertz) early-warning system on the east coast of England. This introduced me to the then super-secret (even by radar standards) world of wave-guides and magnetrons and slowly revolving parabolic dishes scanning the waters of the North Sea in search of downed aircraft and potential invasion forces.

This was but an interlude before moving on to something technologically even more exciting. One day I was called to Group Headquarters and grilled by Wing Commander Edward Fennessey (later Sir Edward, Managing Director of British Post Office Telecommunications). Presumably, like the Warrant Officer at training camp, he was satisfied by what he saw, for soon afterwards I found myself on an airfield in Cornwall with a bunch of wild young scientists and engineers from the Radiation Laboratory of the Massachusetts Institute of Technology. They were demonstrating a brand-new radar system called GCA (for Ground Controlled Approach), designed, for a change, to do something constructive. It could *talk* aircraft down, rather than shoot them down.

The leader of the team, and GCA's inventor, had just left for the United States, on a mission that no one knew anything about. When I caught up with Luis Alvarez some ten years later, he had helped to assemble the atomic bomb and was well on his way to his Nobel

Prize. (I often wonder what Alfred Nobel would have thought of that particular combination. . . .)

Working with the GCA team had a decisive influence on my life. For the first time, I got to know some *real* scientists, and I was also exposed to the most advanced electronic technology. The system which provided information on the aircraft's distance from the desired glide-path operated at the then enormous frequency of 10 Gigahertz (3 centimeters wavelength) and the beams with which it scanned the sky were only a fraction of a degree wide.

Many years later, I was to dedicate my only *non*-science-fiction novel, *Glide Path* "To Luis Alvarez, George Comstock, Richard Gray, and all who worked on AN/MPN-1 XE—wherever they may be." Dr. George Comstock, Luis' deputy, died in 1971, and I have lost touch with Richard Gray (the British "boffin," or civilian scientist who encountered GCA during a visit to the U.S. and realised its potential). But Luis Alvarez still hits the headlines at unpredictable intervals—most recently, in connexion with the theory that the dinosaurs may have been the victims of an asteroid impacting on the earth.

Though the essay that follows can hardly claim to be a technical paper, it serves very well to sum up an era in aviation, electronics—and politics. Few today will understand the reference to Gatow in the opening paragraph; that was the airport in West Berlin which kept the city open during Stalin's unsuccessful attempt to blockade it. All-weather operation of the Berlin Airlift was possible only through the use of GCA; so though the system was too late to have much impact on the war, it played a major role in deciding the peace.

You're on the Glide Path — I Think

NOW that GCA has become thoroughly established as one of the leading blind-approach systems and has been doing yeoman service all over the World—not least at a little place called Gatow—it is perhaps safe to reminisce about some of the early pioneering days, when the idea of talking pilots down the glide path was regarded with the gravest suspicion.

The first GCA unit was built in 1942-43 at the great Radiation Laboratory, Massachusetts Institute of Technology, its inventor being the atomic physicist Dr. (now Professor) Luis Alvarez, who had become tangled up in radar when America entered the War. He was later to be rapidly untangled and directed back into atomic physics when that subject appeared to have some remote connections with warfare.

Most people must by now have seen photographs of the present GCA equipment, even if they have not seen it in actuality; but the prototype was a very different affair. It occupied two vast trucks instead of a single trailer, and was much more impressive and very much more of a nuisance to move. It was also considerably more complicated (someone once counted 500 valves—sorry, tubes—before they got tired), and it needed more operators than the present sets.

These were not fundamental objections, as the Mark I was built entirely for experimental purposes, with no thought of serious operational use. In those days it had still to be shown whether radar could track aircraft accurately enough for the information to be used to land them. And also—equally important !—if pilots would do as they were told when ordered round the sky by disembodied but apparently omniscient voices.

The Beginning

The Mark I was undergoing tests in the States, apparently without arousing any great excitement, when it was discovered almost accidentally by a visiting British V.I.B. (Very Important Boffin). He at once realized its importance and, by what means we know not, succeeded in " capturing " the whole equipment and loading it aboard a British battleship. He also " kidnapped" Dr. Alvarez and his team, whisking them to the United Kingdom on a priority so high that they crowded Bob Hope and Frances Langford off the flying-boat at Shannon.

The equipment was reassembled at Elsham Wolds, then a bomber station, where the first trials were successfully accomplished. Unfortunately, it was not long before some genius decided that the weather at Elsham was altogether too good, and that since GCA was supposed to be a blind-approach system it ought to go to a station in a state of more or less permanent " clamp." So the unit was moved to Davistowe Moor.

We only saw this aerodrome in the rainy season, which possibly does not last the entire year, but when we arrived on the scene as Technical Officer U/T, we found the American scientists amplifying their already excellent vocabularies over expiring transformers, and complaining bitterly that their equipment wasn't built for underwater operation. At night, when the apparatus closed down and cooled off, the all-pervading mist would creep gleefully into every cranny, depositing moisture in high-voltage circuits so that brief but spectacular firework displays would ensue in the morning.

As part of the battle against this insidious enemy electric heaters were installed and switched on at night. One evening, as we were connecting these to the mains in the completely blacked-out hangar, a series of eldritch ululations disclosed the fact that we'd electrified one of the mechanics inside the equipment. We eventually located him by rapid sound-ranging and are still annoyed that we never got a Royal Humane Society medal for hauling him, still in a state of twitch, out of the works. Our tough Canadian Flight Sergeant, who got bitten more or less regularly by the 15,000-volt transmitter power supply, couldn't understand what all the fuss was about.

Luckily, the unit was removed to St. Eval, near Newquay, Cornwall, before the whole apparatus became waterlogged: and it was here that the Mark I saw most of its service with the R.A.F.

Testing an experimental blind-approach system on an operational station had its disadvantages. We had our own little flight of Oxfords and Ansons, which were liable to be making approaches on odd runways—and even downwind on the runway in use—when Flying Control was trying to land a customer !

To make matters worse, since there were no proper hard-standings for the apparatus, the big GCA trucks and their satellite fleet of service trucks, NAAFI vans and visitors' cars had to be sited on one of the out-of-use runways, near the main intersection. All too often a change of wind would demand a hasty retreat by the entire unit—a move which we resisted tooth and nail, since it required readjusting the controls and uncoupling all our cables. There were so many of these—an inch or more thick—linking the vehicles that the site sometimes looked like a rendezvous for amorous squids; but eventually we got so streamlined that we were able to change positions in about twenty minutes.

The Flying Control officers became quite used to seeing what appeared to be an advance party from Bertram Mills's Circus proceeding up the runway, turning on to an intersection, and then proceeding to pitch camp with sublime indifference 100 yards from the edge of the runway in use. Once we miscalculated and found a squadron of Spitfires taking off behind us: luckily, our 20-ton trucks did some rapid footwork and skipped on to the grass in time.

Some of the GCA sites were in more reasonable places on outlying pieces of perimeter track, and one was surrounded by a tasteful tableau of crashed Liberators. We were always very careful to explain to visitors that they had managed to get that way without any help from us.

The original American team was still with us for the early part of the time at St. Eval, although Dr. Alvarez had now returned to the States. Incidentally, Alvarez was very far from the popular conception of a high-powered scientist. He had a pilot's licence and was one of the best, as well as perhaps the first, of GCA controllers.

According to legend, he would calmly continue talking a plane to earth even when cathode-ray tubes were popping in all directions, frenzied mechanics were crawling under his legs, and smoke was gently curling from his meter panel. Moreover, he was an expert at breaking down " sales resistance" —and there was plenty of it in those days, particularly among exponents of rival systems.

When Dr. Alvarez returned to America, some of us guessed the reason; but we did not know until a long time later that he was one of the atom bomb team on Tinian in August, 1945. His deputy, Dr. George Comstock, remained in charge until the rest of the team returned. Our dearest memory of Dr. Comstock is of him, on his last night in England, lying in bed avidly reading something called " The Gamma Ray Murders."

We were very sorry to see the Americans go: and some of our W.A.A.F. operators were quite heart-broken. They were a grand crowd, and taught us a great deal. Our discussions were by no means devoted entirely to waveguides, magnetrons and pulse techniques. We also learnt some interesting songs.

With the assistance of the Americans we had trained a team of R.A.F. mechanics, operators and controllers who were later to form the nucleus of the GCA empire. But we were now very much on our own and could no longer run to the experts when anything went wrong—as it very frequently did. It had never been intended that the laboratory-built Mark I should be used continuously, month after month, for training and for innumerable demonstrations, in a foreign country and run by people who hadn't watched it grow up from a blue-print.

Yet it always managed to be serviceable when A. V. M. Blank or A. C. M. Double Blank arrived in his private Proctor.

Trials and Tribulations

We sometimes thought that everyone in the R.A.F. above the rank of Group Captain had visited us at one time or another. They usually went away thoughtful, if not convinced. There were times when the crowd in the control truck was so thick that mere Air Commodores had to sit outside on the grass, waiting their turns. The operators grew quite accustomed to working with a packed mass of humanity breathing down the backs of their necks.

They also grew quite accustomed to the sudden disappearance of all signals as we switched off to forestall some incipient breakdown. If the weather was dirty and we had an aircraft up at the time, that was just too bad: it would have to ask someone else the way home. As we so often pointed out to the O.C. Flying, it was easy enough to get more aircraft and pilots,

[Published in *The Aeroplane*, September 23, 1949, pp. 441-2]

but there was only one GCA, and we couldn't take risks with it. He rather stubbornly refused to see our point of view.

At St. Eval we made every imaginable mistake, and quite a few others, mastering the technique and developing the RT patter that has now become universally familiar. Nothing could be taken for granted, and we had to learn by trial and error.

No one, for example, seemed sure of the best glide-path: anything between two and five degrees was suggested for different types of aircraft. Changing the glide-path involved mechanical rearrangements in a Heath-Robinsonian apparatus full of gears, clutches, solenoids and selsyn motors. As the GCA was not sited at touch-down, but well up the runway, the radar operator " saw " a distorted picture of the aircraft's approach: the glide-path, in fact, appeared on the screen as an hyperbola instead of a straight line.

This distortion was corrected by most peculiar cams based on a curvilinear spiral co-ordinate system: these revolved once during every approach, except when they fell off their shafts. Changing a glide-path meant changing a cam, but one day the wrong cam was accidentaly left in the machine so that we brought a heavy bomber down a fighter glide-path. Nevertheless the pilot reported an excellent approach, so we decided not to pamper our clients any more, and thereafter everyone came down at 3½ degrees, whether they knew it or not.

The biggest operating boob we ever made on the Mark I might have had serious consequences had our aircraft not carried safety pilots who kept an eye open while the driver was obeying our instructions, and could break off the approach if anything was obviously wrong. One day the observer in the aircraft was a civilian scientist whose progress from station to station was always marked by the trail of mislaid secret documents he scattered in his wake. (If he reads this, we are of course only kidding.)

It was his first approach on GCA, and any faith he had in the system was somewhat shattered when he found his aircraft descending into the sea some miles off the coast while the controller was saying, " On the runway, one mile to go, coming along very nicely. . . ." He stood it as long as he could, then tapped the pilot gently on the shoulder and suggested that the depressingly damp scenery below bore little resemblance to runway 320.

It turned out later that the inexperienced radar operators had picked up the wrong aircraft, and were tracking someone who was making a normal visual approach and was naturally " coming along very nicely," while our own aircraft had been missed altogether. The mistake was, in the long run, a fortunate one, as it focused attention on the problem of identification and resulted in improvements in control technique. But it was some time before we lived it down.

Another slip which might have had equally sad consequences received no such publicity, being covered up by a quick screw-driver adjustment between approaches. We have kept very quiet about it ever since, but it may do no harm to mention it now.

Strange Echoes

In order to check that the radar system was properly lined-up, each runway had at its end a metal reflector or " marker " which acted as a kind of radar mirror and gave a fine signal on the screens. One day a marker fell down and we didn't notice its absence as we found a nice echo more or less in the expected place. Unfortunately, this echo happened to be caused by a Liberator on a hard-standing a hundred feet from the marker, so that in lining up on it we had slewed our glide-path round through several degrees. We discovered that something was wrong when the pilots complained that the approach we gave them passed through the top of a hangar.

At this point it might be as well to reassure any nervous readers by again pointing out that these incidents took place during the training of the first crew and with the first experimental equipment. They were our schoolboy howlers, we learnt a great deal from them, and they never did anybody any harm.

The last incident was by no means the only time when we lost a marker; one day we found that workmen were borrowing them to serve as builder's hods, which they strongly resembled. So eventually we used to send a mechanic out to the runway marker to wave it up and down while we watched to see which radar signal disappeared from the screen.

One day, when the marker was taken down, the echo didn't vanish, and we found that the mechanic was sending back quite a juicy signal himself. We can still remember our surprise as we watched him returning towards us, visible through the open door of the truck, and also as a small blob

creeping across the radar screen. A number of unflattering explanations were offered for this phenomenon, but we never really solved it to our satisfaction. No one else ever gave anything like such a good echo.

We were occasionally troubled by sea-gulls—though not in the usual way. They gave transient echoes which flickered across the screen from time to time: there was no possibility of confusing them with aircraft responses—they were far too feeble—but they puzzled us until we found the explanation.

The resolving power of the Mark I was very great, particularly at short ranges. We had a striking demonstration of this one day when, on the radar screen, we watched our C.O. cycling absent-mindedly down the runway in use, observed the airfield controller emerge rapidly from his kennel, and saw the two signals blend into each other as an animated conversation developed. After a while there was an amœba-like separation of the echoes, the C.O. proceeded blithely on his way, and the controller went back to his Aldis lamp, no doubt thinking that next time he wouldn't bother if a Walls ice-cream tricycle came trundling down the runway.

St. Eval was one of the first airfields to be fitted with FIDO, and the installation was a colossal one, burning, we are afraid to say how many, thousand gallons of petrol a minute. Not only was there a double row of burners the whole length of the main runway, but various sheets of flame branched out at right angles as well. When the whole affair was going full blast it lit up most of Cornwall and caused confusion among all the fire brigades for 50 miles around.

FIDO Plus GCA

For a long time attempts were made to arrange a combined GCA-FIDO landing, but they were foiled by persistently good weather. At last we got what we wanted—a drizzling fog with practically zero visibility. It was so bad, in fact, that the aircraft could never even have taken off without FIDO.

At midnight, all was ready. The scene might have come from Dante's Inferno—there were great sheets of fire roaring on either side, clouds of steam rising into the mist, and a heat like that from an open furnace beating into our faces, for we were only 100 ft. from the nearest burners. The aircraft was standing by, waiting to take off with the Station Commander aboard, and in the GCA trucks the cathode-ray traces were scanning normally, building up the radar pictures on the screens. At that precise moment, the turning gear that rotated the P.P.I. aerial decided it had had enough, and crunched to a halt shedding half its teeth in the process.

The Search or Traffic Control system, with its 360 degrees of vision, was thus completely blind: but the aerials of the landing system were still scanning, giving us a picture some 30 degrees wide centred on the runway and pointing downwind. It was decided to risk it, by keeping the aircraft in the narrow 30-degree sector and using the landing system, which was now all we had, both for control and approach.

As soon as the aircraft took off it of course promptly vanished into our 330-degree blind sector, but we immediately turned it through 180 degrees and it soon reappeared. It was allowed to fly down-wind for a few miles—we dared not let it go too far, as the landing system had a range of less than 10 miles—and then whipped round for an approach. The pilot was unable to land on this run: he found himself at the edge of the runway, but visibility was so bad that he could only see a single line of FIDO burners and didn't know which side of the runway he was! So the manœuvre had to be repeated, and luckily the second approach was successful, despite the attempts of the FIDO-induced gale to push the aircraft off course.

Those were the worst conditions under which the Mark I was ever used. As we took the trucks back to their hangar, visibility was still so bad that the drivers had to be guided by instructions from the running-board; and we could have done with our own radar to get us round the perimeter track.

That exploit was also one of the last high-lights of the Mark I's career. It had already run for six months longer than it had ever been intended to operate, and we are very proud of the fact that in the days before it was finally dismantled it was working as well as it had ever done, thanks to extensive overhauls and partial rebuildings. But the operational Mark IIs were now on the way, and the GCA team was moving to a new airfield all (or nearly all) of its very own.

The Mark I made the trip, but was never reassembled, and finally perished in a cannibal orgy. A long time later we came across the gutted and derelict vehicles in an M.T. park and had a quiet weep inside them, remembering some of the happiest as well as some of the most exasperating hours of our life. *Requiescant In Pace.*—A.C.C.

6 | Linearity Circuits

Keeping the Mark I running (the XE stood for "experimental," which was an understatement) and teaching RAF personnel how to operate it should have been a full-time job, but somehow I found time to start writing serious fiction *and* to produce my longest technical paper. By this time, I had become interested in the mathematics of active, as opposed to passive, circuits— i.e., circuits that contained vacuum tubes as well as resistors, capacitors and inductors. The behaviour of waveforms in such circuits could be described only by differential equations, and my self-acquired knowledge of these was just sufficient to tackle the more elementary examples. The result was a fairly long paper which appeared in *Wireless Engineer* in June 1944, and prompted some correspondence in February 1945.

Even if "Linearity Circuits" was a purely mathematical exercise of little practical value, I look back on it fondly, and its vacuum tube diagrams now make it a quaint period piece. It was my last venture into Higher Electronics because the V2 rocket had now arrived on the stage of history, and my thoughts and energies were now being redirected towards space.

The British Interplanetary Society had been in suspended animation during the war, but now that the end of hostilities was clearly in sight (at least in Europe), we began to think about the future. Much of our propaganda battle had been won—ironically, by our defeated enemies. We would no longer have to convince our critics that big rockets could be built, and could reach space; thousands of them had already done so, in the closing months of the war.

Yet even if we demonstrated, beyond any dispute,

that it was possible to build manned spaceships, they clearly would be extremely expensive; and it seemed unlikely that the necessary funds would be made available purely for exploration or scientific research. In the 1930s, some hopeful experimenters had tried to raise money by launching mail-carrying rockets; the movies of their hilarious disasters still make entertaining viewing. We regarded such publicity stunts with contempt; even if they succeeded, it seemed unlikely that the rocket could ever compete with the airplane for the delivery of mail.

But perhaps there was some other way in which rockets could earn money—money which could be ploughed back into the development of spacecraft, so that men could go on to the Moon and planets. At the various meetings where we would-be astronauts set about restarting the BIS, many crazy schemes were proposed.

Sometime in the winter of 1944–45, I thought of one which seemed a little less crazy than the others.

LINEARITY CIRCUITS *

By Arthur C. Clarke

CONTENTS

1. Introduction

THE earliest time-base circuit used in television and cathode-ray tube technique consisted essentially of a condenser charging through a resistance from a high potential source of supply. At intervals determined either externally or by the circuit itself the condenser would be quickly discharged and the process would recommence. Thus a saw-tooth wave would be produced with a gradual rise followed by a rapid fall of voltage.

The voltage output of such a circuit does not increase linearly with time but obeys an exponential law. Consequently when it is applied to the horizontally deflecting plates of a cathode-ray tube, the spot moves more rapidly at the beginning of the trace than at the end, and thus the picture or signal is distorted.

Numerous circuits of varying degrees of complexity have been devised to correct the exponential output of such a time base, and to make it a linear function of time. Such circuits are generally known as " linearity circuits " and in this paper an attempt has been made to discuss the theory of their operation and to determine their limitations.

Two lines of attack are employed in the investigation. In the first place certain actual or possible circuits are analysed and found to be incapable of producing perfect correction, though sufficiently satisfactory for many practical purposes. Secondly, an enquiry is made into the types of circuit which would be capable of producing perfectly linear voltages.

In attempting to apply any of the results obtained to practical cases, the following points should be noticed :—

* MS. accepted by the Editor, January, 1944.

(a) Except where otherwise stated it is assumed that any valves act as linear amplifiers.

(b) It is assumed that there is no load on the linearity circuit, e.g. that it is working into a valve with zero admittance.

(c) It is not always desirable for a time base to have a linear output : what is more often required is a *controllable* degree of non-linearity to compensate for distortion in subsequent stages. That, rather than the production of perfect linearity, is the purpose of some of the circuits dealt with in this paper.

The discussion is confined to voltage (electrostatic) time bases. Current (electromagnetic) time bases are not considered, but under suitable conditions low impedance valves may be driven by some of these corrected voltage time bases to produce currents for electromagnetic deflection.

2. Acknowledgment

The author would like to acknowledge his debt to O. S. Puckle's " Time Bases " which appeared during the preparation of this article and enabled him to extend considerably the scope of the original enquiry.

3. Integrating and Differentiating Circuits

3.1.—Fig 1 shows the simplest possible form of time base. E is a source of high potential and S is some electronic switching device such as a gas-filled triode or hard-valve trigger circuit. Although the development of the equations in this section will be found in any textbook dealing with transient phenomena, it is given here for completeness and because it is a particularly simple example of the cases dealt with later.

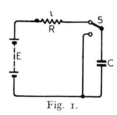

Fig. 1.

The driving voltage E equals the voltages across the resistance and the condenser, i.e.

$$E = iR + \frac{1}{C} \int i \, dt \qquad \cdots \qquad \cdots \quad (3.1)$$

Differentiating to remove the integral

$$\frac{1}{C} i + R \frac{di}{dt} = 0$$

$$\therefore \quad \frac{di}{i} = -\frac{1}{CR} dt$$

[Published in *Wireless Engineer*, June 1944, pp. 256–66. Additional correspondence, February 1945, pp. 72–3]

Integrating,

$$\log i = -\frac{t}{CR} + k$$

When $t = 0$, $k = \log i_0$ where i_0 is the initial current at the moment when the condenser starts to charge. This is obviously E/R since at $t = 0$ there is no charge on the condenser and the full voltage E appears across R.

$$\therefore \quad \log i = -\frac{t}{CR} + \log\frac{E}{R}$$

$$\therefore \quad \log i \cdot \frac{R}{E} = -\frac{t}{CR}$$

$$\text{or} \quad i = \frac{E}{R}\epsilon^{-\frac{t}{CR}} \qquad .. \qquad .. \quad (3.2)$$

To determine the voltage V_c across the condenser at any time it is only necessary to return to Eq. (3.1) from which

$$V_c = E - iR$$

$$= E - E\epsilon^{-\frac{t}{CR}}$$

$$= E\left(1 - \epsilon^{-\frac{t}{CR}}\right) \qquad .. \qquad .. \quad (3.3)$$

When i and V_c are plotted they give the familiar curves in Fig. 2. The shape of the curves depends on the product CR which is known as the "time constant" of the circuit. The smaller CR is, the more rapidly the circuit reaches its final steady state.

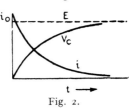

Fig. 2.

Even without mathematics it is obvious that the voltage on the condenser must follow an exponential law. As the condenser charges, the net driving voltage across R decreases and hence the current in the circuit decreases. But the voltage on the condenser is proportional to the integral of current and hence we have a quantity proportional to its own rate of change.

This is the condition which gives rise to an exponential law, whether it be in the case of a cooling body (whose rate of fall of temperature is proportional to its temperature relative to its surroundings) or continuous compound interest, where a sum of money is growing at a rate proportional to itself.

Clearly the only way to prevent an exponential output is to ensure by some means that the charging current is *not* proportional to the driving voltage across R but remains constant. $\frac{1}{C}\int i\, dt$ then equals $\frac{i}{C}t$ and a linear rise is obtained.

Alternatively the exponential rise may be tolerated and an attempt made to remove it in subsequent circuits. If the charging voltage is

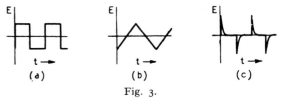

Fig. 3.

very large and the output required is only a small fraction of it, the departure from linearity is small enough to be ignored for many practical purposes. This procedure is sometimes adopted in oscilloscope circuits where high voltages are already available in the C.R.T. supplies. Circuits have also been devised in which fairly low H.T. voltages can be made to behave as very high potential sources by means of negative feedback arrangements. (*See* Section 10.)

3.2. The series condenser-resistance circuit with the output taken across the condenser is known as an integrating circuit since the voltage developed, if sufficiently small, is the approximate integral of the input voltage with respect to time. This follows from the condenser's ability to store charges and will be clear if we consider the case of a square wave applied to the circuit. (Fig. 3a.)

The output is approximately triangular (b),

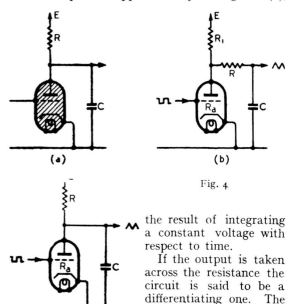

(a)   (b)

Fig. 4

(c)

the result of integrating a constant voltage with respect to time.

If the output is taken across the resistance the circuit is said to be a differentiating one. The differential of a square wave consists of alternating "spikes" of amplitudes plus and minus infinity for a theoretically perfect wave with an instantaneously changing front. In practice pulses with exponential trailing edges (c) are obtained.

The terms differentiating and integrating are used as convenient labels to distinguish between the two types of circuits, even when the values involved are such that the outputs do not approximate to the theoretical triangular waves or narrow spikes.

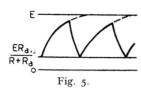

Fig. 5.

4. The Simple Time Base

In practice integrating circuits are used as in Fig. 4 for the production of time bases. In case (a) a gas-filled triode acts as a switch discharging the condenser when the voltage across it has reached a certain value, or on the arrival of a synchronising pulse. The circuit corresponds exactly with Fig. 1, for the gas-filled triode may be assumed to have an infinite resistance when non-ionised and zero resistance when struck.

In (b) the integrating circuit is connected to the anode of a valve into which is fed a square wave or a series of negative pulses sufficient to drive the valve to cut-off. Again the valve may be

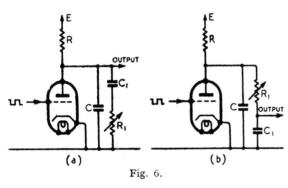

Fig. 6.

considered as acting as a switch. When it is conducting the voltage across the circuit will be $\frac{ER_a}{R_1 + R_a}$ where R_a is the D.C. resistance of the valve. When the valve is cut off by the sudden application of the negative wave the condenser will start to charge up towards the line voltage E thus producing a triangular output.

There is no need to employ two resistances as in Fig. 4 (b), since the anode load of the valve will complete the integrating circuit—Fig. 4 (c).

When the valve is conducting C will be charged up to $\frac{ER_a}{R + R_a}$ volts which will be nearly zero if R is large and, as is usually the case, the valve is

conducting heavily. When the valve is cut off C charges up towards E and the output is a saw-tooth between the limits E and $\frac{ER_a}{R + R_a}$ (Fig. 5).

Whether or not the voltage across C reaches E depends on the duration of the negative wave and the time constant of the circuit. It will be noted that as $R_a \ll R$ the condenser voltage falls back to $\frac{ER_a}{R + R_a}$ very quickly : the time constant on discharging is much shorter than on charging.

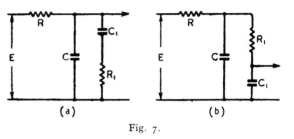

Fig. 7.

For many purposes the valve may be regarded as a pulse or square wave generator of output E driving the integrating circuit and this conception will be used in subsequent analyses.

5. Auxiliary Circuits—Analysis

5.1. A large number of attempts have been made to linearise the output voltage by auxiliary integrating or differentiating circuits and some of the simpler possible arrangements will now be considered. These are not all cases which will necessarily be of practical use but they will serve to demonstrate what happens in the more complicated arrangements.

Regarding the valve in Fig. 6 as a switch with zero D.C. resistance when conducting we may redraw the circuits as shown in Fig. 7 where E is a square wave or pulse generator suddenly applying a voltage E to the circuit at time $t = 0$. If the D.C. resistance of the valve when conducting is R_a, and not zero as assumed, the form of the derived equations is not affected. The only alteration is that E must be replaced by $\frac{ER}{R + R_a}$.

5.2. Both circuits may be represented as drawn in Fig. 8.

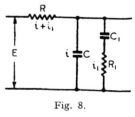

Fig. 8.

We have $\quad E = (i + i_1)R + \frac{1}{C_1}\int i_1 dt + R_1 i_1$

$$\cdots \qquad \cdots \quad (5.1)$$

$$\frac{1}{C}\int i\,dt = \frac{1}{C_1}\int i_1\,dt + R_1 i_1 \quad .. \quad .. \quad (5.2)$$

Differentiating,

$$R\frac{di}{dt} + R\frac{di_1}{dt} + \frac{i_1}{C_1} + R_1\frac{di_1}{dt} = 0 \quad .. \quad (5.3)$$

$$\frac{1}{C}i = \frac{1}{C_1}i_1 + R_1\frac{di_1}{dt} \quad .. \quad .. \quad (5.4)$$

From (5.4)

$$\frac{di}{dt} = \frac{C}{C_1}\frac{di_1}{dt} + CR_1\frac{d^2i_1}{dt^2}$$

Substituting in (5.3)

$$\frac{RC}{C_1}\frac{di_1}{dt} + CRR_1\frac{d^2i_1}{dt^2} + R\frac{di_1}{dt} + R_1\frac{di_1}{dt} + \frac{i_1}{C} = 0$$

$$\therefore \quad CRR_1\frac{d^2i_1}{dt^2} + \left(R + R_1 + \frac{RC}{C_1}\right)\frac{di_1}{dt} + \frac{1}{C}i_1 = 0$$

$$\therefore \quad \frac{d^2i_1}{dt^2} + \left(\frac{1}{CR} + \frac{1}{CR_1} + \frac{1}{C_1R_1}\right)\frac{di_1}{dt} + \frac{1}{CRC_1R_1}i_1 = 0$$
$$.. \quad .. \quad (5.5)$$

This is a linear second order differential equation of the form :—

$$\frac{d^2i_1}{dt^2} + b\frac{di_1}{dt} + ci_1 = 0$$

The solution of such an equation is

$$i_1 = A\epsilon^{\lambda_1 t} + B\epsilon^{\lambda_2 t} \quad .. \quad .. \quad .. \quad (5.6)$$

where A and B are constants determined by the initial circuit conditions and

$$\lambda_1 = \frac{-b + \sqrt{b^2 - 4c}}{2}$$

$$\lambda_2 = \frac{-b - \sqrt{b^2 - 4c}}{2}$$

In the particular case where $\lambda_1 = \lambda_2 = \lambda$ the solution reduces to

$$i_1 = (A + Bt)\epsilon^{\lambda t} \quad .. \quad .. \quad .. \quad (5.7)$$

5.3. The case where $\lambda_1 \neq \lambda_2$ will be considered first. Since the general solution

$$i_1 = A\epsilon^{\lambda_1 t} + B\epsilon^{\lambda_2 t}$$

must be true for all values of time it will be true when $t = 0$.

Then $(i_1)_0 = A + B$

But when $t = 0$ there can be no current flowing in the C_1R_1 branch as there is no voltage across C. Hence $(i_1)_0 = 0$ and $A = -B$.

$$\therefore \quad i_1 = A(\epsilon^{\lambda_1 t} - \epsilon^{\lambda_2 t}) \quad .. \quad .. \quad (5.8)$$

To determine A, we use eqn. (5.4) from which we note that

$$\frac{1}{C}i = \frac{A}{C_1}\left(\epsilon^{\lambda_1 t} - \epsilon^{\lambda_2 t}\right) + AR_1(\lambda_1\epsilon^{\lambda_1 t} - \lambda_2\epsilon^{\lambda_2 t})$$

When $t = 0$ and $i = (i)_0$ we have

$$\frac{1}{C}(i)_0 = AR_1(\lambda_1 - \lambda_2)$$

To find $(i)_0$ we need merely note that at $t = 0$ the full voltage E appears across R since C is uncharged. Hence

$$(i)_0 + (i_1)_0 = \frac{E}{R}$$

but $(i_1)_0 = 0$ and hence $(i)_0 = \frac{E}{R}$ and

$$\frac{E}{CR} = AR_1(\lambda_1 - \lambda_2)$$

$$\therefore \quad A = \frac{E}{CRR_1(\lambda_1 - \lambda_2)}$$

Hence

$$i_1 = \frac{E}{CRR_1(\lambda_1 - \lambda_2)}(\epsilon^{\lambda_1 t} - \epsilon^{\lambda_2 t}) \quad .. \quad (5.9)$$

5.4. Before considering the type of output voltage that will be produced by this current it is necessary to investigate the nature of λ_1 and λ_2. They must clearly be negative but they may be unreal.

This would be the case if $4c > b^2$.

Then

$$\frac{4}{CRC_1R_1} > \left(\frac{1}{CR} + \frac{1}{CR_1} + \frac{1}{C_1R_1}\right)^2$$

$$\therefore \quad 4CRC_1R_1 > (CR + C_1R_1 + C_1R)^2$$

Putting $CR = T$ and $C_1R_1 = T_1$

$$4TT_1 > (T + T_1 + C_1R)^2$$

$$4TT_1 > (T + T_1)^2 + C_1^2R^2 + 2C_1R(T + T_1)$$

$$\therefore \quad 0 > (T - T_1)^2 + C_1^2R^2 + 2C_1R(T + T_1)$$

As all the terms on the right-hand side must be positive, this is impossible and hence $b^2 > 4c$.

Thus λ_1 and λ_2 are real negative quantities and in addition the case $\lambda_1 = \lambda_2$ cannot arise, since b^2 would then equal $4c$. The solution

$$i_1 = (A + Bt)\epsilon^{\lambda t}$$

need not therefore be considered.

5.5. As i_1 in Fig. 8 has been determined we can now consider the type of output voltage it will produce. Taking case (a) of Fig. 7 first the voltage produced is

$$v = i_1 R_1 + \frac{1}{C_1}\int i_1\,dt$$

$$= AR_1(\epsilon^{\lambda_1 t} - \epsilon^{\lambda_2 t}) + \frac{A}{C_1}\int(\epsilon^{\lambda_1 t} - \epsilon^{\lambda_2 t})\,dt$$

$$= AR_1(\epsilon^{\lambda_1 t} - \epsilon^{\lambda_2 t}) + \frac{A}{C_1}\left(\frac{1}{\lambda_1}\epsilon^{\lambda_1 t} - \frac{1}{\lambda_2}\epsilon^{\lambda_2 t}\right) + K$$

$$= A\left(R_1 + \frac{1}{C_1\lambda_1}\right)\epsilon^{\lambda_1 t} - A\left(R_1 + \frac{1}{C_1\lambda_2}\right)\epsilon^{\lambda_2 t} + K$$

When $t = \infty$ the exponential terms will have vanished and K must therefore be equal to the final output voltage, which is E. Thus the output of the circuit is

$$v = E + A\frac{(R_1C_1\lambda_1 + 1)}{C_1\lambda_1}\epsilon^{\lambda_1 t} - A\frac{(R_1C_1\lambda_2 + 1)}{C_1\lambda_2}\epsilon^{\lambda_2 t}$$

$$= E + A'\epsilon^{\lambda_1 t} - A''\epsilon^{\lambda_2 t} \quad \dots \quad \dots \quad (5.10)$$

where A' and A'' are constants such that $E + A' = A''$.

5.6. Case (b) of Fig. 7 gives a very similar result. Here

$$v = \frac{1}{C_1}\int i_1\, dt$$

$$= \frac{A}{C_1}\int (\epsilon^{\lambda_1 t} - \epsilon^{\lambda_2 t})\, dt$$

$$= \frac{A}{C_1}\left(\frac{\epsilon^{\lambda_1 t}}{\lambda_1} - \frac{\epsilon^{\lambda_2 t}}{\lambda_2}\right) + K$$

where as before $K = E$.

$$\therefore \quad v = E + \frac{A}{c_1\lambda_1}\epsilon^{\lambda_1 t} - \frac{A}{c_1\lambda_2}\epsilon^{\lambda_2 t} \quad \dots \quad (5.11)$$

which is of the same form as eqn. (5.10).

5.7. The voltages defined by eqns. (5.10) and (5.11) are not simple exponential functions but are the results of combining exponential curves of different time constants and initial amplitudes.

Examples of such composite functions are shown in Fig. 9. By varying A', A'', λ_1 and λ_2 the output voltage may reach its final value E by an infinite number of routes.

It can be readily shown that no combination of the constants can produce a linear rise. The proof is as follows.

5.8. If a linear rise is to be produced it is necessary to satisfy the equation

$$A\epsilon^{at} + B\epsilon^{bt} = kt$$

Expanding

$$A\left(1 + at + \frac{a^2t^2}{2} + \frac{a^3t^3}{3!} \dots \right)$$

$$+ B\left(1 + bt + \frac{b^2t^2}{2} + \frac{b^3t^3}{3!} \dots \right) = kt$$

Equating coefficients

$$A + B = 0$$
$$Aa + Bb = k$$
$$Aa^2 + Bb^2 = 0$$

This can only be true if $A = -B$, $a = b$, in which case the original function vanishes completely, giving us the helpful result that a linear output can be obtained only if it is infinitely small.

Nevertheless the presence of an auxiliary circuit may produce a slight improvement in linearity at the beginning of the voltage rise, as shown in

Fig. 9 where the dotted lines indicate the shape of the exponential curves which would rise to 70% of the final voltage in the same time as the composite function.

Thus by varying C_1 and R_1 the linearity of the output may be controlled to a certain extent. The degree of control depends in a complex manner on the circuit parameters and the duration of the applied square wave.

It is not profitable to carry the general analysis further than this and to attempt to find values of C_1 and R_1 which give the "most linear" rise as they will vary with the amplitude of output required. However much the initial slope of the curve be altered, it is bound eventually to make an asymp-

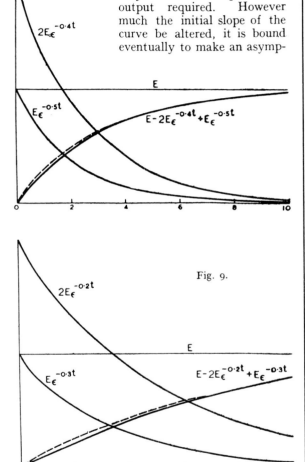

Fig. 9.

totic approach to E and so will have to depart from the linear condition.

6. Auxiliary Circuits—Further Analysis

6.1. A slightly different type of circuit may be constructed in which the integrating circuit

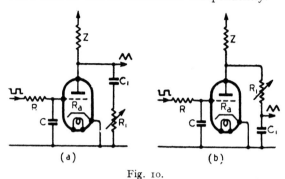

precedes the valve and the correcting circuit follows it, as shown in Fig. 10.

This differs from the cases in Fig. 6 because the two circuits are isolated from each other by the valve and so can be considered independently.

Fig. 10.

The valve and integrating circuit can be regarded as an exponential wave generator driving the correcting circuit and the usual valve equivalent circuit (Fig. 11) can be employed. A further simplification can be obtained by the use of Thévenin's Theorem* which results in the circuits shown in Fig. 12.

Here, $e = \dfrac{vZ}{Z + R_a}$ and $R' = \dfrac{R_a Z}{Z + R_a}$

Now v and hence e is an exponential wave and we may write

$$e = E(\mathrm{I} - \epsilon^{-\lambda t})$$

where $\lambda = \dfrac{\mathrm{I}}{CR}$

Then

$$e = i(R_1 + R') + \frac{\mathrm{I}}{C_1}\int i\, dt$$

$$\therefore \quad E(\mathrm{I} - \epsilon^{-\lambda t}) = i(R_1 + R') + \frac{\mathrm{I}}{C_1}\int i\, dt$$

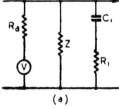

Fig. 11.

Differentiating,

$$E\lambda\epsilon^{-\lambda t} = (R_1 + R')\frac{di}{dt} + \frac{i}{C_1}$$

$$\therefore \quad \frac{di}{dt} + \frac{\mathrm{I}}{(R_1 + R')C_1}i = \frac{E\lambda\epsilon^{-\lambda t}}{R_1 + R'} \qquad .. \ (6.1)$$

* Often so-called but originally due to Helmholtz.—Ed.

This is a linear first order differential equation of the form

$$\frac{di}{dt} + ai = b . f(t)$$

and may be solved by multiplying by an integrating factor, which in this case is ϵ^{at}

$$\therefore \quad \epsilon^{at}\frac{di}{dt} + \epsilon^{at}ai = b\epsilon^{(a-\lambda)t}$$

$$\therefore \quad \frac{d}{dt}(i\epsilon^{at}) = b\epsilon^{(a-\lambda)}$$

$$\therefore \quad i\epsilon^{at} = b\int\epsilon^{(a-\lambda)t}\, dt$$

$$= \frac{b}{a-\lambda}\epsilon^{(a-\lambda)t} + K$$

$$\therefore \quad i = \frac{b}{a-\lambda}\epsilon^{-\lambda t} + K\epsilon^{-at}$$

To determine K we put $i = i_0$ when $t = 0$ and thus

$$i_0 = \frac{b}{a-\lambda} + K$$

But i_0 is zero since when $t = 0$, the driving voltage e is also zero.

$$\therefore \quad K = -\frac{b}{a-\lambda}$$

Thus we have

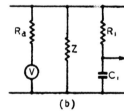

Fig. 12.

$$i = \frac{b}{a-\lambda}(\epsilon^{-\lambda t} - \epsilon^{-at}) \qquad .. \qquad .. \ (6.2)$$

where $a = \dfrac{\mathrm{I}}{C_1(R_1 + R')}$ and $b = \dfrac{E\lambda}{R_1 + R'}$

The output voltage e_0 is given by

$$R_1 i + \frac{\mathrm{I}}{C_1}\int i\, dt \qquad .. \qquad .. \qquad .. \ (6.3)$$

in case (a) and by

$$\frac{\mathrm{I}}{C_1}\int i\, dt \qquad .. \qquad .. \qquad .. \qquad .. \ (6.4)$$

in case (b).

Considering eqn. (6.3) first we have

$$e_0 = \frac{bR_1}{a-\lambda}(\epsilon^{-\lambda t} - \epsilon^{-at}) + \frac{\mathrm{I}}{C_1}\frac{b}{a-\lambda}\left[\int\epsilon^{-\lambda t}dt - \int\epsilon^{-at}dt\right]$$

$$= \frac{b}{a-\lambda}\left[R_1(\epsilon^{-\lambda t} - \epsilon^{-at}) + \frac{\mathrm{I}}{C_1}\left(-\frac{\mathrm{I}}{\lambda}\epsilon^{-\lambda t} + \frac{\mathrm{I}}{a}\epsilon^{-at}\right)\right] + K$$

$$= K + A'\epsilon^{-\lambda t} + A''\epsilon^{-at} \qquad .. \qquad .. \ (6.5)$$

Eqn. (6.4) gives a precisely similar result on integration : both functions are of the type discussed in Sections 5.6 and 5.7 and the same conclusions apply to them. The auxiliary circuits can vary and to some extent improve the linearity of the output, but cannot completely correct the charging characteristic of the original integrating circuit.

6.2. In all the above cases no account has been taken of the steady charge which will accumulate on C. This is a constant term which will disappear when the initial circuit equations are differentiated and so does not affect the form of the solution.

7. Auxiliary Circuits—Conclusions

7.1. The above discussions can be generalised to cover all possible correcting circuits using valves acting purely as linear amplifiers and working into condenser-resistance networks. *Once an exponential wave had been produced any subsequent linear circuits can only differentiate or integrate it—and the differential or integral of an exponential function is still exponential.*

7.2. Similar arguments apply when the circuit contains inductances, as in the case of Blumlein's time-base in which the condenser is charged through a resistance and inductance in series. The inductance limits the initial charging current and so the voltage across the condenser is nearly linear with respect to time, being actually the rising front of a damped sine wave. It is clear that no finite number of inductances can be combined in any linear circuit to produce a perfect sawtooth. Each LC circuit would contribute its characteristic frequency, but the linear sawtooth requires an *infinite* number of frequencies for its production.

8. Valves in Linearity Circuits

A number of important circuits have been devised in which valves are used to improve the linearity of the time base. The valve may be used for three purposes—

    (a) as a constant-current device
    (b) to provide negative feedback
    (c) as a non-linear amplifier.

In cases (a) and (b) the valve may also be regarded as acting as a non-linear device by behaving, for example, as a non-ohmic resistance.

9. Constant-Current Devices

One of the most important cases is that of the constant-current pentode which may be used to replace the resistance through which the condenser charges (Fig. 13). If the voltage across the pentode is not allowed to fall below " A " the current remains substantially constant and the

condenser may charge up to 80–90 per cent. of the supply voltage before non-linearity becomes noticeable. The pentode behaves as though it has a very high A.C. or slope resistance—$\dfrac{dV_a}{dI_a}$—while its D.C. or static resistance, V_a/I_a, is relatively small and so it passes a considerable current.

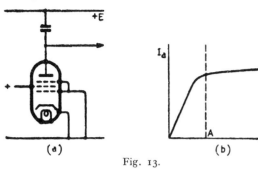

Fig. 13.

Results may be still further improved by the use of a cathode resistance to produce negative feedback. Feedback is also employed in Bedford's circuit (*see* Section 11).

10. Cathode-Follower Time Base

The cathode-follower time base (Fig. 14) uses negative feedback to produce constant current operation with an ordinary triode. In a cathode-follower a negative signal produces a slightly smaller negative output, a positive signal a slightly smaller positive output. Thus the potential difference between grid and cathode is almost constant whatever excursions the two electrodes make. Accordingly in the circuit of Fig. 14 a nearly constant current

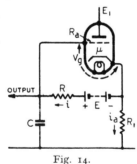

Fig. 14.

must flow through R, and hence C must charge up at a linear rate.

The general circuits equations are:

$$V_g = E - iR \qquad .. \qquad .. \qquad .. \quad (10.1)$$

$$E = i(R + R_1) - i_a R_1 + \frac{1}{C} \int i\, dt \ .. \quad (10.2)$$

$$i_a = \frac{E_1 + \mu V_g}{R_a + R_1} \qquad .. \qquad .. \quad .. \quad (10.3)$$

From (10.1) and (10.3)

$$i_a = \frac{E_1 + \mu E - \mu i R}{R_a + R_1} \qquad .. \qquad .. \quad (10.4)$$

From (10.2)

$$(R + R_1) \frac{di}{dt} - R_1 \frac{di_a}{dt} + \frac{i}{C} = 0$$

$$\therefore \quad (R + R_1) \frac{di}{dt} + \frac{\mu R R_1}{R_a + R_1} \frac{di}{dt} + \frac{i}{C} = 0$$

$$\therefore \quad \left[R + R_1 + \frac{\mu R R_1}{R_a + R_1}\right] \frac{di}{dt} + \frac{i}{C} = 0$$

This is of the form

$$a \frac{di}{dt} + \frac{i}{C} = 0$$

which has the solution [*see* equation (3.2)]

$$i = I \epsilon^{-\frac{t}{ac}}$$

To find I put $t = 0$. Then from (10.2) and (10.4), if the initial value of i is i_0,

$$E = i_0 (R + R_1) - i_a R_1$$

$$\therefore \quad i_0 (R + R_1) - \left(\frac{E_1 + \mu E - \mu i_0 R}{R_a + R_1}\right) R_1 = E$$

$$\therefore \quad i_0 \left(R + R_1 + \frac{\mu R R_1}{R_a + R_1}\right) = E + \frac{E_1 + \mu E}{R_a + R_1} . R_1$$

$$\therefore \quad i_0 \left[(R + R_1) (R_a + R_1) + \mu R R_1\right] = E (R_a + R_1) + R_1 (E_1 + \mu E)$$

$$\therefore \quad i = \frac{E (R_a + R_1) + R_1 (E_1 + \mu E)}{(R + R_1) (R_a + R_1) + \mu R R_1} \epsilon^{-\frac{t}{ac}} \quad \cdots \quad \cdots \quad (10.5)$$

where $a = \frac{(R + R_1) (R_a + R_1) + \mu R R_1}{R_a + R_1}$

This somewhat unwieldy expression may be simplified for the case when $R_1 = R_a$
Then

$$i = \frac{2 E R_a + R_a (E_1 + \mu E)}{2 R_a (R + R_a) + \mu R R_a} \epsilon^{-\frac{t}{ac}}$$

$$= \frac{2 E + E_1 + \mu E}{2 (R + R_a) + \mu R} \epsilon^{-\frac{t}{ac}}$$

where a has now reduced to $R + R_a + \mu R/2$

Now the output of the time base circuit is the voltage across C which is $\frac{1}{C} \int i dt$

$$= \frac{1}{C} . \frac{E + \mu E/2 + E_1/2}{R + R_a + \mu R/2} \int \epsilon^{-\frac{t}{ac}} dt$$

$$= - \left[E + \frac{\mu E}{2} + \frac{E_1}{2}\right] \epsilon^{-\frac{t}{ac}} + K$$

When $t = 0$ this expression equals zero.

Hence $K = E + \frac{\mu E}{2} + \frac{E_1}{2}$ and the output voltage equals

$$\left(E + \frac{\mu E}{2} + \frac{E_1}{2}\right) (1 - \epsilon^{-\frac{t}{ac}}) \quad \cdots \quad (10.6)$$

Comparing this result with eqn. (3.3) it will be seen that the condenser appears to be charging from a source of e.m.f. $E + \mu E/2 + E_1/2$. As μ may be very high, the effective charging voltage can thus be several hundred times E.

11. Bedford's Circuit.

11.1. Bedford has designed a useful circuit in which a variable degree of linearity may be obtained by feedback. The charging pentode V_1 has its cathode connected to a tapping A on the cathode resistance of the amplifying valve V_2. As the voltage at the anode of V_1 falls, so will that at the grid of V_2 and hence at A. Thus the voltage across the pentode tends to remain constant, producing an improvement in linearity. By varying the position of A, the output voltage may be made to follow an infinite variety of curves and nonlinearity of any subsequent stages may be corrected.

It might be thought that by a proper choice of resistances and tapping points perfect linearity could be obtained, but as will be shown in the following analysis, this is not the case.

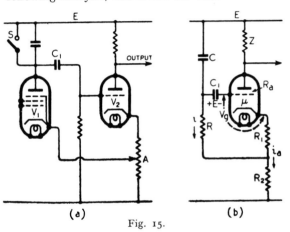

Fig. 15.

The circuit has been redrawn in Fig. 15 (b) with the pentode V_1 regarded as a simple resistance. If the time constant of the coupling circuit is long compared with the repetition period the condenser C_1 may be regarded as carrying a constant voltage equal to that of the supply.

The circuit equations are then

$$i_a = \frac{E + \mu V_g}{Z + R_a + R_1 + R_2} = \frac{E + \mu V_g}{Z_1} \quad \cdots \quad (11.1)$$

$$iR = i_a R_1 + E + V_g \quad \cdots \quad \cdots \quad (11.2)$$

$$\frac{1}{C} \int i dt + iR + (i + i_a) R_2 = E \quad \cdots \quad (11.3)$$

From (11.1)

$$i_a Z_1 = E + \mu V_g$$

$$\therefore \quad V_g = \frac{i_a Z_1 - E}{\mu}$$

From (11.2)

$$i = E \frac{(\mu - 1)}{\mu R} + \frac{(\mu R_1 + Z_1)}{\mu R} i_a$$

From (11.3)

$$\frac{i}{C} + \frac{R di}{dt} + \left(\frac{di}{dt} + \frac{di_a}{dt}\right) R_2 = 0$$

$$\therefore \quad (R + R_2) \frac{di}{dt} + R_2 \frac{di_a}{dt} + \frac{i}{C} = 0$$

$$\therefore \quad (R + R_2) \frac{(\mu R_1 + Z_1)}{\mu R} \frac{di_a}{dt} + R_2 \frac{di_a}{dt}$$
$$+ \frac{E}{\mu CR}(\mu - 1) + \frac{\mu R_1 + Z_1}{\mu CR} i_a = 0$$

$$\therefore \quad [C(R + R_2)(\mu R_1 + Z_1) + \mu CRR_2] \frac{di_a}{dt}$$
$$+ (\mu R_1 + Z_1) i_a = E(1 - \mu) \quad (11.4)$$

This is of the form

$$a \frac{di_a}{dt} + b\, i_a = c \quad .. \quad .. \quad .. \quad (11.5)$$

For i_a to be a linear function of time equation (11.5) must reduce to

$$a \frac{di_a}{dt} = c$$

Hence $b = \mu R_1 + Z_1 = 0$

or $\qquad \mu = -\dfrac{Z_1}{R_1}$

This condition is not physically realisable as it implies that a negative signal on the grid increases the anode current. The meaning of the solution is as follows.

Since $\quad i_a = \dfrac{E + \mu V_g}{Z_1} \quad$ the voltage across R_1 is

$$i_a R_1 = \frac{ER_1}{Z_1} + \frac{\mu V_g R_1}{Z_1}$$

$$= \frac{ER_1}{Z_1} - V_g$$

if the above hypothetical condition were possible.

Thus

$$i_a R_1 + V_g = \frac{ER_1}{Z_1} = \text{a constant.}$$

But $i_a R_1 + V_g$ is the voltage across R, so this is the condition for a constant charging current.

11.2. It is also instructive to consider the circuit by the familiar *reductio ad absurdum*

method of Euclid. Let us suppose that a perfectly linear output is being produced by the triode. Then V_g and i_a must both be linear with respect to time. Hence the voltage across R must be linear and so must be the current i through it which is charging C. The voltage across the condenser, which is obtained by integrating the current i with respect to time, is therefore proportional to t^2 and so is not linear but parabolic.

We thus have three voltages V_C, V_R and V_{R2}, two of which are linear and one of which is parabolic, adding up to a constant voltage E. This is obviously impossible except in the special and

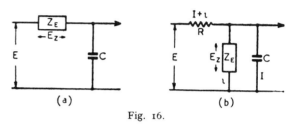

(a)   (b)

Fig. 16.

practically unrealisable case discussed in Section 11.1.

In practice, since R is not an ohmic resistance but a constant current pentode contributing its share to the linearity of the circuit, an almost perfect sawtooth output can be obtained. The main disadvantage of the circuit is that it requires four valves, allowing for two in the switching circuit.

We have seen that none of the circuits so far considered are capable, even in theory, of generating perfectly linear outputs. We will now approach the problem from the reverse direction and, assuming that such outputs are available, will discuss the types of circuits that must have produced them, with a view to seeing if any of them are physically realisable.

12. Non-Linear Impedance

A number of resistors employed in electrical engineering, such as " Metrosil " and other surge-arresting materials, do not obey Ohm's Law except over small ranges but have non-linear current-voltage characteristics. This raises the question : what must be the characteristic of a resistance employed in an integrating circuit if it is to produce a linear output ?

There are two possible simple circuit arrangements, series and parallel, as shown in Fig. 16. The requirements of both circuits are that the resistance Z vary with the voltage E_z across it in such a way that the current charging the condenser remains constant. We will assume that the value of the resistance is Z_E when the voltage across it is E_z.

In case (a) the resistance of Z must obviously be directly proportional to the voltage across it, since it is required to pass a constant current. A resistance obeying the law $Z_E = kE_z$, even over a limited range, does not seem very likely to be realised in practice. The commercial non-linear resistors obey laws of the form $Z_E = kE_z^{-4}$ and only depart from linearity at fairly high voltages. However, it would be rash to assume that no substance could be found to obey this direct proportionality law over a voltage range which would make it useful for commercial television purposes.

In case (b) we have

$$E = (I + i)R + iZ_E$$

where I is a constant which must equal E/R, from a consideration of the initial conditions when there is no charge across the condenser.

Thus

$$E = \left(\frac{E}{R} + i\right) R + iZ_E$$

Whence

$$Z_E = -R.$$

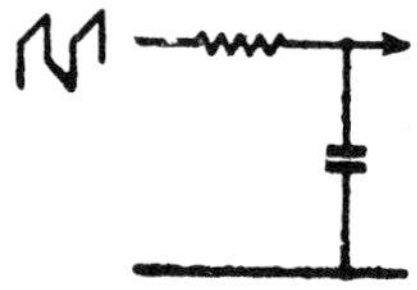

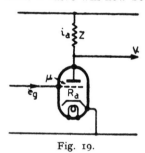

Fig. 17.

Although negative resistances independent of frequency may be realised in practice, for example in the case of the transitron, they require valve circuits, and it does not appear profitable to pursue the parallel circuit case any further.

13. The Integrating Amplifier

It has so far been assumed that the input to the integrating circuit is a constant voltage or a square wave. If, however, the input voltage is rising steadily at the correct rate, it may force a constant current through the circuit and so produce a perfectly triangular output across the condenser.

The required input voltage may clearly be obtained by taking an ordinary integrating circuit driven by a square wave and feeding the output back into the circuit. The input may then be regarded as a square wave surmounted by a triangular wave. The square wave component will produce the constant current through the resistance . and the triangular component will appear across the condenser. Clearly the theoretical gain of the feedback loop should be unity.

This is the principle of the integrating amplifier of Beale and Stansfield which consists of a two-. stage amplifier with an integrating circuit between the stages (**Fig. 18**).

Although it would appear that the circuit is liable to go into self-oscillation, according to Puckle there is no danger of this occurring in normal use owing to the fact that gain at low frequencies is reduced in the RC couplings between

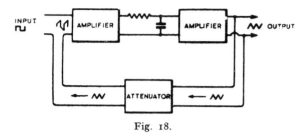

Fig. 18.

the stages. With proper adjustment of the feedback an almost perfectly linear output may be obtained.

14. The Logarithmic Amplifier

14.1.   We will conclude this paper by investigating the case of the non-linear valve amplifier. It has already been mentioned that linearity circuits are usually employed to correct for distortion in subsequent stages so that the ultimate result on the face of the cathode-ray tube is a linear trace. Amplifying valves with curved characteristics may be deliberately used to produce a linear output from an exponential input and the gain law of such a valve will now be considered.

14.2.   In the circuit of Fig. 19 e_g is the input which is assumed to be of exponential form. The output voltage V is assumed to be linear and the amplification factor μ is therefore a function of e_g which is to be determined.

Fig. 19.

The circuit equations are

$$V = i_a Z = \frac{\mu e_g Z}{Z + R_a} = \mu e_g Z_1 \text{ say.}$$

$$e_g = E(1 - \epsilon^{-\lambda t})$$

$$\mu = \phi(e_g)$$

$$V = kt$$

where k and λ are constants.

Then $kt = \mu e_g Z_1$

$$\therefore \qquad \mu = \frac{kt}{e_g Z_1} \qquad \cdots \qquad \cdots \qquad \cdots \quad (14.1)$$

Now $1 - \dfrac{e_g}{E} = \epsilon^{-\lambda}$

$\therefore \qquad \lambda t = -\log\dfrac{E - e_g}{E} = \log\dfrac{E}{E - e_g}$

$\therefore \qquad t = \dfrac{1}{\lambda}\log\dfrac{E}{E - e_g} \qquad .. \qquad .. \quad (14.2)$

Hence from (14.1)

$$\mu = \dfrac{k}{\lambda Z_1}\dfrac{1}{e_g}\log\dfrac{E}{E - e_g} \qquad .. \qquad .. \quad (14.3)$$

Now $\qquad i_a = \mu e_g \dfrac{Z_1}{Z}$

Therefore from (14.3)

$$i_a = \dfrac{k}{\lambda Z}\log\dfrac{E}{E - e_g} \qquad .. \qquad .. \quad (14.4)$$

14.3. In Fig. 20 μ and i_a have been plotted against e_g. Since eqn. (14.3) becomes indeterminate when $e_g = O$, we must write

$$\mu = -\dfrac{k}{\lambda Z_1}\dfrac{1}{e_g}\log\left(1 - \dfrac{e_g}{E}\right)$$

$$= -\dfrac{k}{\lambda Z_1}\dfrac{1}{e_g}\left[-\dfrac{e_g}{E} - \dfrac{1}{2}\left(\dfrac{e_g}{E}\right)^2 - \dfrac{1}{3}\left(\dfrac{e_g}{E}\right)^3 \ldots\right]$$

$$= \dfrac{k}{\lambda E Z_1} \quad \text{when } e_g = 0$$

This quantity has been put equal to unity in drawing the curves in Fig. 20.

Although the scales used in Fig. 20 are quite arbitrary, since the constants k, λ, Z, Z_1, and E may have any value, the required shape of the valve characteristic is clearly brought out. The $i_a - v_g$ curve is very similar to that of the ordinary variable-mu or super-control valve.

It would thus appear that by careful choice of the circuit constants a useful improvement in linearity might be obtained by employing a

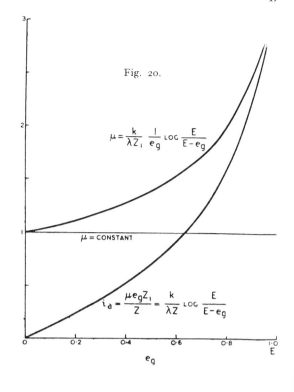

Fig. 20.

variable-mu amplifier or a valve with a similar logarithmic characteristic. This use of a non-linear amplifier was suggested by Bedford and Stevens (British Patent 474623), and a similar idea has been used by Jenkins (*see* Puckle, p. 85).

When television sets are mass-produced, it might be well worth while to design special valves for the amplification of exponental time-bases, if none of the existing types could be found with the required logarithmic characteristic.

"Linearity Circuits"

To the Editor, "Wireless Engineer"

SIR,—In A. C. Clarke's very interesting article on "Linearity Circuits" in the June, 1944, issue of *Wireless Engineer* a slip seems to have occurred

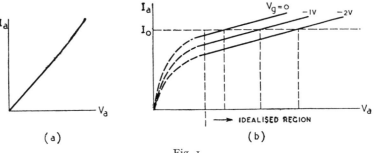

Fig. 1.

in Section 11 on Bedford's circuit. The author arrives at the conclusion that no perfect linearity can be achieved even with Bedford's circuit. Whilst I admit that owing to valve characteristic curvature no perfection can ever prevail, I should like to show briefly that under quite reasonable assumptions perfect linearity can be achieved.

To start with, a pentode cannot be actually replaced by a simple ohmic resistance. A glance at Fig. 1(a) which gives the characteristics of a resistance, and Fig. 1(b) giving that of a pentode will demonstrate my statement. The reason is that in a pentode A.C. and D.C. resistances are two entirely different quantities, with an ohmic resistance they are identical.

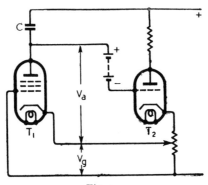

Fig. 2.

Furthermore, Bedford's circuit does not depend on an attempt to keep the anode voltage constant, as the author explains in sub-section 11.1 of his paper, but to keep the anode current I_0 constant by means of counteracting the dropping anode voltage V_a by a positively increasing grid voltage V_g (see Fig. 2).

Therefore Figs. 15(a) and (b) of Mr. Clarke's paper are not electrically equivalent, and consequently the mathematical derivation does not hold for Bedford's circuit.

If, however, one assumes that the pentode I_a/V_a characteristic in its operating range can be well approximated by a family of straight, parallel and equidistant lines as shown in Fig. 1(b) and, if one further assumes a linear triode amplifier T_2—the cathode resistance considerably helps in this assumption—it is easy enough to show that Bedford's circuit can give a perfectly linear saw tooth.

The important point is to have a constant current I_0 charging the condenser C. Then the anode voltage will decrease linearly. As can be seen from Fig. 1(b) these two conditions viz., constant current I_0 and linearly decreasing anode voltage V_a, call for a linear increase in grid voltage V_g, which in turn is automatically produced across the cathode resistance of T_2, since its grid is fed by the perfect linear saw tooth. There is no contradiction in this simple proof.

I should like to express my thanks and appreciation to the author for, what I should almost call the theorem that an exponential wave cannot be linearised by passive linear circuits. I think that such realisation will save many a useless effort to future time base designers.

G. L. HAMBURGER.

London, W.2.

[A copy of the above letter was sent to the author of the article whose reply we publish below —ED.]

To the Editor, "Wireless Engineer"

SIR,—The analysis I gave was based on the condition when the grid of the pentode is returned to its cathode and hence there is no alteration of grid voltage. In this case perfect correction is not possible and my conclusion stands, though I was careful to point out that since R is not an ohmic resistance but a constant current pentode the results are better than the simple theory predicts. The circuit, however, is inferior to the true Bedford circuit in which the grid is taken to earth, and I am grateful to Mr. Hamburger for showing that under these conditions true linearity is theoretically and for all likely purposes practically possible. I append an analysis deriving the necessary circuit conditions.

I would like to bring my paper up to date by mentioning that a number of patents have recently appeared on the use of Thermistors (temperature sensitive resistances) in time-base circuits. Though I have no further details this appears to be a rather

[Published in *Wireless Engineer*, February, 1945, pp. 72—3]

prompt verification of the prophecy in Section 12 concerning the possible future use of non-linear resistances.

I thank Mr. Hamburger for his appreciation of my " theorem " and will be very pleased if it does prove of value to time base designers.

ARTHUR C. CLARKE.

Appendix to A. C. Clarke's article, " Linearity Circuits," referred to in the above letter.

We wish to determine the condition for constant current through the pentode. If V_a, V_g, V_g' and I_a are the alternating voltages and currents in the circuit given below, and μ_p the amplification factor of the pentode, we have :—

$$\frac{V_a}{V_g} = \mu_p \qquad \qquad \qquad (1)$$

$$V_a = V_g' + I_a R_1 \qquad \qquad (2)$$

$$I_a = \frac{\mu V_g'}{R_a + Z + R_1 + R_2} = \frac{\mu V_g'}{Z_1} \qquad (3)$$

$$V_g = I_a R_2 \qquad \qquad \qquad (4)$$

From 1, 2 and 4,

$$\frac{V_a}{V_g} = \mu_p = \frac{V_g' + I_a R_1}{I_a R_2} = \frac{V_g'}{I_a R_2} + \frac{R_1}{R_2}$$

From 3,

$$V_g' = \frac{I_a Z_1}{\mu}$$

$$\therefore \quad \mu_p = \frac{Z_1}{\mu R_2} + \frac{R_1}{R_2}$$

$$\therefore \quad \mu \mu_p R_2 = Z_1 + \mu R_1 \qquad \qquad (5)$$

These conditions appear to be physically realisable. Taking μ_p as 1,000 and μ as 20 gives

$$Z_1 + 20 R_1 = 2 \times 10^4 R_2$$

Since $Z_1 = Z + R_a + R_1 + R_2$ this may be written quite accurately

$$Z + R_a + 20 R_1 = 2 \times 10^4 R_2.$$

$Z + R_a$ would probably be of the order of 6×10^4 ohms. Then

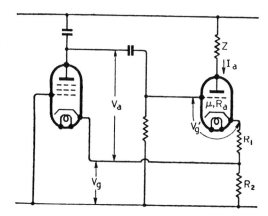

$$60,000 + 20 R_1 = 2 \times 10^4 R_2$$

$$\therefore \quad 3,000 + R_1 = 1,000 R_2$$

From this we conclude that if R_1, for example, is one thousand ohms, R_2 will be four ohms for the case under consideration. It is best, therefore, to split the cathode resistance of the triode between a resistor and a low value potential divider, the latter being at the earthy end of the circuit. It must be noted, however, that practical solutions of equation 5 may not be possible for all values of μ_p and Z_1.

IV | The Beginnings of Satellite Communications

7 | *The Space-Station: Its Radio Applications*

For more than twenty years, I was under the impression that the first reference to the geostationary communications satellite network was in my *Wireless World* article of October 1945. Great was my surprise when, in 1968, the engineering staff of the Sri Lanka Broadcasting Corporation discovered a letter I had published eight months earlier, in the February issue, and which I had completely forgotten.

Under the heading "V2 for Ionospheric Research?" I pointed out that the German long-range rocket falling on London at that very moment could be used "in an immediate post-war research project" to carry scientific instruments to the E, F1 and perhaps F2 layers. With the development of a second stage, orbital velocity could be reached, and it would be possible to have an instrumented payload:

> . . . circling the earth perpetually outside the limits of the atmosphere and broadcasting information as long as the batteries lasted. Since the rocket would be in brilliant sunlight for half the time, the operating period might be indefinitely prolonged by the use of thermocouples and photoelectric elements.

> Both of these developments demand nothing new in the way of technical resources; the first and probably the second should come within the next five or ten years. However, I would like to close by mentioning a possibility of the more remote future—perhaps half a century ahead.

> An "artificial satellite" at the correct distance from the earth would make one revolution every 24 hours; i.e., it would remain stationary above the same spot and would be within optical range of nearly half the earth's surface.

Three repeater stations, 120 degrees apart in the correct orbit, could give television and microwave coverage to the entire planet. I'm afraid this isn't going to be of the slightest use to our post-war planners, but I think it is the *ultimate* solution to the problem.

That "perhaps half a century ahead" (i.e., 1995) certainly makes me look a dyed-in-the-wool conservative. But please remember that when I wrote this letter, the war in Europe was still in progress, and after *that* no one could guess how long it would take to deal with Japan. And, of course, I was still thinking in terms of large, *manned* space stations; the transistor and its progeny still lay in the future.

Another person who was thinking on similar lines was the late George O. Smith, radio engineer and science-fiction writer, whose *Venus Equilateral* series started with "QRM—INTERPLANETARY" in the October 1942 *Astounding Science Fiction* and continued through thirteen stories in three years. They concerned a radio relay station at the Trojan position sixty degrees ahead of Venus, positioned there to maintain communications between Earth and Venus when the sun blocked the direct path between the two planets. As I wrote in my introduction to *The Complete Venus Equilateral* (Ballantine Books, 1976):

> Though there had been many tales about "space stations" long before the Venus Equilateral series (Murray Leinster's "Power Planet" is a classic example from the early thirties), George Smith was probably the first writer—certainly the first technically qualified writer—to spell out their uses for space communications. It is therefore quite possible that these stories influenced me subconsciously when, at Stratford-on-Avon during the closing months of the war, I worked out the principles of synchronous communications satellites now embodied in the global Intelsat system. Appropriately enough, the person who pointed this out to me is another long-time science fiction fan: Dr. John Pierce, instigator of the Bell Laboratories program that led to Echo and Telstar.*

At this point, a few more historical footnotes are in order. I have sometimes been credited with the discovery of the stationary orbit itself, which of course is ridiculous. No one could have "discovered" this, since its existence was perfectly obvious from the time of Newton (indeed, of Kepler!), I will be astonished if it has not often appeared in astronomical literature—perhaps when Asaph Hall discovered the satellites of

---

*See *The Beginnings of Satellite Communications* by J.R. Pierce, San Francisco Press, 1968. As I contributed the Preface, I have no hesitation in stealing John's title for this chapter.

Mars in 1877. The small outer moon Deimos is not far beyond the stationary orbit, and Phobos is well inside it.

The Russian pioneer Tsiolkovski took the concept for granted but did not develop it; radio, of course, was in its infancy when he was writing around the turn of the century. Not until 1928 did the somewhat shadowy and mysterious Austrian Captain H. Potočnik, writing under the name Hermann Noordung, develop the engineering aspects of the manned space-station in great detail—*and place it in the stationary orbit*. He naturally assumed that there would be radio links between Earth and station.

Though I was quite unaware of this in 1945 (never having seen his books at the time, still less dreaming that he would be my houseguest six years later), Hermann Oberth appears to have been the first person specifically associating space-stations and communication. In his first book, *The Rocket Into Planetary Space* (1923), he did so in a very interesting way:

> With their powerful instruments they would be able to see fine detail on earth and could communicate by means of mirrors reflecting sunlight. This might be useful for communication with places on the ground which have no cable connexions and cannot be reached by electric waves. Since they, provided the sky is clear, could see a candle flame at night and the reflection from a hand mirror by day, if they only knew where and when to look, they could maintain communications between expeditions and their homeland, far distant colonies and their motherland, ships at sea. . . . The strategic value is obvious especially in the case of war in areas of low population density. . . .

This quotation (translation by Willy Ley, from his *Rockets, Missiles and Men in Space*, Viking, 1968) is truly impressive, and also a reminder of the primitive state of radio at the beginning of the 1920s, before the enormous and unexpected potential of short waves had been discovered. Willy Ley once remarked to me: "Do you realise why Oberth never invented the radio relay satellite? Because when he was writing, the radio-telegraphy stations had long-wave antennas that covered square kilometres of ground." However, this hardly seems a good enough explanation, in view of the fact that even by 1923 Oberth had conceived of orbiting solar reflectors 100 kilometres across, to melt icebergs and alleviate winter in high latitudes!

On May 25, 1945 I composed a four-page memorandum setting out in concise form the whole concept of geostationary relay satellites, and carefully typed the four or five copies my Remington Noiseless Portable could manage. The top one I sent to businessman Ralph Slazenger (of the well-known sporting goods firm), who had joined us in our attempts to revive the British Inter-planetary Society. Luckily, he kept it carefully and many years later returned it to me in immaculate condition. It is now in the National Air and Space Museum, Washington, D.C.; for the 1979 World Advisory Radio Conference (WARC 79) in Geneva, INTELSAT reproduced several thousand copies, so perfectly that they cannot be distinguished from the original. As Exhibit A at the INTELSAT stand, I signed these for hours on end for visiting VIP's.

The Space-Station: Its Radio Applications

1. *The space station was originally conceived as a refueling depot for ships leaving the Earth. As such it may fill an important though transient role in the conquest of space, during the period when chemical fuels are employed. Other uses, some of them rather fantastic, have been suggested for the space station, notably by Hermann Noordung.[1] However, there is at least one purpose for which the station is ideally suited and indeed has no practical alternative. This is the provision of world-wide ultra-high-frequency radio services, including television.*

2. *In the following discussion the word "television" will be used exclusively but it must be understood to cover all services using the u.h.f. spectrum and higher. It is probable that television may be among the least important of these as technical developments occur. Other examples are frequency modulation, facsimile (capable of transmitting 100 000 pages an hour[2]), specialized scientific and business services, and navigational aids.*

3. *Owing to bandwidth considerations television is restricted to the frequency range above 50 Mc/sec and there is no doubt that very much higher frequencies will be used in the immediate future. The American Telephone and Telegraph Company are already building an experimental network using frequencies up to 12 000 megacycles.[3] Waves of such frequencies transmitted along quasi-optical paths and accordingly receiver and transmitter must lie not far from the line of sight. Although refraction increases the range, it is fair to say that the service radius for a television station is under 50 miles. (The range of the London service was rather less than this.) As long as radio continues to be used for communication, this limitation will remain, as it is a fundamental and not a technical restriction.*

4. *Wide-band frequency-modulation, one of the most important of radio developments, comes in the same category. FM can give much better quality and freedom from interference than normal amplitude-modulation, and many hundreds of stations are being planned for the post-war years in America alone. The technical requirements of FM make it essential that only the direct signal be used, and ionospheric reflexions cannot be employed. The range of the service is thus limited by the curvature of the Earth, precisely as for television.*

5. *To provide services over a large area it is necessary to build numerous stations on high ground or with radiators on towers several hundred feet high. These stations have to be linked by landline or subsidiary radio circuits. Such a system is practicable in a small country such as Britain, but even here the expense will be enormous. It is quite prohibitive in the case of a large continent and it therefore seems likely that only highly populated communities will be able to have television services.*

6. *An even more serious problem arises when an attempt is made to link television systems in different parts of the globe. Theoretical studies[2] indicate that using a radio relay system, repeater stations will be necessary at intervals of less than 50 miles. These will take the form of towers several hundred feet high, carrying receivers, amplifiers and transmitters. To link regions several thousand miles apart will thus cost many millions of pounds, and the problem of trans-oceanic services remains insoluble.*

7. *In the near future, the large airliners which will fly great circle routes over oceans and uninhabited regions of the world will require television and allied services and there is no known manner in which these can be provided.*

8. *All these problems can be solved by the use of a chain of space stations with an orbital period of 24 hours, which would require them to be at a distance of 42 000 km from the centre of the Earth (Fig. 1). There are a number of possible arrangements for such a chain but that shown is the simplest. The stations would lie in the Earth's equatorial plane and would thus always remain fixed in the same spots in the sky, from the point of view of terrestrial observers. Unlike all other heavenly bodies they would never rise nor set. This would greatly simplify the use of directive receivers installed on the Earth.*

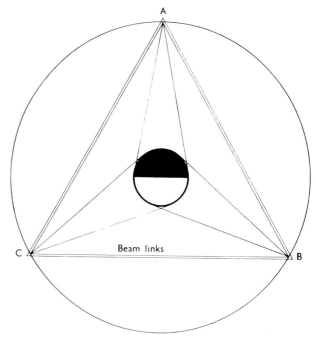

Fig. 1.

9. *The following longitudes are provisionally suggested for the stations to provide the best service to the inhabited portions of the globe, though all parts of the planet will be covered.*

> 30 E—Africa and Europe.
> 150 E—China and Oceana.
> 90 W—The Americas.

10. *Each station would broadcast programmes over about a third of the planet. Assuming the use of a frequency of 3000 megacycles, a reflector only a few feet across would give a beam so directive that almost all the power would be concentrated on the Earth. Arrays a metre or so in diameter could be used to illuminate single countries if a more restricted service was required.*

Six copies typed: privately circulated May 1945. Top copy now in National Air and Space Museum, Smithsonian Institution, Washington, D.C. [Reprinted in *Spaceflight*, Vol. 10, no. 3, March 1968, pp. 85–6]

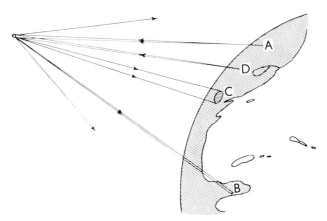

Fig. 2. Programme from A being relayed to point B and area C. Programme from D being relayed to whole hemisphere.

11. *The stations would be connected with each other by very-narrow-beam low-power links, probably working in the optical spectrum or near it, so that beams less than a degree wide could be produced.*

12. *The system would provide the following services which cannot be realized in any other manner:—*

   (a) *Simultaneous television broadcasts to the entire globe, including services to aircraft.*

   (b) *Relaying of programmes between distant parts of the planet.*

13. *In addition the stations would make redundant the network of relay towers covering the main areas of civilization and representing investments of hundreds of millions of pounds. (Work on the first of these networks has already started.)*

14. *Fig. 2 shows diagrammatically some of the specialized services that could be provided by the use of differing radiator systems.*

15. *The numerous technical problems involved in this communication system cannot be discussed here but it can be stated that none of them present any difficulties even at the present time, thanks to the development of hyperfrequency engineering. It is hoped to discuss them in a later paper when security conditions permit.*

16. *The receiving equipment at the Earth end would consist of small parabolas perhaps a foot in diameter with dipole pickup. These would be sufficiently directive to prevent interference in the three doubly-illuminated zones. They would be aimed towards the station with the least zenithal distance and once adjusted need never be touched again. Mobile equipment would require automatic following which presents slight mechanical complications (a few valves and a servo motor) but no technical difficulties.*

17. *The efficiency of the system would be nearly 100%, since almost all the power would fall on the service area. A preliminary investigation shows that the world broadcast would require about 10 kilowatts, while the beam relay services would require only fractions of a kilowatt. These powers are very small compared with present-day broadcasting stations, some of which radiate hundreds of kilowatts. All the power required for a large number of simultaneous services could be obtained from solar generators with mirrors about 10 metres in radius, assuming an efficiency of about 40%. In addition, the conditions of vacuum make it easy to use large and fully demountable valves.*

18. *No communication development which can be imagined will render the chain of stations obsolete and since it fills what will eventually be an urgent need, its economic value will be enormous.*

19. *For completeness, other major uses of the station are listed below:—*

(a) Research—*Astrophysical, Physical, Electronic.*

These applications are obvious. The space-station would be justified on these grounds alone, as there are many experiments which can only be conducted above the atmosphere.

(b) Meteorological.

The station would be absolutely invaluable for weather forecasting as the movement of fronts, etc., would be visible from space.

(c) Traffic.

This is looking a good deal further ahead, but ultimately the chain will be used extensively for controlling and checking, possibly by radar, the movement of ships approaching or leaving the Earth. It will also play an extremely important role as the first link in the solar communication system.

REFERENCES

1. Noordung, Hermann, "Das Problem der Befahrung des Weltraums."
2. Hansell, C. W., "Radio-Relay-Systems Development." (*Proceedings of the Institute of Radio Engineers*, March 1945, pp. 156–168.)
3. Guy, Raymond F., Address to I.R.E., Philadelphia, 7 December 1944.

8 | *Extra-Terrestrial Relays*

The *Wireless World* paper was written in late June and submitted to the RAF censor on July 7; he took less than a month to approve it—a suspiciously short period of time, I have often thought. It was sent to *Wireless World* on August 13, and accepted on September 1 for publication in the October issue. I had originally given it the forthright and uncompromising title "The Future of World Communications," but the editor changed it to the more informative "Extra-Terrestrial Relays." He would have been surprised to know that, thirty-seven years in the future, most of the human race would be familiar with the abbreviation *E.T.*

And I've just autographed a copy for Steven Spielberg, to await his arrival here to film the sequel to *Raiders of the Lost Ark*.

EXTRA-TERRESTRIAL RELAYS
Can Rocket Stations Give World-wide Radio Coverage?

ALTHOUGH it is possible, by a suitable choice of frequencies and routes, to provide telephony circuits between any two points or regions of the earth for a large part of the time, long-distance communication is greatly hampered by the peculiarities of the ionosphere, and there are even occasions when it may be impossible. A true broadcast service, giving constant field strength at all times over the whole globe would be invaluable, not to say indispensable, in a world society.

Unsatisfactory though the telephony and telegraph position is, that of television is far worse, since ionospheric transmission cannot be employed at all. The service area of a television station, even on a very good site, is only about a hundred miles across. To cover a small country such as Great Britain would require a network of transmitters, connected by coaxial lines, waveguides or VHF relay links. A recent theoretical study[1] has shown that such a system would require repeaters at intervals of fifty miles or less. A system of this kind could provide television coverage, at a very considerable cost, over the whole of a small country. It would be out of the question to provide a large continent with such a service, and only the main centres of population could be included in the network.

The problem is equally serious when an attempt is made to link television services in different parts of the globe. A relay chain several thousand miles long would cost millions, and transoceanic services would still be impossible. Similar considerations apply to the provision of wide-band frequency modulation and other services, such as high-speed facsimile which are by their nature restricted to the ultra-high-frequencies.

Many may consider the solution proposed in this discussion too far-fetched to be taken very seriously. Such an attitude is unreasonable, as everything envisaged here is a logical extension of developments in the last ten years—in particular the perfection of the long-range rocket of which V2 was the prototype. While this article was being written, it was announced that the Germans were considering a similar project, which they believed possible within fifty to a hundred years.

Before proceeding further, it is necessary to discuss briefly certain fundamental laws of rocket propulsion and "astronautics." A rocket which achieved a sufficiently great speed in flight outside the earth's atmosphere would never return. This "orbital" velocity is 8 km per sec. (5 miles per sec), and a rocket which attained it would become an artificial satellite, circling the world for ever with no expenditure of power—a second moon, in fact. The German transatlantic rocket A10 would have reached more than half this velocity.

It will be possible in a few more years to build radio controlled rockets which can be steered into such orbits beyond the limits of the atmosphere and left to broad-cast scientific information back to the earth. A little later, manned rockets will be able to make similar flights with sufficient excess power to break the orbit and return to earth.

There are an infinite number of possible stable orbits, circular and elliptical, in which a rocket would remain if the initial conditions were correct. The velocity of 8 km/sec. applies only to the closest possible orbit, one just outside the atmosphere, and the period of revolution would be about 90 minutes. As the radius of the orbit increases the velocity decreases, since gravity is diminishing and less centrifugal force is needed to balance it. Fig. 1 shows this graphically. The moon, of course, is a particular case and would lie on the curves of Fig. 1 if they were produced. The proposed German space-stations would have a period of about four and a half hours.

It will be observed that one orbit, with a radius of 42,000 km, has a period of exactly 24 hours. A body in such an orbit, if its plane coincided with that of the

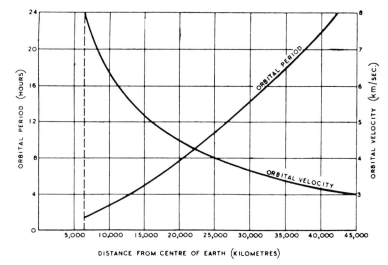

Fig. 1. **Variation of orbital period and velocity with distance from the centre of the earth.**

[Published in *Wireless World*, October 1945, pp. 305–8]

earth's equator, would revolve with the earth and would thus be stationary above the same spot on the planet. It would remain fixed in the sky of a whole hemisphere and unlike all other heavenly bodies would neither rise nor set. A body in a smaller orbit would revolve more quickly than the earth and so would rise in the west, as indeed happens with the inner moon of Mars.

Using material ferried up by rockets, it would be possible to construct a "space-station" in such an orbit. The station could be provided with living quarters, laboratories and everything needed for the comfort of its crew, who would be relieved and provisioned by a regular rocket service. This project might be undertaken for purely scientific reasons as it would contribute enormously to our knowledge of astronomy, physics and meteorology. A good deal of literature has already been written on the subject.[2]

Although such an undertaking may seem fantastic, it requires

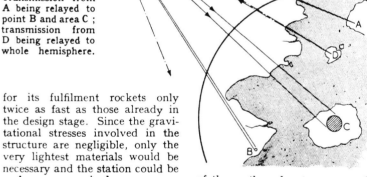

Fig. 2. Typical extra-terrestrial relay services. Transmission from A being relayed to point B and area C; transmission from D being relayed to whole hemisphere.

for its fulfilment rockets only twice as fast as those already in the design stage. Since the gravitational stresses involved in the structure are negligible, only the very lightest materials would be necessary and the station could be as large as required.

Let us now suppose that such a station were built in this orbit. It could be provided with receiving and transmitting equipment (the problem of power will be discussed later) and could act as a repeater to relay transmissions between any two points on the hemisphere beneath, using any frequency which will penetrate the ionosphere. If directive arrays were used, the power require-

ments would be very small, as direct line of sight transmission would be used. There is the further important point that arrays on the earth, once set up, could remain fixed indefinitely.

Moreover, a transmission received from any point on the hemisphere could be broadcast to the whole of the visible face of

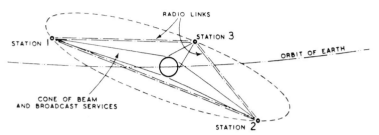

Fig. 3. Three satellite stations would ensure complete coverage of the globe.

the globe, and thus the requirements of all possible services would be met (Fig. 2).

It may be argued that we have as yet no direct evidence of radio waves passing between the surface of the earth and outer space; all we can say with certainty is that the shorter wavelengths are not reflected back to the earth. Direct evidence of field strength above the earth's atmosphere could be obtained by V2 rocket technique, and it is to be hoped that someone will do something about this soon as there must be quite a surplus stock somewhere! Alternatively, given sufficient transmitting power, we might obtain the

necessary evidence by exploring for echoes from the moon. In the meantime we have visual evidence that frequencies at the optical end of the spectrum pass through with little absorption except at certain frequencies at which resonance effects occur. Medium high frequencies go through the E layer twice to be reflected from the F layer and echoes have been received from meteors in or above the F layer. It seems fairly certain that frequencies from, say, 50 Mc/s to 100,000 Mc/s could be used without undue absorption in the atmosphere or the ionosphere.

A single station could only provide coverage to half the globe, and for a world service three would be required, though more could be readily utilised. Fig. 3 shows the simplest arrangement. The stations would be arranged approximately equidistantly around the earth, and the following longitudes appear to be suitable:—

30 E—Africa and Europe.
150 E—China and Oceana.
90 W—The Americas.

The stations in the chain would be linked by radio or optical beams, and thus any conceivable beam or broadcast service could be provided.

The technical problems involved in the design of such stations are extremely interesting,[3] but only a few can be gone into here. Batteries of parabolic reflectors would be provided, of apertures depending on the frequencies employed. Assuming the use of 3,000 Mc/s waves, mirrors about a metre across would beam almost all the power on to the earth. Larger reflectors could be used to illuminate single countries or regions for the more restricted services, with consequent economy of power. On the higher frequencies it is not difficult to produce beams less than a degree in width, and, as mentioned before, there would be no physical limitations on the size of the mirrors. (From the space station, the disc of the earth would be a little over 17 degrees across). The same mirrors could be used for many different transmissions if precautions were taken to avoid cross modulation.

It is clear from the nature of the system that the power needed will be much less than that required for any other arrangement, since all the energy radiated can be uniformly distributed over the service area, and none is wasted. An approximate estimate of the power required for the broadcast service from a single station can be made as follows:—

The field strength in the equatorial plane of a $\lambda/2$ dipole in free space at a distance of d metres is

$$e = 6.85\,\frac{\sqrt{P}}{d}\ \text{volts}\,/\,\text{metre, where}$$

P is the power radiated in watts.

Taking d as 42,000 km (effectively it would be less), we have $P = 37.6\,e^2$ watts. (e now in μV/metre.)

If we assume e to be 50 microvolts/metre, which is the F.C.C. standard for frequency modulation, P will be 94 kW. This is the power required for a single dipole, and not an array which would concentrate all the power on the earth. Such an array would have a gain over a simple dipole of about 80. The power required for the broadcast service would thus be about 1.2 kW.

Ridiculously small though it is, this figure is probably much too generous. Small parabolas about a foot in diameter would be used for receiving at the earth end and would give a very good signal/noise ratio. There would be very little interference, partly because of the frequency used and partly because the mirrors would be pointing towards the sky which could contain no other source of signal. A field strength of 10 microvolts/metre might well be ample, and this would require a transmitter output of only 50 watts.

When it is remembered that these figures relate to the broadcast service, the efficiency of the system will be realised. The point-to-point beam transmissions might need powers of only 10 watts or so. These figures, of course, would need correction for ionospheric and atmospheric absorption, but that would be quite small over most of the band. The slight falling off in field strength due to this cause towards the edge of the service area could be readily corrected by a non-uniform radiator.

The efficiency of the system is strikingly revealed when we consider that the London Television service required about 3 kW average power for an area less than fifty miles in radius.[5]

A second fundamental problem is the provision of electrical energy to run the large number of transmitters required for the different services. In space beyond the atmosphere, a square metre normal to the solar radiation intercepts 1.35 kW of energy.[6] Solar engines have already been devised for terrestrial use and are an economic proposition in tropical countries. They employ mirrors to concentrate sunlight on the boiler of a low-pressure steam engine. Although this arrangement is not very efficient it could be made much more so in space where the operating components are in a vacuum, the radiation is intense and continuous, and the low-temperature end of the cycle could be not far from absolute zero. Thermo-electric and photo-electric developments may make it possible to utilise the solar energy more directly.

Though there is no limit to the size of the mirrors that could be built, one fifty metres in radius would intercept over 10,000 kW and at least a quarter of this energy should be available for use.

The station would be in continuous sunlight except for some weeks around the equinoxes, when it would enter the earth's shadow for a few minutes every day. Fig. 4 shows the state of affairs during the eclipse period. For

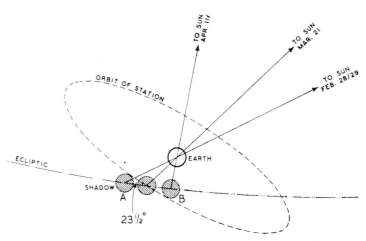

Fig. 4.   Solar radiation would be cut off for a short period each day at the equinoxes.

this calculation, it is legitimate to consider the earth as fixed and the sun as moving round it. The station would graze the earth's shadow at A, on the last day in February. Every day, as it made its diurnal revolution, it would cut more deeply into the shadow, undergoing its period of maximum eclipse on March 21st. on that day it would only be in darkness for 1 hour 9 minutes. From then onwards the period of eclipse would shorten, and after April 11th (B) the station would be in continuous sunlight again until the same thing happened six months later at the autumn equinox, between September 12th and October 14th. The total period of darkness would be about two days per year, and as the longest period of eclipse would be little more than an hour there should be no difficulty in storing enough power for an uninterrupted service.

Conclusion

Briefly summarised, the advantages of the space station are as follows :—

(1) It is the only way in which true world coverage can be achieved for all possible types of service.

(2) It permits unrestricted use of a band at least 100,000 Mc/s wide, and with the use of beams an almost unlimited number of channels would be available.

(3) The power requirements are extremely small since the efficiency of "illumination" will be almost 100 per cent. Moreover, the cost of the power would be very low.

(4) However great the initial expense, it would only be a fraction of that required for the world networks replaced, and the running costs would be incomparably less.

Appendix—*Rocket Design*

The development of rockets sufficiently powerful to reach "orbital" and even "escape" velocity is now only a matter of years. The following figures may be of interest in this connection.

The rocket has to acquire a final velocity of 8 km/sec. Allowing 2 km/sec. for navigational corrections and air resistance loss (this is legitimate as all space-rockets will be launched from very high country) gives a total velocity needed of 10 km/sec. The fundamental equation of rocket motion is [2]

$$V = v \, log_e R$$

where V is the final velocity of the rocket, v the exhaust velocity and R the ratio of initial mass to final mass (payload plus structure). So far v has been about 2-2.5 km/sec for liquid fuel rockets but new designs and fuels will permit of considerably higher figures. (Oxyhydrogen fuel has a theoretical exhaust velocity of 5.2 km/sec and more powerful combinations are known.) If we assume v to be 3.3 km/sec, R will be 20 to 1. However, owing to its finite acceleration, the rocket loses velocity as a result of gravitational retardation. If its acceleration (assumed constant) is a metres/sec.[2], then the necessary ratio R_g is increased to

$$R_g = R \, \frac{a + g}{a}$$

For an automatically controlled rocket a would be about $5g$ and so the necessary R would be 37 to 1. Such ratios cannot be realised with a single rocket but can be attained by "step-rockets"[2], while very much higher ratios (up to 1,000 to 1) can be achieved by the principle of "cellular construction"[3].

Epilogue—Atomic Power

The advent of atomic power has at one bound brought space travel half a century nearer. It seems unlikely that we will have to wait as much as twenty years before atomic-powered rockets are developed, and such rockets could reach even the remoter planets with a fantastically small fuel/mass ratio —only a few per cent. The equations developed in the appendix still hold, but v will be increased by a factor of about a thousand.

In view of these facts, it appears hardly worth while to expend much effort on the building of long-distance relay chains. Even the local networks which will soon be under construction may have a working life of only 20-30 years.

References

[1] "Radio-Relay Systems," C. W. Hansell. *Proc. I.R.E.*, Vol 33, March, 1945.
[2] "Rockets," Willy Ley. (Viking Press, N.Y.)
[3] "Das Problem der Befahrung des Weltraums," Hermann Noordung.
[4] "Frequency Modulation," A. Hund. (McGraw Hill.)
[5] "London Television Service," MacNamara and Birkinshaw. *J.I.E.E.*, Dec., 1938.
[5] "The Sun," C. G. Abbot. (Appleton-Century Co.)
[7] *Journal of the British Interplanetary Society*, Jan., 1939.

I do not recall *any* reaction, positive or negative, to this article; certainly there was no serious adverse criticism because by this time the release of atomic energy had convinced most people that science could do virtually anything. Later I was to learn that it had had a considerable influence in all sorts of places. Thus, Robert P. Haviland of the General Electric Company wrote (*Journal of the Astronautical Sciences*, January–February 1968, Vol. XV no. 1, p. 35):

> In 1944, while on duty in the Navy Department, I did a study on the future of rockets, which led to a study of space flight. But the main question was, "Why bother?" About this time a paper by a young RAF officer by the name of Clarke appeared in the British journal, *Wireless World*, which gave an answer important to the Navy—improved communications. As a result, a formal program was established. This program did not go far, but it had surprising results; I believe it was a major factor in the acceptance, in just ten years, of the need for an artificial earth satellite.

The United States Navy's interest, I later discovered, was responsible for the first presentation of the concept to the general public. Someone at the lab passed my article on to William S. Barton, the science reporter of the *Los Angeles Times*, and he wrote it up in the issue for February 3, 1946. Knowing nothing whatsoever about me, he was forced to guess, and headlining me as "Scientist who fought V2 rockets," he scored two complete misses. But the rest of the article, illustrated by a somewhat imaginative space-station, was reasonably accurate, and Barton made the point that "local scientists, far from laughing at the proposal, consider it actually possible of future realization."

Sputnik was still almost twelve years ahead. TELSTAR five years after that—and Early Bird, the first commercial geostationary communications satellite, was launched just twenty years after the publication of my paper.

I have often been asked—usually pityingly—why I made no attempt to patent the communications satellite. Perhaps the most truthful answer is that I never really expected to see it in my lifetime; I also (though in more cynical moments I am sceptical about this) seem to recall thinking that it was an idea for all humanity, so I should publish to prevent anyone else from taking out a patent. As indeed I did. . . .

That was clearly underlined for me in 1961 when my friend, the science-fiction writer Theodore L. Thomas, using his pen name Leonard Lockhard, published the slightly nonfact article "The Lagging Profession" in *Analog* Magazine (Vol. LXVI, no. 5, January 1961). Here he described a meeting with "Helix Spardleton, Esquire, patent attorney extraordinary" and myself, at which I learned (1) even if I had tried to patent communications satellites in 1945, the patent would have been rejected because the required technology did not yet exist, and (2) the patent wouldn't have been worth getting because its life would only have been seventeen years. I quote Helix Spardleton's exact words: "There is one consolation. Even if you had patented your communications system back in—oh, say 1947—the patent would expire in 1964. That's only four years from now, so you probably would not have made any money on the patent anyway."

How right he was; on that scenario, the patent would have expired the year before Early Bird was launched.

Yet, as things have turned out, I can honestly say that I don't give a damn. (Though I suppose that if I had not done well in other fields, by this time I might have been a typical embittered inventor, waving protest banners outside COMSAT headquarters.) Someone once described a patent as "a license to be sued"; and I know few worse ways of spending one's time than in lawyer's offices. I have been quite content to leave the responsibility to the Pierces and the Rosens, while I have had the fun.

And rather more of the credit, I suspect, than I really deserve.

For earlier versions of this account, which may differ in minor details, see the essay "A Short Pre-History of Comsats, Or, How I lost a Billion Dollars in My Spare Time" (in the book *Voices From the Sky*, 1966) and the speech "Voices From the Sky" in *Spaceflight*, Vol. 10 no. 3, March 1968, pp. 78–84.

V | Rockets and Warfare

9 | *The Rocket and the Future of Warfare*

My contact with real scientists and the most modern technology while working on GCA made me determined not to go back to auditing government accounts. Though I was not sure what I would do for a living in the postwar world, I had proved that I could make a modest income from writing; and if all else failed, I could always go back to the farm. . . .

So it needed little persuasion from my two closest friends, A.V. ("Val") Cleaver—later head of the Rolls-Royce Rocket Division—and Flight-Sergeant Johnnie Maxwell, RCAF, to talk me into resigning from civil service and going to college so that I could get a proper scientific education. There were grants available for this purpose (the British equivalent of the U.S. "G.I. Bill"), and I promptly applied for one. I was swiftly rejected, on very reasonable grounds. These grants were to help students whose education had been interrupted by the war—and definitely not for the benefit of already established civil servants who merely felt like a change of career.

I do not recall being unduly depressed by this verdict, which was quickly overtaken by other events. In the summer of 1945—while I was still in uniform—I received a letter from RAF Corporal Eric Burgess containing some interesting news.

As a schoolboy space enthusiast in the thirties, Eric had received nationwide publicity by launching small powder rockets in defiance of the 1875 Explosives Act—legislation designed to promote industrial safety by regulating the manufacture of fireworks. Hauled into court, Eric had made a great impression on the magistrate by his eloquent defence of astronautical research, and was discharged with a caution.

As might be expected from this debut, his subsequent career has been rather interesting. He has written numerous books and countless articles on astronomy and astronautics, and was for a while science writer on the staff of the prestigious *Christian Science Monitor*. In addition, he has coauthored several NASA publications, such as *Pioneer: First to Jupiter, Saturn and Beyond* (NASA SP-446) as well as *Flight to Mercury* (written with JPL Director Bruce Murray). Quite recently, he published *Celestial Basic*, a book and two diskettes of computer programmes giving a whole variety of astronomical events for thousands of years, past and future. I have run them on my APPLE II, and am overawed by the work and skill that must have gone into them. (I have never been able to write more than five lines of BASIC without disaster.) His latest book (1982), *By Jupiter: Odyssey to a Giant* can serve as a very useful nonfiction companion to *my* latest 'last' book. . . .

But back in 1945 Eric was still in the RAF, and, with half a dozen other space enthusiasts, we were in constant correspondence over plans to revive the astronautical movement. (These eventually succeeded, in the revival of the British Interplanetary Society.) During the course of this, he foolishly told me; "Do you know that the *Royal Air Force Quarterly* is offering a prize for the best essay on 'The Rocket and the Future of Warfare'?"

He should have kept his mouth shut. If he'd done so, *he* would have won first prize (forty pounds)—instead of second (fifteen pounds). . . .

My contribution was written in November 1945 and appeared in the March 1946 issue of the *Quarterly*. Almost four decades later, I had occasion to refer to it again, when addressing the United Nations Disarmament Committee in Geneva as Sri Lankan delegate (August 3l, 1982).* Much of it, alas, has turned out to be all too accurate.

---

*See "War and Peace in the Space Age," reprinted in *1984: Spring*.

The Rocket and the Future of Warfare

Cease ! Drain not to its dregs the urn
  Of bitter prophecy.
The world is weary of the past,
Oh, might it die or rest at last !
                          —SHELLEY.

I.—INTRODUCTION

In the following essay an attempt has been made to trace to its logical conclusion the development of rockets and guided weapons. So many possibilities are opened up by these new techniques that the discussion has necessarily been restricted to very general terms. Such a treatment is indeed inevitable in an age when at any moment some new discovery may cause a complete technical revolution.

Inevitably the atomic bomb has loomed large in the discussion. The world has recognized instinctively the bond between the two subjects, and any portrayal of the future that was not dominated by the fact of atomic energy could well be likened to " Hamlet " without the Prince.

The rocket is now making its third and probably final appearance on the field of warfare. After its original employment by the Chinese in the thirteenth century it was used sporadically by various Western countries for over five hundred years without attaining any great importance. At the end of the eighteenth century it reappeared, somewhat surprisingly, in India, where Tippoo Sahib employed it against the British with considerable effect. Inspired—or provoked—by this example, Sir William Congreve developed the war rocket in this country until it became a serious rival to the smooth-bore guns of the day, and for a while every army in Europe had a corps of rocket artillery.

With the development of rifled artillery the rocket was soon completely eclipsed and for nearly a hundred years it was used only for signalling, life-saving and a few other specialized applications. It played very little part in the 1914 war and its spectacular return in the early 1940's has been due to the mastery of new engineering techniques and a greater appreciation of its potentialities. Even ten years ago few believed that the rocket would ever again play any major part in warfare, yet to-day it is challenging both artillery and aircraft and promises to be a decisive weapon in any future war.

The rocket has so many applications that their classification is a matter of some difficulty, but the scheme adopted in Table I will be used throughout this essay. Under two of the main headings a sub-division is made into " Piloted " and " Guided " rockets, and at this point it may be as well to consider the position of pilotless aircraft generally.

The only P.A.Cs. used in this war have been flying bombs of various kinds, culminating in the famous V1. It seems likely that such machines will be used for (*a*) delivering explosives at a distant spot; (*b*) reconnaissance; and (*c*) destruction of enemy aircraft by collision or the launching of short-range projectiles. At the end of the war the Germans had in use or advanced development rockets carrying out all these functions, and any P.A.Cs. produced in the future would almost certainly be jet- or rocket-propelled. Thus the distinction between pilotless aircraft and rockets is likely to disappear, and accordingly no separate analysis will be made, although the subject of pilotless fighters will be touched upon in Section VII.

II.—FUNDAMENTALS OF ROCKET PROPULSION

The two dominant characteristics of the rocket are its enormous rate of power generation (a thousand or more times as great as that of a conventional engine of similar size) and its independence of any external medium for fuel, support or thrust. The first property enables it to achieve very high speeds and accelerations; the second permits it to travel in the rarefied air of the upper atmosphere, or in no air at all. Also as a result of the second property the rocket has no recoil and this gives it an important and in some cases overwhelming advantage over ordinary artillery.

The performance of a rocket depends upon certain technical considerations which will now be briefly outlined. The most important of these is the jet velocity, which in turn depends upon the type of fuel used and the efficiency of the motor. For the most powerful chemical fuels this velocity has a theoretical maximum of about 12,000 miles an hour. V2, which represents an early stage in rocket development (comparable, according to its designer, with that of the aeroplane at the close of the last war) had a jet velocity of 4,700 miles an hour.

Given a rocket motor with a certain performance, there are two ways in which it can be used. It may be employed to drive a projectile or aircraft at a certain velocity which is then maintained

[Published in the *Royal Air Force Quarterly*, March 1946, pp. 61–9]

as long as the fuel supply lasts—usually a matter of seconds or at most a very few minutes. Air resistance prevents the machine from reaching more than a fraction of its theoretical speed, and the flight or trajectory ends soon after the failure of the fuel supply. Consequently this is a short-range, low-altitude application of the rocket in which the maximum speeds attained are usually less than the velocity of sound.

The second case is fundamentally different and so far has had only one representative, the long-range rocket A4 (V2). Here the motor is used to impart the greatest possible velocity to a machine which for most of its journey is travelling as a free projectile, at such a height that air resistance is almost negligible. In this case alone is the rocket being used efficiently: the " atmospheric " applications are all extremely wasteful of fuel and are only justified by high performances which can be obtained in no other way. A good example of

this is the Me.163. In vacuum, where its motor could still operate, though of course the control surfaces would be useless, this machine would attain a speed of 2,700 miles an hour when it had burnt all its fuel. In actual practice, once it has reached about 600 miles an hour all the remaining fuel is used to overcome drag.

When air resistance is neglected, it is not difficult to design a rocket travelling at up to twice the velocity of its exhaust—in other words, at about 10,000 miles an hour in the case of present fuels and motors. Greater speeds can in theory be obained by increasing the fuel load, but there is obviously a limit to the amount of fuel a rocket of a given size can carry, even if the whole of the payload is sacrificed. A rocket capable of travelling at three times the velocity of its jet would have to consist of 95 per cent. fuel by weight— hardly a practical proposition, to say the least.

These figures, however, give only part of the

TABLE I

CLASS	PROTOTYPE	ULTIMATE DEVELOPMENT
A. SHORT RANGE.		
(1) Artillery	Katushka, etc.	Little change if still required.
(2) Anti-tank	Bazooka, etc.	
(3) Airborne Rockets ...	R/Ps.	Radar-controlled launching turrets. Proximity fuzing.
(4) Anti-aircraft	Z-guns	None; superseded by B.2.
(5) Rocket Boosters ...	JATOs.	Little change.
B. MEDIUM RANGE.		
PILOTED		
(1) Interceptor Fighter ...	Me. 163, Natter	Eventually superseded by B.2.
GUIDED		
(2) Anti-aircraft	Wasserfall, Rheintochter, X.4, etc.	Radar-controlled homing rockets capable of very high accelerations, fitted with anti-jammers, proximity fuzes, I.F.F. Designed to attack bombers and long-range rockets. Ground or air launched.
C. LONG RANGE.		
GUIDED		
(1) Rocket Bomb	A.4. A.9.+A.10. (Two-step transatlantic rocket)	(1) Step-rocket of world range with chemical fuels. Speeds up to circular velocity (5 m.p.s.) Atomic warhead. (2) Atomically-driven rocket travelling on powered trajectories at speeds up to 1 per cent. of velocity of light.
PILOTED		
(2) Reconnaissance ...	DFS. 228	Television-carrying winged projectile. Later super-seded by guided version.
(3) Bomber	—	Winged rocketship with speeds up to circular velocity. Used for launching rocket bombs.
D. INFINITE RANGE.		
Interplanetary Rocket ...	—	" Spaceship." Evolved from C.3.

story, for in addition to the loss due to air resistance a rocket has to expend fuel to support itself against gravity. This fuel could otherwise have been used to increase the machine's final velocity, and when these two losses are taken into account the A4 rocket has a " velocity budget " something like that below :

			m.p.h.
Air resistance loss	...	...	1,000
Gravitational loss	...	...	1,100
Actual velocity	...	...	3,400
Theoretical velocity	...		5,500

Very long-range rockets would derive considerable advantage from mountain-top launches, since the air density is approximately halved at an altitude of four miles. The gain would be two-fold, for not only would air resistance be lessened but higher accelerations would be possible with a consequent reduction of gravitational loss. This point has strategic implications which will be mentioned later.

The range achieved by a rocket depends on its velocity when the fuel is burnt, for after that point it behaves as a normal projectile. A rocket which attained a speed of five miles a second (18,000 miles an hour) would have infinite range, since it would never return to the earth : such high speeds are, however, unnecessary, for, as Perring has pointed out,[1] the range of a rocket can be greatly increased by the use of wings which come into play at the end of the free trajectory and enable the machine to enter a high-speed glide. The German A9 rocket had an 800-mile trajectory, after which it entered its glide at 8,000 miles an hour and so achieved a total range of 3,000 miles. Speeds of about four miles a second (14,000 miles an hour) would suffice for the greatest possible terrestrial ranges, and such speeds can be attained by " step-rockets " launched if necessary from high altitudes.

Having sketched in the technical background, we can now consider in detail the various applications of the rocket to warfare, in the order laid down in Table I.

III.—Short-range Rockets

Rockets of this class have played a considerable part in the late war, particularly when used by aircraft for ship or ground attack. They have the great advantage of producing no recoil and so requiring only very light launching equipment. It is thus possible to concentrate very large numbers of projectors in a single place and so lay down short-range barrages of an intensity impossible by other means. Batteries of this type (" Katushka ") were used by the Russians at Stalingrad and mobile installations were employed later in the war for saturation bombardment preceding attacks or landings. For this application the short range and inaccuracy of the weapon do not matter, and if barrages are ever again used in warfare they are more likely to be provided by rockets than by other forms of artillery.

The rocket's absence of recoil has made it possible to design weapons of great fire power which can be operated by a very small crew or even by a single man. The " bazooka " anti-tank gun is the best example of this and may well mark the beginning of the end of tank warfare. A few infantrymen can now destroy the largest tank and it must be remembered that whereas the bazooka is only at the beginning of its development the amount of armour a tank can carry appears to be nearing its limit.

The rocket mine would seem to be a particularly effective anti-tank weapon, now made possible by the invention of " zero length " launchers. It would consist of a short launching rack buried vertically in the ground and, although it would not be as easy to install as a normal mine, it would be a great deal more effective against armoured vehicles.

The airborne rocket has already had a revolutionary effect on aircraft fire power and the process will continue. The largest gun (75-mm.) so far installed in an aircraft weighed 760 lb. and fired a 15-lb. shell containing only 1.5 lb. of explosive. These 760 lb. could have been replaced by twelve 60-lb. rockets of far greater destructive power, and when they had been discharged the aircraft's performance would not have been reduced by the dead weight of the gun. It has been stated that the fire power of a rocket-carrying Mosquito equals that of a 6-inch gun cruiser, and there is no limit to the size of projectile that can be launched from an aircraft, so long as it can be lifted off the ground. Aircraft fitted with such weapons could prevent all movement of armoured vehicles except those supported by air cover.

The development of air-to-air rockets appears to have lagged, although the Germans used them fairly effectively against American bomber formations. These weapons will come into prominence as engagements are opened at greater ranges and a possible line of development is the heavily armed " destroyer " fitted with rocket-launching turrets. The rockets would be aimed by radar and detonated by proximity fuses when they approached their targets. The larger projectiles might even be guided, either from the launching plane or from the ground.

Such " flying destroyers," if indeed they ever appear, are likely to represent a transitional stage in warfare and will be rapidly superseded by the weapons discussed in the next section.

Before leaving the subject of short-range rockets mention should be made of assisted take-off units (" Jato's "), which have been extensively used during the war. These units permit a considerable increase in take-off weight and hence performance, and they can also be used to reduce the length of runway an aircraft needs to become airborne. Both these applications are of great practical importance and rocket-assisted take-off may become standard practice for large aircraft.

IV.—Medium-range Rockets

We now come to a class of machine which was beginning to appear at the end of the war and promises to revolutionize air fighting as we know it to-day. This is the medium-range rocket interceptor, of which both piloted and guided versions were under intensive development by the Germans at the end of hostilities in Europe.

The piloted machines will be considered first: one, the Me.163, actually became operational, and a second, the " Natter," was undergoing flight tests when the war ended. Both were manned rockets of very short endurance (about five minutes under full power), but with phenomenal rates of climb. The Me.163 could reach 40,000 feet in three minutes, while the Natter could do so in little over a minute.

There is no doubt that such machines will be developed intensively in the future and they may be expected completely to supersede the conventional interceptor fighter. Their high rate of climb would enable them to remain on the ground until the attacking bombers were only a few miles away. They would then go almost vertically into action, break off the engagement and return to earth.

Such machines, themselves launching rocket projectiles into the bomber streams, present a very considerable problem to the attacker. They could be countered only by heavy barrages from " destroyers " of the type envisaged in the preceding section, or by the use of such enormous speeds that interception was impossible. This in turn means the superseding of the bomber by the long-range rocket, and at this stage the human pilot begins to disappear from the picture.

The human body can withstand only limited accelerations, can respond to only a few stimuli at a time, and has comparatively slow reactions. The speed of attack is steadily increasing and the 3,400 miles an hour of A4 is merely the beginning. Against such speeds men can never hope to fight. Skill and courage and resolution—in the end all are of no avail, for there comes at last a time when only machines can fight machines.

At the close of the war the Germans were working desperately on a large number of guided rockets, such as " Wasserfall," " Schmetterling " and " Rheintochter." Some of these had been tested and claims of one contact in four had been made with experimental models. These missiles were to be controlled from the ground by radio and directed into the bomber streams, where they would home on their targets by radar or infra-red detectors. They would be capable of very high speeds—up to the velocity of sound—and when they are perfected it is difficult to see how the conventional bomber can hope to ward off such attacks. No doubt elaborate counter-measures would be tried, such as those employed in the radar war, but it is impossible to jam the whole radio spectrum. Automatically homing rockets might be deceived for a while, but there would be no effective defence against a ground-controlled projectile carrying A.I. and television and homing on the hundreds of kilowatts of heat thrown out by the bombers' engines. Such machines have already been developed and do not represent any great advance on existing technique.

These weapons mark the end of the man-carrying fighter—but not necessarily the end of the fighter pilot, who represents a complex of skills difficult to replace by machinery. There have already been several examples of missions largely controlled from the ground (*e.g.,* oboe bombing, radar-controlled fighter sweeps) and the remotely controlled fighter, operated by a pilot many miles away, is a logical development to which we will return later.

Guided missiles are peculiarly adapted to naval operations, and for defensive purposes may well replace fighter aircraft at an early date. Large and vulnerable carriers will no longer be required purely to provide fighter cover, and the necessity of getting all aircraft safely down after an action will disappear, thus giving the fleet much greater freedom of action. Guided rockets could also to a large extent replace heavy guns for long-range engagements, with a consequent saving of weight of many thousands of tons in the case of a capital ship.

The guided rocket appears to be the only conceivable defence against the long-range rocket bomb, and this possibility will be discussed in Section V.

V.—Long-range Rockets

We saw in Section II that by increasing its speed sufficiently a rocket can be given even antipodal ranges, although at the expense of very small payloads. So far, the only long-range rocket has been A4, which had a maximum speed of

3,400 miles an hour and a range of 220 miles. The Germans had planned to increase that range to 3,000 miles by giving A4 wings and launching it from a much larger " booster " rocket (A10) which would have weighed about 85 tons. This " step-rocket " principle is very important and is one way of circumventing the velocity-payload law.

There is at present no defence against such projectiles once they have been fired, and their launching sites are much less vulnerable than airfields to enemy attack. Although no detailed analyses of costs have yet been made, it appears that with conventional explosives rockets may be more economical than bombers for short ranges (say up to 400 miles). Cleaver[2] has pointed out the enormous saving in man power required for a rocket offensive as compared with heavy bomber operations, and rockets can, of course, be mass-produced extremely cheaply.

With present techniques it would require a rocket weighing about 100 tons to deliver a payload of one ton at a distance of 3,000 miles, about 70 per cent. of this weight being fuel. As atomic bombs weigh only a few hundred pounds and can never be much larger—though they will be far more efficient—it seems impossible to make any convincing case for the very heavy bomber.

The main objection to the rocket as a long-range weapon is its inaccuracy, but that is a defect which will certainly be overcome in time by the use of target-locating devices, radio lattices or television. It would be virtually impossible to jam a rocket controlled by a locked microwave beam from a high-altitude relay aircraft several hundred miles away, particularly as the radio control might only be required for a very few seconds when the projectile was nearing its target. It will also be possible to develop entirely self-contained controls similar to those used in the later A4's fired against London. They would comprise course integrators which could be set for any required destination and could not be affected by any external means. Once it had been launched only actual collision could deflect such a projectile from its target.

Against such weapons no complete defence would be possible. The only defence of any kind would be the guided rocket, and one can visualize the development of small machines capable of accelerations of 100 g. or more and homing on radiation, radar or even local gravity fields. They would be equipped with various types of I.F.F. to prevent them attacking each other. The possibilities here are endless: one might suggest, for example, the injection of suitable metals into the blast coupled with spectrum analyzers for interrogation.

However, even these machines would have little chance of intercepting, in a matter of seconds, projectiles travelling at 3,000 or more miles an hour.

As many have pointed out, the rocket is the ideal means of delivering atomic explosives and may soon prove the only method that can be used without the destruction of the attacker. A second important advantage, not so far emphasized, is that the enormous impact velocity of the rocket greatly simplifies the detonation problem if a ground-burst is required. The sub-critical masses have only to be placed on the axial line and they will be united at a speed which will prevent premature detonation and make unnecessary the complicated " gun " arrangements in the present atomic bombs.

Should it become possible to build atomically *propelled* rockets with motors of no more than the efficiency of the Hiroshima bomb (about 0.1 per cent.), the resulting jet velocities would be many millions of miles an hour, and the theoretical limit is the velocity of light itself. Although, of course, such speeds would be out of the question inside the atmosphere, it would be relatively easy to design rockets flying under continuous thrust at very high accelerations along constantly " randomed " paths. The interception of such machines by any material projectile would be virtually impossible, since even if they could be detected their destinations could not be foreseen until it was too late.

The Germans had one variety of long-range piloted rocket actually constructed at the end of the war, but this type of machine appears to have few military advantages for a number of reasons —not the least of them being the difficulty of providing for the safe return of the crew. Such machines might be valuable for reconnaissance, but even here they would ultimately be superseded by the guided rocket carrying television equipment.

The true " rocket bomber " (*i.e.,* a manned rocket delivering explosive loads and capable of returning to its base) appears to have no advantages over the long-range guided rocket, and suffers from serious drawbacks, particularly vulnerability and low performance, since it has to carry a much greater weight of fuel as well as the equipment needed by the crew. However, General Arnold, in a report to the United States Secretary for War, has suggested that such machines would be required to launch rockets from unexpected quarters if the defence against long-range projectiles became too effective. These machines would be true " spaceships," travelling in trajectories outside the atmosphere.

This argument does not seem to be valid, since

guided rockets could be designed to follow courses at least as tortuous as those of manned machines, and at much greater speeds.

It is interesting to note that such machines could not employ bombs in the ordinary sense of the word, since any part of the load would share the ship's orbital motion and so be incapable of falling back to the earth.

VI.—Infinite Range

A rocket which attains a speed of five miles a second above the atmosphere would never return to earth, but would continue to circle it for ever in an astronomical orbit. At a somewhat higher speed (seven miles a second) the rocket would escape from the earth's gravitational field completely and recede into space.

While chemical fuels are employed these velocities can only be achieved by " step-rockets " of very small payload, and such machines are likely to be of scientific value only. The advent of the atomic drive would, however, change the picture completely, for if conversion efficiencies of 0.1 per cent. were achieved, fuel loads of only a few per cent. would be ample for journeys to the nearer planets. It is not intended to more than mention these spectacular possibilities here, but they will be an immediate outcome of any harnessing of atomic power to rocket propulsion. When that time comes—and it may be only a few years away—vistas are opened before which the imagination falters. The least of the achievements we may expect to see is the establishment of stations in closed orbits at heights of a thousand miles or more, circling the world in periods of a few hours like artificial moons. The Germans were indeed planning such stations, and they present an attractive solution to the problem of world surveillance and control.

These latter suggestions may appear to many to be so fantastic as to be unworthy of serious consideration. But they are the logically inevitable outcome of one aspect of atomic energy, and as such cannot be ignored in any discussion striving for completeness.

VII.—The Shape of Future Wars

We have now completed our detailed survey of the rocket's applications to warfare and can step back to take the broader view. One's first reaction to the new orders of magnitude presented by the combination of the rocket and atomic power is one of incredulity, but the technological nightmare which any future war will inevitably bring cannot be dispelled by closing one's eyes. All the weapons we have described can be built and will be if they are required. Most, indeed, already exist at this moment in prototype form. We may well

be thankful to the Germans—little though they deserve our gratitude—for showing so clearly what lies ahead for the world if war continues. Their A4's, Natters and Wasserfalls point a lesson which the human race must learn now, for there may be no second chance. It will be a little late when the dust of all man's treasures incarnadines the sunsets of the world.

It has been said that no weapon is decisive, and that to every form of attack there is some defence. Whatever truth these statements may once have had, they belong to an age which has passed. In the guided rocket the Germans may have had the answer to the heavy bomber, but it came too late to prevent the destruction of their cities. During the interval between the adoption of a new weapon and its countering, the damage done to the material structure of civilization grows steadily greater, and there must come a time at last when breakdown occurs. The present state of Germany shows how nearly that point had been reached even with the weapons of the pre-atomic age.

No instrument of war has ever been conceived that lends itself so perfectly as the rocket to treacherous, unheralded and possibly overwhelming attack. There is a tendency to imagine that the very extent of their devastation would deter an aggressor from using the most powerful weapons of all. So pathetic a belief denies the facts of history, for ruthless men will use every means of warfare that comes to hand so long as it promises military advantage. However, it by no means follows that the new weapons need rely on annihilation to produce decisive results. The combination of rocket and atomic explosive raises the possibility of an entirely new type of warfare—radiation war.

It has been revealed that the temperature of an atomic bomb is of the order of several million degrees. All reports have emphasized the intolerable brilliance of the explosion, but it is seldom realized that only an infinitesimal fraction of the radiation lies in the visible spectrum at all. By far the greater part of the energy radiated lies around a peak nearly ten octaves higher, and the total rate of dissipation is about a million million times as great as that from an equal area of the sun's surface. *In other words, the bomb acts as an X-ray generator of unimaginable power.*

Many of the casualties at Hiroshima were due to radiation alone, and many who were not killed outright were permanently blinded. If bombs are developed for their actinic output rather than their explosive power, and detonated perhaps ten miles above the ground, they could interdict enormous areas. No one would dare to venture into the open if at any moment of the night or day they might be struck down by a searing blast of radiation. Above all, crops could be blasted with such a weapon and all agricultural processes brought to a standstill. This alone would be enough to decide the outcome of a war.

It is perhaps here, rather than in its more commonly discussed uses, that the long-range rocket presents the most terrifying possibilities. If such a thing can ever exist, here would seem to be the ultimate weapon. It need have no great accuracy, and even if it were intercepted the resulting explosion would be none the less effective. A rocket every few hours would inhibit outdoor life or movement over perhaps thousands of square miles.

Such attacks might in time assume even more vicious forms. The rockets might be detonated nearer to the ground to induce artificial radioactivity which would compel the evacuation of the areas affected. Neutron and gamma-ray warheads might be developed against which only great thicknesses of rock could provide protection. And most terrible of all would be the threat —even if it were no more than that—of X-ray mutation. This might well daunt a race which would fight to the death against ordinary weapons.

To-day our reaction to such ideas is one of horrified disbelief, but horror is a singularly ineffective safeguard. The repugnance men once felt for flame-throwers and gas warfare did not prevent or even notably retard their adoption. Total war is bounded only by the limits of man's material powers, and those limits are swiftly receding towards infinity.

What part armed forces as we know them to-day will play in any major war between great powers will depend on how far the technological revolution has advanced. The statement that armies and navies are obsolete is certainly not true at the present day nor is it likely to be for many years to come. Countries may be defeated by long-range weapons, but they must then be occupied even if there is no land fighting. The invasion of Japan by unsupported newspaper correspondents, to quote Seversky, shows that this stage is perhaps already here.

The great capital ship, the protection of which has become such an increasing burden, has had its demise predicted so often that any further prophecies of doom are apt to be discounted. The carrier-borne fighter has provided the fleet with air cover, and guided missiles may give warships still more effective protection against aircraft. But the long-range rocket will be able to seek out moving targets at least as readily as fixed ones, for no radar camouflage can conceal a battle fleet steaming across the open sea. It is now possible, in a fraction of a microsecond, to liberate in a single spot enough energy to lift a million-ton fleet vertically a dozen miles.* What effect such forces will have when released beneath the ocean has yet to be seen, but they must surely spell the end of any relatively compact formations of heavy ships.

Navies will be needed for the transfer of supplies in any foreseeable future, but the fear of radar reconnaissance followed by sudden annihilation may force them underseas. The invention of the Walter engine has made this technically possible and any surface craft may be small, high-speed units powered by similar motors. The superseding of heavy guns by precision guided rockets would indeed make large warships unnecessary, since vessels of all sizes but the very smallest could have equal fire power.

An important naval development will probably be the mobile rocket launcher, almost certainly a submersible. Its purpose would be to approach an enemy country and fire long-range rockets at selected targets, perhaps along trajectories that would make the victim suspect some entirely innocent neighbour. Such a scheme would have an irresistible attraction to certain types of mind: the treachery required involves no more than a straight-line extrapolation through Pearl Harbour.

The effect of the new weapons on field armies is more difficult to analyze. Any nation fearing invasion would use its long-range weapons to the uttermost against approaching armies, knowing that the opportunity would pass when the battle had been joined. It is difficult to see how any assault could be launched in the face of weapons that have already destroyed a hundred thousand lives in an instant of time, and it seems more than likely that the armies would not in fact move forward until the issue had been decided.

Armies will, of course, still be required for many types of fighting. No one imagines that long-range rockets would have assisted greatly in the Burma campaign. But it must not be forgotten that the very existence of the new weapons makes improbable such campaigns as the long struggle for air bases witnessed in the Pacific. Much of the bloody " island-hopping " of the Eastern War would have been unnecessary had the Allies possessed the means of delivering bomb loads accurately at ranges of three thousand miles.

The status of air forces has already been touched upon in earlier sections. For the near

---

* The output of the Hiroshima bomb was of the order of ten million mile-tons.

future we can visualize the development of small, high-speed forces for specialized precision bombing, but for the heavy bomber there seems no future at all. Not only will it be superseded by more effective methods of attack, but the defence against it appears to be in sight.

Troop and equipment carriers will certainly be needed, perhaps on the largest scale, but they could only be used in areas where the danger from guided missiles was small, since they would be even more vulnerable than bombers. Once they had landed their material it would at once come under bombardment: probably these forces would be used to move armies forward when it was clear that the initial long-range attack had been successful.

The fighter, as a defensive weapon, will give way to the guided rocket in the relatively near future. For long-range offence it may play a considerable part for many years, until automatic and remote controls have reached a very high degree of perfection. But ultimately even here it will be superseded, for there are no limits to what may be done by machines, whereas there are very definite limits to men's physical powers—in particular their ability to withstand high accelerations. There is also a psychological factor of some importance to be considered in this case. Men— at least normal men—will not risk their lives on dangerous missions when they know that the same operation can be carried out by controllers sitting in safety before television screens.

Combat between remotely controlled machines is a possibility but not a very likely one, for such aircraft would rely on their speed to avoid situations where they had to fight. The problem of designing purely automatic—as opposed to remotely controlled—fighters capable of more than holding their own against piloted machines is one of extreme difficulty but great technical interest. With any automatic equipment there comes a stage when further complexity defeats its own end, but often by the time this point is reached the designer is unable or unwilling to stop. This tendency was noticeable in certain aspects of Allied radar, and was still more prominent in German V-weapon research. Therefore it should not be assumed that a device will never be developed simply because it is excessively complex or of little military value.

All possible combat manœuvres can be analyzed and recorded by suitable coding in machines of the punched-card type. It is conceivable that "battle integrators" may be constructed along these lines, capable of making operational decisions in a matter of milliseconds according to changing combat conditions. Recent advances in mathematical logic and the calculus of state-

ment, coupled with the rise of operational research, suggest the development of calculators capable of solving both tactical and strategic problems. These machines might be used in conjunction with automatic and guided weapons to wage an altogether new type of warfare which would be too swift and complex for detailed human control. This prospect—the apotheosis of mechanized war—is perhaps as far as imagination dare go at the present day.

VIII.—The Problem of Defence

The increasing disparity between offence and defence has become steadily more apparent in the course of this analysis. It cannot be too strongly emphasized that ultimately, as has been stated in the Washington Declaration, effective defence will be impossible against the weapons that man's expanding knowledge will put into his hands. The human race will shortly possess the power to interdict surface life over the greater part of the globe and, to quote the Smyth Report on Atomic Energy, civilization may soon have the means to commit suicide at will. The problem that now confronts us is not one of defence but of survival.

It is sometimes suggested that a war with long-range weapons might result in a stalemate when the contestants had retreated underground beyond the reach of each other's arms. Such a move would appear to be the only answer to the threat of atomic bombs, but it may be doubted whether a highly industrialized civilization could live permanently underground. The prospect is not, to say the least of it, an attractive one, and the difficulty of food production would set a practical limit to the length of time such an existence was possible. This, apart from any other considerations, would make prolonged warfare with atomic weapons out of the question. Nor does it in fact follow that adequate protection could be obtained in this way. The penetrating power of a rocket falling from a hundred miles or more is enormous and would enable atomic warheads to be exploded at a considerable depth. Such "ground depth charges" could collapse or severely damage any cavity that could be built without an impossible amount of labour.

Once the location of an underground city or production centre had been discovered it would be doomed. Absolute secrecy would be impossible and sooner or later the approximate site would be found. This would be followed by low-altitude reconnaissance with geophysical surveying instruments which would locate the exact position of the cavity. Only in the heart of large mountains could complete safety be guaranteed against the weapons which may be available in another decade.

The British Empire, with its great distances and vast areas of territory, is probably the least vulnerable target in the world. On the other hand, the British Isles themselves would be indefensible in the face of long-range attack with atomic weapons. If the defence of the Empire is to be considered in isolation, apart from any other security scheme, the removal to Canada of the Central Government and the Service Departments must be carried out as a permanent measure. It would be impossible to do this after a war had started, and there would certainly be insufficient prior warning to enable such a vast transfer of administration to be made.

Whether the units of the Empire could retain any degree of co-ordination under the impact of this type of warfare is open to doubt, but in such a matter detailed prediction is impossible. The more closely one examines the problem the more convinced one becomes that security, like peace, is indivisible and that even a political organism as large as the Commonwealth could not hope to survive by its own efforts. One returns again to the conclusion that the only defence against the weapons of the future is to prevent them ever being used. In other words, the problem is political and not military at all. *A country's armed forces can no longer defend it; the most they can promise is the destruction of the attacker.*

In such circumstances the statement that the United Nations Organization is the last hope of mankind is literally and terribly true. It is therefore necessary to consider in what way the rocket can be used as an instrument of world rather than regional security.

Now that the world possesses rockets and atomic bombs mankind has a tendency to discount the weapons of which it was so terrified a few years ago. Therefore even if there is no intention of using them except as a last resort, the World Security Council should for psychological reasons possess long-range atomic rockets. However, the weapons which it would use if force proved necessary would be the air contingents of its members, employing ordinary explosives and machines of the type that exist to-day. Behind these would be the threat, never materializing save in dire emergency, of the mightier forces against which there could be no defence.

Not more than twenty launching sites with interlocking circles of fire should be sufficient to give world coverage. The sites would be on mountains, for the reasons mentioned in Section II, and would be staffed by men drawn from every nation. It would be the aim to inculcate in these men a supra-national outlook. This is by no means impossible even to-day, as the International Red Cross has shown, and this viewpoint is becoming more widespread in spite of superficial appearances to the contrary. The fact that the personnel required would be largely scientific would assist the realization of this aim.

These launching sites would have to be supported by a research organization of such a calibre that no individual nation could hope to match it. This body might in time act as the nucleus around which the scientific service of the World State would form, perhaps many years in advance of its political realization.

The necessity for these measures should be kept under continual review, for the world would never feel completely at ease while they existed. A heavily armed police force decreases rather than increases the citizen's sense of security—but, on the other hand, we must recognize that the world to-day resembles the lawless Middle West of the last century, in which an unarmed sheriff would have had little chance of enforcing order. When a world economic system is functioning smoothly, when all standards of living are approaching the same level, when no national armaments are left—then the launching sites could be dismantled.

Only along these or similar lines of international collaboration can security be found: any attempt by great powers to seek safety in their own strength will ultimately end in a disaster which may be measureless.

Upon us, the heirs to all the past and the trustees of a future which our folly can slay before its birth, lies a responsibility no other age has ever known. If we fail in our generation those who come after us may be too few to rebuild the world when the dust of the cities has descended and the radiation of the rocks has died away.

REFERENCES

[1] " A Critical Review of German Long-range Rocket Development," by W. G. A. Perring, F.R.Ae.S.

[2] " Bombers or Rockets? " by A. V. Cleaver, *Flight,* 19th July, 1945.

VI | *Amateur Astronomer*

10 | *The Astronomer's New Weapons*

"The Rocket and the Future of Warfare"—although it has never been reprinted until now—had a decisive effect on my career. Its success gave me more confidence as a writer, at a critical time; but even more important, it got me into the University, by a curious chain of events.

Prime Minister Winston Churchill, to his great surprise, had just been ejected from office by the nation he had led to victory. A new Labour government was in power, and the traditional Speech to the Throne at the opening of Parliament was read by a promising young MP with a distinguished war record, Captain Raymond Blackburn. He later made several references to the role of rockets, so I sent him my paper—a move which led to an invitation to the House and a meeting with the War Minister. Blackburn and I became friends, and when my application for a university grant was turned down, I promptly appealed to him for assistance. In a very short time, my grant was approved, and I applied for admission to King's College, London. I have always been very grateful to Raymond Blackburn for his intervention, and am happy to have resumed contact with him after almost thirty years.

King's was my second choice: I wanted to take astronomy, a neglected subject then only on the syllabus of University College. But there was no room for me at U.C., so King's it was, and I have never regretted the outcome. Not wishing to specialise, I took the B.Sc. General Degree in Physics, Pure Mathematics and Applied Mathematics, and graduated with First Class Honours in 1948. In my final year I was able to take the astronomy course at University College—but to my disappointment, found it extremely dull. The introductory lectures were all devoted to a boring and specialised subject, the errors of the telescope, and I quickly got tired of writing out pages of uninteresting and, worse *ugly* mathematics. I was glad to leave after only one term.

(Yet I have sometimes wondered if my astronomy tutor knew exactly what he was doing; this may have been his subtle method of separating the boys from the men. *And* from the girls; if my memory is correct, one of them is now among the most distinguished in her field.)

During my two years at King's, I filled in the worst gaps in my knowledge of mathematics, but also found time to do a surprising amount of writing (including the novel *Prelude to Space*, written in just twenty days during my first summer vacation, 1947—but not sold until 1950). I was also very active in both the British Interplanetary Society and the British Astronomical Association, being on the Council of both. I rarely missed a meeting—and even more rarely remained inconspicuous when I did attend.

My first address to the B.A.A.—"The Astronomer's New Weapons"—was delivered in June 1945, while I was still in RAF uniform. Although the war in the East was still in progress (no one knew then how swiftly Luis Alvarez and his colleagues would bring it to an abrupt end), much of the secrecy surrounding radar had been lifted, and I was able to talk freely about future technical developments. Many of these have indeed come true, for just about this time the foundations of radio astronomy were being laid. People like Bernard Lovell were looking wistfully at the big radar dishes that would soon be scrap metal, and wondering how they could get their hands on a few of them.

The Astronomer's New Weapons

Electronic Aids to Astronomy

1. *Introduction.*—The revolutionary advances of electronics, culminating in the invention of radar, has given science a whole armoury of new weapons, some of which would have seemed flatly impossible even ten years ago. The purpose of this article is to discuss the application of some of these devices to astronomical research. At the present time it is necessary to be rather vague as far as details are concerned, but it is hoped to give some conception of the instruments which will, in theory at least, be available to the next generation of astronomers. Whether astronomers will be able to afford them, or will be able to persuade people to build them, is another matter.

As far as the author is aware most of these ideas (except where stated) are original, but he will be rather surprised if a number of them have not been tried already and perhaps reported elsewhere.

2.1. *Photo-cell Circuits.*—The photo-electric cell, which can detect and measure very faint radiation from the infra-red to far into the ultra-violet, was one of the first electronic devices to be employed by astronomers. It has been used for measuring star magnitudes, for mapping isophotal contours, and for determining the limits of extensive nebulæ. These applications, however, by no means exhaust its possibilities, some of which will now be discussed.

2.2. *Automatic Following.*—When making long-exposure photographs it is necessary to guide the telescope by means of an auxiliary telescope, as the clock drive cannot correct for such errors as refraction and possible flexure of the telescope (though this is being done with the 200-inch reflector). It is possible to devise a photo-electric circuit which will keep the telescope fixed on a star, or even on a body which is moving relatively to the star-field. The circuit is, in principle, not unlike that used in radio to keep a receiver automatically tuned to a particular station (Automatic Frequency Control). If the telescope wanders away from the star, the light falling on the cell will

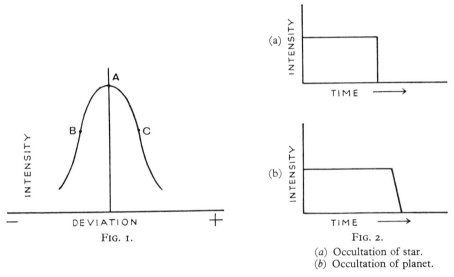

FIG. 1.

FIG. 2.

(*a*) Occultation of star.
(*b*) Occultation of planet.

follow a curve like that in fig. 1. Should the intensity drop to the points B or C, the resulting fall in voltage would cause a motor to operate, restoring conditions to the point A.

The device would have to be "phase sensitive" to distinguish between the arithmetically identical conditions at B and C, and it would have to be allowed a certain small movement about A for the sake of stability. A large telescope that started to "hunt" would be a terrifying sight!

2.3. *Timing of Occultations and Transits.*—Photo-electric cells have been used for this purpose for some time and can eliminate the "personal equation" from such observations. Either a disappearance or a reappearance can be registered automatically on a microchronograph.

This technique might be used for measuring the diameters of very small bodies, perhaps bodies showing no visible disk (e.g. asteroids and the smaller satellites of Jupiter and Saturn). Such occultations, unlike those of stars, would not be instantaneous, but if viewed on a high-speed oscilloscope should give the curve (*b*) of fig. 2. From the light-curve it would then be a simple matter to determine the body's angular diameter. Diversity reception (see paragraph 2.5) might be necessary to obtain the required accuracy.

2.4. *Meteor and Auroral Studies.*—A photo-electric device can if necessary keep watch on the whole of the sky or on any portion of it. It would be fairly easy to construct a "meteor detector" which would work in conjunction with an automatic camera. The device would be insensitive to absolute levels of intensity, but would use what are known as "differentiating circuits" (circuits producing voltages proportional to time-rate of change) to detect sudden alterations of light.

[Published in the *Journal of the British Astronomical Association*, August 1945, Vol. 55, no. 6, pp. 143–7]

When such a change occurred, the camera would be operated and all but the initial portion of the meteor track recorded.

The same device could also be used to count the number of meteors in a given area of sky. No doubt the instrument would be bothered by aircraft lights, not to mention rocket jets, but so will astronomers generally!

The rather vexed question of lunar meteors might also be settled by such an instrument, which could detect any sudden changes of light from the darkened portion of the Moon. Unless, as Pickering has suggested, the Moon has a very tenuous but extremely deep atmosphere, there should be many meteor impacts visible from the Earth. If this point could be settled one way or the other it would be a valuable contribution to selenology.

One would also expect the Moon to have auroral displays, and a photo-cell working in conjunction with a spectrograph as a very sensitive detector of the characteristic auroral lines might be able to give information on this point.

2.5. _Planetary Studies._—An analysis of the light-curves of selected portions of a planet, using a very slow time-base, might give information regarding the physical structure of its surface, at least to the extent of distinguishing between rough and smooth terrain. Though the Moon is the obvious choice for such experiments, Mars and Mercury might also give results.

Some crude experiments by the author, using a three-inch refractor and an RCA 931 nine-stage electron multiplier followed by an oscilloscope amplifier giving an overall amplification of several hundred million, showed that quite simple equipment should suffice for such an investigation. However, in view of the long-period fluctuations to be expected, a direct-current recording amplifier of the type used in electro-encephalography is desirable.

To reduce light variations due to the Earth's atmosphere, the principle of "diversity reception," used in transatlantic telephony, could be employed. This would involve the use of a number of photo-cells, separated by several yards or even miles. Their voltage outputs would be combined by suitable mixing circuits, and in this way random atmospheric fluctuations would tend to cancel out, leaving only the true variations due to the body under examination.

The rotation periods of asteroids and satellites could be determined by the study of their light-curves.

3.1. _Television Devices._—Under this heading are included all devices which form images by electronic means. Chief of these are the iconoscope (television camera) and the electron microscope. In the iconoscope, a light image is projected optically on to a photo-sensitive screen and the resulting "electron image" is scanned, amplified and reproduced on the screen of a cathode-ray tube perhaps miles away. In the case of the electron microscope, the original image is itself electronic, being formed by the passage of an electron beam through the object under examination. The image is again amplified and projected on to a fluorescent screen.

The iconoscope has no greater resolving power than the telescope, since it uses optical systems to form its primary image. However, it can be used to reproduce images from radiation beyond the visible spectrum, e.g. in the infra-red. This is the principle of the so-called "electron telescope," which can see through fog or in complete darkness.

The electron microscope, on the other hand, has a far greater resolving power than the optical microscope, owing to the extreme shortness of matter waves for high-velocity electrons. By its aid it may ultimately be possible to see single molecules or even atoms, and it is one of the most striking examples in the history of science of the way in which an apparently insuperable physical barrier can be circumvented. But it is difficult to see how it can be used for direct astronomical observation. Although crude electron images may be formed in space by natural means, they would not survive their passage through the Earth's magnetic field and atmosphere.

3.2. _Electron Telescope Applications._—Although the electron telescope offers no hope of increased magnification, since it can only convert optical images which have already passed through the atmosphere, it has several interesting applications.

At the moment the photographic plate is more sensitive than the iconoscope, but the latter is only at the beginning of its development. Ultimately it may enable us to amplify images too faint to be recorded photographically, thus increasing the efficiency and effective aperture of our telescopes, with all that that implies in cosmological research.

An adaptation of the electron telescope, the "coronograph," has already been used for the examination of the Sun's corona. In this case we are dealing with an image parts of which are so much brighter than the rest that the faint regions are obliterated. By electronic means it is possible to increase the contrast so that an image of the corona can be obtained. This device would also have applications in nebular and auroral studies, and in special cases where it is necessary to examine a faint object very close to a brilliant one (e.g. Sirius B).

3.3. _Star Counting._—Star counting is important but excessively tedious, and it is possible not only to use an iconoscope to do this automatically, but also to _count all the stars between definite magnitude limits, and those alone._ Such an instrument would be designed on the following lines, and would work on photographs or, with further development, through the telescope directly.

The star-field would be projected on the iconoscope screen and the resulting electron image scanned by a cathode-ray beam in the usual way (fig. 3). Each star will produce a voltage pulse (fig. 4 (_a_)) proportional to its intensity or magnitude, and these pulses would be greatly amplified. They would then pass through a limiting or "clipping" circuit—a kind of electrical guillotine— which would make them all of the same amplitude (fig. 4 (_b_)). The pulses would then go to an electrical counter, which would thus record the total number of stars in the field. Such counters can easily deal with a million pulses a second, so that the scanning speed would only be limited by the sensitivity of the iconoscope. It will be noticed that differences in magnitude will not affect the result of the counting.

To count the stars within definite magnitude limits a slightly different technique would be used. Fig. 5 (the magnitudes are arbitrary and do not indicate the sensitivity that would be

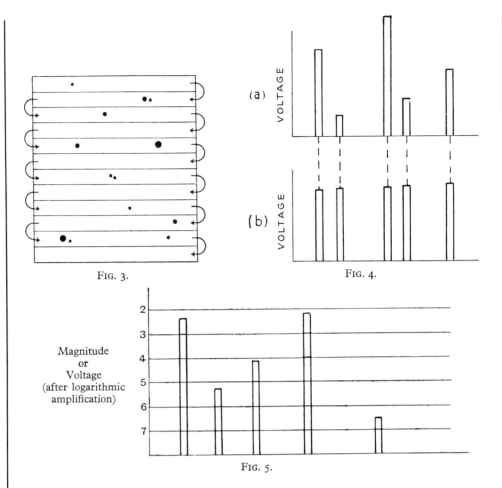

FIG. 3.

FIG. 4.

Magnitude
or
Voltage
(after logarithmic
amplification)

FIG. 5.

expected) shows the voltage output of the device. It is very easy to design circuits which will only respond to voltages *above* a certain amplitude, and such a circuit could be set so that the counter would receive pulses only from stars above any desired magnitude. By repeated countings, reducing the limit a magnitude at a time, a complete analysis of the field could be made in a matter of minutes.

It is possible, although a little more difficult, to arrange for the counter to register only stars between two pre-set magnitudes, or below instead of above a definite limit, down to the threshold sensitivity of the apparatus.

The counter would obviously be in difficulties when dealing with very crowded star-fields, in which the images overlapped extensively. However, a correcting factor could be determined experimentally by scanning artificial fields and the results would still be of statistical value. A useful check could be made by re-scanning the field at right angles.

4.1. *Radar Devices.*—The principles of radar are now well known and have been publicly described (Smith-Rose, *Wireless World*, 1945 Feb.–Mar.), though frequencies, powers and ranges cannot be quoted. The technique was first developed for ionospheric sounding and involved transmitting short pulses of energy and timing the return of the echoes, which are usually displayed on a cathode-ray tube together with the original transmitted pulse. By comparing the echoes against artificial calibrating signals at known ranges, the distance of the reflecting object can be calculated. Bearings are obtained by using the directive effects of various aerial arrays.

Although aircraft can be detected at very great distances (it has, for example, been revealed that the Germans used to observe British bomber fleets marshalling over their bases), it might seem rash to suppose that the same technique could be used in astronomical research. However, experimental evidence shows that this is the case. Radio echoes of several seconds' delay—corresponding to distances greater than that of the Moon—have been well established. A series of experiments carried out by Professor Stormer and Dr. van der Pohl in 1928, using powerful signals from the Eindhoven transmitter, revealed echoes of from three to fifteen seconds' delay, the majority having a delay of eight seconds (equivalent distance 744,000 miles). Echoes have also been reported with delays of up to twelve *minutes* (equivalent distance 68,000,000 miles); but these very long delay echoes have not been confirmed, and it is difficult to see how they were possible with the low powers available at the time (1931).

These echoes are presumably from ionised layers formed in space by electron streams from the Sun, and they demonstrate that it is possible to send radio waves through the ionosphere and to receive them again after they have traversed astronomical distances.

Since these experiments were carried out, the power and sensitivity of radio equipment has been increased by several orders of magnitude. Using existing techniques and even existing

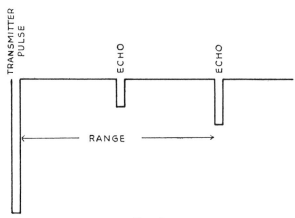

FIG. 6.

apparatus there should be no difficulty in receiving echoes from the Moon.   As time-intervals of a millionth of a second can be easily measured on the cathode-ray tube, it would thus be possible to measure the Moon's distance to a fraction of a mile.

The same technique could be extended to the nearer planets, and even to the Sun, thus determining the solar parallax with an accuracy far beyond that of any previous measurement, for the precision of the system would be independent of range.   There is no theoretical reason why the Sun's distance should not be determined to within a mile by this method, though of course such an accuracy would be physically meaningless since the Sun is not a stable body.

It is very much to be hoped that after the war suitable high-powered radar equipment may be made available for research of this nature.

Apart from its use for ranging purposes, radar might teach us something of the nature of planetary surfaces, since the type of echo received would vary according to the nature of the reflector.   In particular, it might be possible to determine if the surface of Venus is largely aquatic or not.

5. *Miscellaneous.*—In this section are collected a number of techniques and discoveries which may lead to important developments in the fullness of time.

5.1. *Cosmic Static.*—In 1932, Jansky of the Bell Telephone Laboratories discovered that some of the background noise always present in radio reception originated in outer space, and directional studies over a period of time showed that the source of this "star static" lay in the Milky Way, altogether external to the solar system.   More recent studies by Reber (*Ap. J.*, 1944 November) have mapped out the noise levels in the northern hemisphere.

The origin of this radiation is unknown, and it has been attributed to thermal agitation of atoms in interstellar space.   The preparation of "noise maps" may yield valuable information regarding such dispersed matter: certainly the subject is one which deserves attention and may produce unexpected results.

5.2. *Meteor Whistles.*—It has now been established that meteors can affect short-wave radio reception by producing distinctive "whistles" of rapidly changing pitch.   As the meteor passes through the atmosphere it produces a trail of ionisation which reflects radio waves, and the interference of direct and reflected waves at a point not far from the transmitter can produce a heterodyne whistle.   The frequency of the whistle depends on the difference in path lengths, and the rate of change of pitch is proportional to the meteor's velocity.

This discovery suggests interesting possibilities in meteor research, particularly if more direct techniques based on radar principles are employed.

6.1. *Conclusions.*—This is not intended to be a complete survey of a very new field, and not all the suggestions diffidently put forward may prove to be practicable.   But the writer believes that electronics may do for astronomy what it has already done for microscopy, and perhaps these notes may prompt others to make further investigations into this fascinating subject.   There should be some excellent bargains in electronic equipment at the end of the Japanese War.

11 | *Astronomical Radar*

With the relaxation of wartime security, I was able to be much more explicit than in the last article, and I quickly took advantage of my new-found freedom. And one prediction—that it would be possible to receive radar echoes from the Moon—had already come true within a matter of months.

"Astronomical Radar" is, of course, now only of historic interest—but history *is* interesting. Even more important, it is often the best guide to the future. The final paragraph of my last article for *Wireless World* has already come true, beyond my wildest dreams.

ASTRONOMICAL RADAR

SINCE the early days of radar, suggestions that echoes might be obtained from the moon have often been put forward but were probably not taken very seriously by most people until Sir Edward Appleton in the Thirty-sixth Kelvin Lecture to the Institution of Electrical Engineers[1] stated categorically that the feat was possible. Its actual accomplishment less than a year later by the United States Signal Corps is typical of the speed of technical progress in these days.

The problems that had to be overcome in carrying out this epoch-making experiment are of considerable interest, and although no full technical report seems to have been published yet, a good deal of general information is now available. The equipment used was a standard Army early-warning set, working on the rather old-fashioned frequency of 111.6 Mc/s. For the experiment a special aerial system was constructed, employing sixty-four dipoles in an eight by eight array. This large aerial was somewhat unwieldy, and apparently incapable of movement in elevation. At any rate the experiments all appear to have been carried out when the moon was on the horizon, and the fact that the greatest possible ionospheric attenuation would then have taken place did not prevent success.

Echoes from terrestrial objects (including aircraft) even at maximum range return to the receiver within a very few milliseconds of the transmitted pulse, and it is possible to use pulse-recurrence frequencies sufficiently high to give an apparently continuous trace on the C.R.T. This means that even if the signal/noise ratio is as low as one to one, the relatively steady echo can be distinguished from the noise appearing

at random along the trace. The "integrating" effect of a long-afterglow tube also increases the discrimination against noise. However, when echoes are being received from the moon the time-lag is multiplied a thousand-fold and the spot on the C.R.T. must take 2½ seconds to traverse the

(Above) Aerial system of the 111-megacycle equipment used in the American experiment.

(Left) U.S. Signal Corps photo showing C-R trace of lunar echo.

screen. The picture is no longer continuous, and a fairly high signal/noise ratio is needed for good results.

It is well known that the noise generated in the first stage of a radio receiver is proportional to the square-root of the band-width. As radar pulses have to be a microsecond or less in duration to obtain accurate ranging, band-widths of several megacycles are needed to pass them without distortion. However, in these pioneer experiments extreme range accuracy was not attempted, and

the band-width was reduced to the extraordinary figure of fifty *cycles*. This reduction in the pass-band would give a theoretical improvement in signal/noise ratio of two or three hundred to one over a standard radar set, but must have introduced very great difficulties in connection with receiver and transmitter stability. The Doppler effect due to the earth's rotation would have sufficed to move the signal right out of the receiver pass-band, and adjustments had to be made to allow for this continually changing quantity.

The pulse recurrence frequency used was about twelve a *minute*, and this combined with the very wide pulse-width of 0.2-0.5 second meant that the transmitter was operating one second in every ten, as compared with about one in every thousand for normal radar. This very greatly reduced the pulse

power that could be employed, and only three to five kilowatts peak was actually radiated—a most surprising figure in these days of megawatt valves.

The Signal Corps' experiment was carried out under Lt.-Col. J. H. De Witt at the Evans Signals Laboratories, Belmar, N.J. First contact was made with the moon at 11.58 a.m. on January 10, 1946, only ten minutes after moonrise. (It has also been reported that echoes have been received just before moonrise. This can be easily explained by refraction, which is sufficient at optical frequencies to make the whole moon "visible" to radar when it

[Published in *Wireless World*, October 1946, p. 321–3]

is actually below the horizon.

The feat is all the more remarkable when one considers that it was achieved by an almost standard Army installation, and it is tempting to consider what might be done with specially designed equipment.

The first obvious step is to move into the microwave region and employ a parabolic array which will throw all the power on to the moon. The moon's angular diameter is half a degree, and the beam-width of the Belmar aerial must have been at least six to eight degrees so that considerably less than one per cent of the modest power transmitted ever reached the target. At a wavelength of ten centimetres, a parabolic mirror smaller than the Camp Evans aerial would have focused almost all the power on the moon and given a ten-fold increase in signal strength.

Increasing Pulse Power

Although the disadvantages of low pulse-recurrence frequency have been pointed out, if photographic integration of the echoes is used these can be overcome even if there are long gaps between pulses. Since magnetrons are now available with peak outputs of over two megawatts[2], a tremendous increase in range should be easily obtainable. Using intervals between pulses of a minute or more, the magnetrons could be operated at even greater overloads than normal. Indeed, if planetary ranging is to be attempted "single-shot" working would be inevitable, as the table below shows.

Minimum Echo Times.

Moon ..	.. 2.56	seconds
Venus ..	.. 4.5	minutes
Mars ..	.. 6.2	,,
Mercury	.. 8.8	,,
Sun ..	.. 16.6	,,
Jupiter	.. 1 hr. 6 mins.	
Outer Planets	2-10 hours	

As the writer has pointed out elsewhere,[3] long-range radar sounding has scientific implications of the greatest importance. The most fundamental measure in astronomy is the distance of the earth from the sun, and hitherto this has been deduced by most elaborate observations spread over a large portion of the globe, and requiring months of analysis before the results can be extracted. It would not be necessary to receive direct echoes from the sun to measure this distance: if the nearer planets could be ranged this would give the scale of the solar system and the sun's distance could then be calculated without difficulty. At its nearest Venus is some 25,000,000 miles from the earth and has an apparent diameter of over a minute of arc—almost enough to show a disc to the naked eye were it not then lost in the sun's glare.

It can be shown[1] that the transmitter power required to produce a given echo from a spherical body in free space is proportional to the following quantity:—

$$\frac{R^4 \lambda^2}{a^4 r^2 \rho}$$

where R is the distance of the body, r its radius, ρ its reflection coefficient, a the diameter of the array, and λ the wavelength. Taking the figures for the Belmar experiment (R = 250,000, r = 1,000 miles) and assuming that a and ρ are unchanged but that a wavelength of 10 centimetres is used, it is possible to get a rough estimate of the power needed to range the other planets. For Venus at its nearest R is 25,000,000 miles and r is nearly 4,000 miles. Hence the peak power needed would be 7,000 times that required for the Belmar experiment, or about 35 megawatts.

This is rather a lot of power, to say the least, but before seeing how we can whittle it down let us consider another example which gives a somewhat surprising result.

Solar Radar

The sun is 400 times as far away as the moon, but its radius is 400 times as great—by that extraordinary coincidence which makes total eclipses possible. Thus to reach it with 10-centimetre waves we need increase our power by only 180 to a level of 0.9 MW—much less than was needed by Venus at a quarter of the distance. Though these figures are, of course, very rough, they represent maximum values and probably give a fair idea of the orders of magnitude involved.

A power of 0.9 MW is within present limits, but 35 MW is rather more than we can hope to generate for some time—though seeing what has happened in the last few years it would be unwise to be dogmatic on this point. However, there are two ways of improving the situation, as may be seen from the equation above. If we could triple the size of the array, this would at once bring the power down to less than half a megawatt. A 150-foot mirror would be a considerable piece of engineering, but as it could be laid on the ground and elevated at one end its construction would not present any insuperable difficulties, especially as it could be made of metallized fabric stretched over a suitable framework. With such an array, it would be possible to receive echoes from Mars when powers of 20 MW are available.

Light-ray Echoes

The second alternative is a decrease in wavelength. It is presumably only a matter of time before the powers now available at 10 centimetres can be obtained at still higher frequencies, but there seem good arguments for moving right down the spectrum into the optical region, at any rate for short-range (!) lunar working. During the war, gas-discharge tubes were developed which gave light pulses of such intensity that aircraft could take night photographs of ground objects. By discharging condensers through such tubes and focusing the light on the moon, it might be possible to make a very simple and efficient pseudo-radar system. The detector would be a photo-multiplier cell with a filter to pass only the light of the—if possible—monochromatic flash. The analogy with a narrow-bandwidth radar system would then be perfect, and when one considers that a 1,000-volt condenser discharging at a rate of 100 amps represents a pulse-power of 100 kW the possibilities are impressive.

The ultimate range and accuracy of "astronomical radar" cannot be easily decided, but an increase of bandwidth to a few hundred cycles would give range accuracy of a thousand miles, which means an error of only 0.001 per cent in the radius of the earth's orbit. This is a far greater degree of precision than has ever been available before and there is probably little point in increasing it. However, Appleton has made the interesting suggestion that radar might be used to check the heights of the lunar mountains, and this would require megacycle band-widths and the type of trace expansion used in gun-laying radar. It might even be possible, by a careful choice of frequencies, to discover if the moon has an ionosphere—though probably any frequencies which could penetrate our E and F layers would make short work of the moon's defences.

Quite recently the somewhat surprising fact has been revealed that the Federal Telephone and Radio Corporation is now seriously considering the use of the moon as a reflector for radio transmissions when normal S.W. links are broken by severe ionospheric disturbances. Henri Busignies, Technical Director of Federal, has calculated that at the minimum economic band-width (about 500 cycles) something like 100kW (continuous wave) power would be needed to provide a reliable service. Powers of this order can now be generated at frequencies of up to 600Mc/s by tubes of the "resnatron" type.[4] Only low speeds of working could be used on this system, and there would be other practical limitations: for example, the moon must be visible at both stations simultaneously. However, the plan is a very interesting one, perhaps a forerunner of the space-station relay-chain recently described by the writer.[5]

To end, if possible, on a slightly more speculative note, the question asked of the *Wireless World* "Brains Trust" some years ago[6] appears to have been answered in good measure. Interplanetary radio communication is an immensely simpler task than radar contact since only a square law of distance is involved. Even the present Signal Corps equipment gives a field-strength on the moon equivalent to that of a medium-power local station!

When the fuels and motors are available, Zworykin's suggestion that remotely-controlled rockets carrying televisors be sent round the moon will present no major difficulties from the communications side, whatever other problems may arise. But those hopeful individuals who expect to see radar meteor-detectors for spaceships are certainly doomed to disappointment, since the average meteor is far smaller than a rifle-bullet and travels fifty times as fast. One could scarcely detect such an object—still less determine whether it were on a collision course—more than a fraction of a second before impact, which would be of no practical use whatsoever. Fortunately meteors large enough to be dangerous are excessively rare: as lethal agents they are much less effective than motor cars and similar hazards of everyday life.

It is quite certain that an era is now beginning in which co-operation between radio engineers and astronomers may produce some spectacular and perhaps quite unforeseen results. When one remembers how radar was the child of pure radio research, who would dare to say what the third generation may not bring?

Addendum.—Since this article was written, the Bell Telephone Laboratories have announced the development of "metal lenses" which can produce microwave beams down to a *tenth of a degree* in width. They are constructed of arrays of metal strips mounted in front of a horn radiator about twelve feet across and appear to be much smaller than the equivalent parabolic mirrors.

This important discovery may mean that the high-gain arrays needed for astronomical radar may be nothing like as large as those envisaged—or alternatively much greater ranges may be attainable with the same apertures.

It is also of interest to note that the optical "radar" system proposed above is already in use in the "Cloud Range Meter" (*Wireless Engineer* Abstracts, No. 1943, July, 1946). This device consists of two parabolic mirrors, one with a high-voltage spark at its focus and the other carrying a photoelectric cell. Echoes are displayed as deflections on an A-scope as in normal radar.

Further details of this instrument are given in the *General Electric Review* for April, 1946.

References

[1] Sir Edward Appleton: Scientific Principles of Radiolocation; *J.I.E.E.*, Pt. 1, September, 1945.
[2] *Wireless World*; May, 1946.
[3] *Journal of the British Astronomical Association*; September, 1945.
[4] *Waves and Electrons*; April, 1946 (p. 169).
[5] *Wireless World*; October, 1945.
[6] *Wireless World*; November, 1942.

12 | *Stationary Orbits*

"Stationary Orbits" is an interesting example of rediscovering the wheel, yet it contains some novel features that I have never seen elsewhere. They are due to my longtime friend and colleague in the British Interplanetary Society, R.A. Smith (1902–59).

Ralph Smith was one of the most enthusiastic prewar members of the BIS; trained as an engineering and architectural draftsman, his artistic skills played a major role in putting our ideas across to the general public. His drawings of space vehicles, lunar bases and space-stations contributed greatly to my own book, *The Exploration of Space* (1951); later we collaborated on *The Exploration of the Moon* (1954). Many of his remarkable illustrations, which anticipated almost all the developments which occurred in the twenty years after his untimely death, were later collected by the BIS in the volume *High Road to the Moon* (1979).

In addition to his artistic talents, Ralph Smith had an astonishing insight into the practical engineering problems of space travel, and eventually earned his living in the nascent British rocket industry. Early in 1947, he came to me with a striking—and to me quite novel—idea. He had discovered, without mathematics but by arguments based on elementary gravitational theory,that there were two points, on either side of the Moon, where a satellite could remain fixed on the Earth-Moon line.

I could detect no flaw in his logic, and set out to find the location of these points, discovering both an analytic and graphical method of doing so. Fortunately, both gave the same result.

The British Astronomical Association published this

paper in its *Journal* for December 1947, and on checking the results thirty-five years later, I am surprised to see how accurate they are—despite an unnoticed approximation that I had made.* The inner point is actually 64,516 km from the Moon compared with my 64,000 km; the outer at 58,020 km compared with the 58,000 km given. Presumably, the complex roots, which I did not investigate, define the Trojan points. (But why are there *four* of them? I leave that as an exercise for the student.)

Today, thanks to the publicity generated by Dr. Gerard O'Neill's space colonisation projects (see for example his book *The High Frontier*), everybody has heard of the Lagrangian points; L1 is the inner one, L2 that beyond the Moon, while L4 and L5 are the leading and trailing Trojan positions. (Lonely L3 is also in the Earth-Moon line, but exactly opposite the Moon in its orbit, and slightly more distant from the Earth.) There is an active L5 Society seeking to exploit this desirable piece of real estate, though it has always seemed to me that L1 and L2 would be more useful places; L2, as I suggested in *Interplanetary Flight* as long ago as 1950, would be an ideal location for a Farside radio/TV relay. This idea was developed in detail twenty years later by Robert W. Farquhar of the Goddard Space Flight Center ("The Utilization of Halo Orbits in Advanced Lunar Operations," NASA TN D-6365, July 1971).

*The body would not be revolving around the Earth, but the centre of mass of the Earth-Moon system. I must also apologise for my careless use of the term "centrifugal force," for which I have frequently criticised engineers. There is, of course, no such thing; if it *did* exist, and gravity balanced it, then there would be no resultant force—and the body would move in a straight line, not a closed orbit.

Stationary Orbits

1. *Introduction.*

When one body revolves around another in a circular orbit, the period may be found very simply by considering the fact that the outward centrifugal force—mv^2/r—acting on the body due to its motion must equal the inward gravitational attraction of the primary. If G is the surface gravity of the central body, R its radius, D the distance of the satellite and T its period, this gives us the relation

$$\left(\frac{2\pi D}{T}\right)^2 \frac{1}{D} = G\frac{R^2}{D^2}$$

Hence

$$T^2 = \frac{4\pi^2 D^3}{GR^2} \quad \ldots \text{ Eq. 1.}$$

which is, of course, Kepler's Third Law as applied to circular orbits.

It is always possible to discover an orbit in which a satellite would revolve with the same period as its primary's "day". Such an orbit may be termed a "stationary" one since a body occupying it would appear fixed in the sky of its primary and would neither rise nor set. Putting $T = 24$ hours or $84,000$ secs. in Equation 1, we see that for the Earth the radius of this particular orbit is a little over $42,000$ kms.

Two interesting cases actually exist in the Solar System where the conditions for a stationary orbit have been nearly realised. For Mars ($G = 3.73 \times 10^{-3}$ km./sec., $R = 3,400$ km., $T = 24$ hrs. 37 min.) the radius of such an orbit would be $20,500$ kms. The orbit of Deimos is $23,500$ kms. in radius, so this little moon moves only very slowly across the Martian sky. Its orbital period is actually 30 hrs. 21 mins., and it remains above the horizon for about two days at a time.

A similar state of affairs is found in the Jovian satellite system—despite the fact that Jupiter has a day of 9 hrs. 50 mins., the shortest axial period of any major planet. The tiny satellite *V* revolves around its primary in 11 hrs. 57 mins., so that four days of Jupiter time elapse between its rising and setting.

These "stationary" orbits, in particular the 24 hour orbit for Earth, will one day be of the very greatest technological importance, and their applications for physical research, surveying, meteorological and radio-relay purposes have been extensively discussed in the literature of astronautics. The whole question of artificial satellites for the Earth has been dealt with at length by Oberth and von Pirquet, and as is now well-known, their establishment was one of the long-term projects of German rocket research. After his capture by the Allies, Professor von Braun, director of V.2 development, stated his belief that such stations would be built for rocket refuelling purposes in about fifty years. More recently the United States Army has made some spectacular predictions about the military uses of space-stations, and General Arnold touched on an aspect of the subject in his celebrated "Third Report to the Secretary for War".

2. *Orbits in the Earth-Moon Field.*

It was recently pointed out to the writer that other types of stationary orbit could exist in the Earth—Moon system if allowance were made for the combined gravitational fields of both bodies. As it has proved possible to find the positions of these orbits by rather simple mathematics, it is felt that the following treatment may be of some interest.

Let us consider a body *S* revolving around the Earth in an orbit beyond the Moon (Fig. 1). Because of its increased distance, the body's orbital period would normally exceed that of the Moon. However, if the Moon happened to lie between the body and the Earth, the two gravitational fields would be added and so the body's orbital speed would have to be increased for it to maintain its position. Theoretically, a distance could be found at which the body would

[Published in the *Journal of the British Astronomical Association*, December 1947, Vol. 57, no. 6, pp. 232–7]

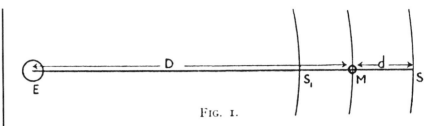

Fig. I.

revolve with the same period as the Moon, and so might always be hidden from the Earth.

A second and still more interesting case arises if we place our "sub-satellite" between the Earth and the Moon, remembering that now the fields oppose each other so that the body's orbital speed can be reduced.

The problem of locating these orbits may be approached in two ways, the first by direct mathematical analysis and the second by a semi-graphical method which throws a good deal of light on the physical processes involved. Both will therefore be given in detail.

3·1. *Case A—Orbit beyond the Moon.*

Let G, g be surface gravities of Earth and Moon respectively, R, r their radii, D the mean Earth-Moon distance, d the distance between Moon and body, T period of Moon and body.

Then the gravitational acceleration at the body due to the combined fields will be:—

$$\frac{GR^2}{(D+d)^2} + \frac{gr^2}{d^2}$$

The centrifugal acceleration due to the body's revolution around the Earth is:—

$$\left[\frac{2\pi(D+d)}{T}\right]^2 \frac{1}{(D+d)} = \frac{4\pi^2(D+d)}{T^2}$$

These must be equal, hence

$$\frac{GR^2}{(D+d)^2} + \frac{gr^2}{d^2} = \frac{4\pi^2(D+d)}{T^2}$$

Now from (I), $T^2 = \dfrac{4\pi^2 D^3}{GR^2}$

Hence

$$\frac{GR^2}{(D+d)^2} + \frac{gr^2}{d^2} = \frac{GR^2(D+d)}{D^3} \quad \ldots \text{ Eq. II.}$$

If we put $a = gr^2/GR^2$, $d = kD$, this reduces after cross-multiplication to:—

$$k^5 + 3k^4 + 3k^3 - a(1+k)^2 = 0$$

Since $g/G = 0.16$, $R = 6,300$ kms., $r = 1,760$ kms., $a = 1.2 \times 10^{-2}$ very nearly.

Hence $k^5 + 3k^4 + 3k^3 - 1.2 \times 10^{-2}(1+k)^2 = 0$ . . . Eq. III.

There is only one positive real root for this quintic, the value of which is approximately $k = 0.16$. This corresponds to a point $0.16 \times 384,000$ or $64,000$ kms. beyond the Moon.

3·2. *Case B—Orbit between Earth and Moon.*

With the same notation as before, we have

$$\frac{GR^2}{(D-d^2)} - \frac{gr^2}{d^2} = \frac{GR^2}{D^3}(D-d)$$

Hence $k^5 - 3k^4 + 3k^3 - 1\cdot2 \times 10^{-2}(1-k)^2 = 0 \ldots$ Eq. IV.

This again has only one real root, $k = 0\cdot15$, which corresponds to an orbit 58,000 kms. inside the Moon's.

4. *Graphical Solution.*

The gravitational accelerations due to the Earth and the Moon at distances x from their centres are given by

$$G_E = \frac{GR^2}{x^2} = \frac{3\cdot97}{x^2} \times 10^4 \text{ cms./sec.}^2 \left.\right\}$$
$$g_m = \frac{gr^2}{x^2} = \frac{4\cdot75}{x^2} \times 10^2 \text{ cms./sec.}^2 \left.\right\} \quad x \text{ in } 1,000 \text{ kms.}$$

If we plot these two fields in the region of the Moon, we obtain the curves shown in Fig. 11. Curve A represents the slowly falling Earth's field, curve B the symmetrical and rapidly decreasing field of the Moon. The total resultant field (curve C) is the algebraic sum of the two, and falls to zero at the so-called "neutral point" about 38,000 kms. from the Moon. At this point the two fields cancel, but beyond the Moon they add and at great distances the Earth's field is predominant.

The summation curve C shows very clearly how the Earth's gravitational field is distorted in the region of the Moon, and from it we can find the positions at which a body would have the same period as the Moon. For the total gravitational field must then be equal to $g_x = v^2/x$, where v is the velocity of the body and x its distance from the Earth. This equals

$$\left(\frac{2\pi x}{T}\right)^2 \frac{1}{x} = \frac{4\pi^2 x}{T^2}$$

Substituting from (1) for T, we have

$$g_x = \frac{GR^2 x}{D^3} = 7 \cdot 10^{-4} x \text{ cms./sec.}^2, \text{ very nearly.}$$

The points where this straight line cuts the curve C will correspond to the orbit required. Plotting this line gives us XX', which intersects C at 58,000 and 64,000 kms. from the Moon, thus confirming the results already obtained.

The line also passes through curve A when $d = 0$, as would be expected since this corresponds to the position and period of the Moon itself. The graphical method also shows (as is indeed physically obvious) that only two solutions are possible and that no other roots of the quintics in Section 3 need be investigated.

5. *Stability of Orbits.*

The important question now arises: are these orbits stable when allowance is made for the perturbing effects of the Sun? If we calculate the value of the Sun's gravitational field at the Earth's orbit, we find that it amounts to $0\cdot594$ cms./sec.^{2} and is constant to within $\pm 0\cdot003$ cms./sec.^{2} over the whole width of the Moon's orbit. This very small cyclical variation of 1% would eventually disturb the orbits, but they would certainly be stable for many revolutions even if not over astronomical periods of time. From the engineering point of view— which is the one I am most concerned with—all these perturbing accelerations are quite negligible, being of the order of a microgravity. Even for a body of several hundred tons mass they could be completely neutralised by the ejection of a few kilograms of matter a day.

6. *Conclusions.*

The above treatment, it should be emphasised, only applies to *circular* orbits and the corresponding analysis for elliptic orbits is far more complicated.

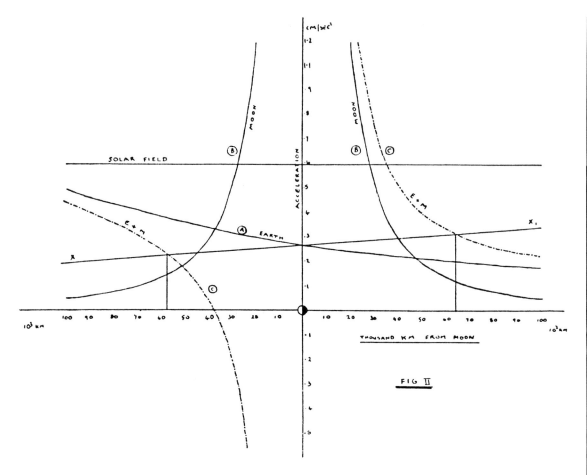

FIG II

It is in fact a degenerate case of the three-body problem and has been treated by Lagrange. The Trojan or equilateral orbits form a related case which may also occur in the Earth-Moon system.

There is no reason to suppose that these orbits are temporarily occupied by any bodies at the moment, though this is not quite impossible. No doubt there are many small meteors in various orbits around the Earth, and from time to time the possibility of a second Moon has been raised (e.g. by the French astronomer Petit). If there is a body in the inner orbit, it could hardly be more than a kilometer in diameter or it would have been detected long ago. A satellite in the outer orbit would, however, be hidden from the Earth for most, if not all, of the time.

References.

1. H. H. Arnold: *Third Report of the Commanding General of the United States Army Air Forces.*
2. A. C. Clarke: *"Extra-terrestrial Relays".* (Wireless World, October 1945).
3. Willy Ley: *Rockets and Space-travel.* (Viking Press, N.Y., 1947.)
4. Hermann Oberth: *Wege zur Raumschiffahrt.* (Munich, 1929. Edwards Bros., Ann Arbor, U.S.A., 1944.)
5. F. R. Moulton: *Introduction to Celestial Mechanics.* Macmillan, 1935.)

13 | *The Radio Telescope*

A few years later, I wrote a short survey paper for the British Astronomical Association on the rapidly developing science of *radio* (as opposed to radar) astronomy. It also provides a striking reminder of how far we have gone in only three decades.

About twenty years after this paper was published, I was lecturing in Ohio when one of the audience came up to me and said: "I wonder if you know my name. I'm Grote Reber." I've never forgotten the moment when I met the man who, single-handedly, started an entire new science.

The Radio Telescope

The progress of astronomy is largely a record of instrumental developments which have, time and again, completely revolutionised the science. Whenever existing techniques have reached their limits, some new and unsuspected invention has opened up vast fields of hitherto unimagined knowledge. We can be fairly sure, for example, that the Oriental star-gazers who founded astronomy never dreamed that one day a few pieces of glass in a tube would make the Moon appear big enough to fill the sky: and we have all heard of the philosopher who remarked, a century or so ago, that if one thing was certain it was that we could never tell the composition of the stars!

The telescope and the spectroscope, with the photographic plate a good third, are the great instrumental landmarks in astronomy. They arrived with fairly decent intervals between them, so that each was thoroughly developed before the next appeared on the scene. It is somewhat typical of our age that in the new revolution now upon us a whole group of inventions has arrived almost simultaneously, each opening up propects so dazzling that future generations may have the impression that astronomy didn't really begin until the middle of the twentieth century—though some quite useful pioneering work was done before then by a few enthusiasts with incredibly primitive instruments and techniques.

In this paper I hope to give a brief survey of what has been done in one of the most promising of the new techniques—that of radio-astronomy. A good deal has been published on the subject, but mostly in the form of original contributtions scattered through scientific literature. This is a very unoriginal contribution which has merely gathered some of the sources together as a sort of "progress report" which will probably be out-of-date before it is delivered.

I would like to emphasise that I am going to write about *radio* and not *radar* astronomy. In the latter case we send signals into space and get echoes back from nearby objects such as meteor trails or the Moon. These techniques have already been well described by Dr. Lovell and his associates in the *Journal*. In the case of radio-astronomy we are picking up *signals*, and not echoes, from very much more remote objects—stars and perhaps even extra-galactic nebulae.

It is very seldom realised what a small portion of the electromagnetic spectrum has so far been used for astronomical reseach. This is partly due to the limitations of our eyes, but more fundamentally to the fact that the atmosphere itself is quite opaque except to a band of frequencies about an octave wide in the "optical" region, of which our eyes can perceive about half (Fig. 1). Until now all our knowledge of celestial bodies has had to come through that narrow slit.

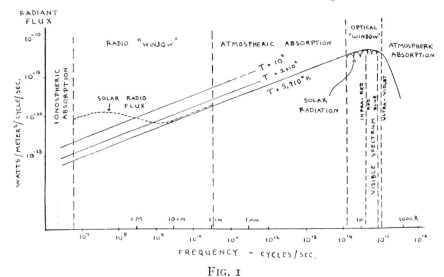

FIG. 1

(Reproduced from *Electronics* by kind permission of McGraw-Hill Publishing Company)

[Published in the *Journal of the British Astronomical Association*, April 1949, Vol. 59, no. 5, pp. 156–9]

Futher down the frequency range, however, the atmosphere becomes transparent again and passes a band of radio-frequencies about $3\frac{1}{2}$ times as wide as the "optical" one—nearly ten times as wide as the visual band. It is this unexplored region that astronomy is now entering for the first time.

The discovery that radio waves come from space was made by Karl Jansky on a frequency of 20 megacycles/sec. (15 meters) in 1931. Jansky proved that this radiation originated in the Sagittarius region of the Milky Way, but nothing further came of this work until the War, when the development of much more sensitive receivers and better aerial systems made more detailed investigations possible. The early aerial systems had very large "beam-widths" (i.e. they received signals over a wide arc) and hence poor resolving power. Even now the angular resolution of a radio telescope is incomparably inferior to that of an optical instrument, though this is not as serious a disadvantage as might be thought. Resolution depends on the number of wavelengths in the instrument's aperture, and few radio arrays have apertures of even 100λ, whereas a telescope may have an aperture of a million λ or more. Hence the best radio instruments cannot, without special techniques, distinguish between sources less than a degree or so apart.

Nevertheless it has been possible to make fairly detailed maps of the sky showing the regions from which the radio signals are most intense. Perhaps the word "signals", like "canali", may conjure up more than it is intended to, so the word "noise" is preferable. If one listens to the receiver when it is tuned into one of these cosmic sources, the result is exactly like the familar rushing sound from a powerful radio when the volume control is turned full up but no station is coming in. Indeed, some of the noise one hears then is extraterrestrial, though it is swamped by the inevitable circuit noise in the set itself.

The "noise maps" prepared by Jansky and others (notably Reber, working on 160 and 480 megacycles/sec.) showed a very strong correlation between radio intensity and the visible distribution of matter in the Milky Way. This is well shown in Fig. 2. (The small circle in the upper left hand corner indicates the beam-width of the apparatus), and it is an interesting thought that we might have been able to discover the Milky Way even if we could never see the stars! The coordinates of the North Pole of the radio-noise system have been ascertained and agree well with the generally accepted figures for the Galaxy:—

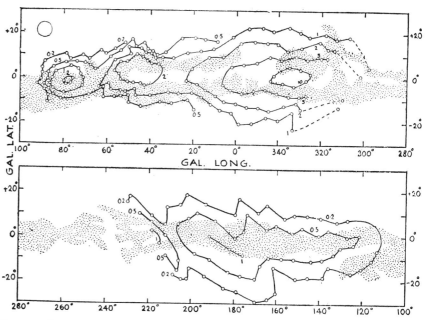

FIG. 2. Contour lines of equal radio intensity at 160 mc./sec. Data by Reber
(*From Journal R.A.S. Canada*)

	R.A.	Dec.
Visual	12h. 40m.	+ 28°
160 Mc/s	12h. 34m.	+ 27°
480 Mc/s	12h. 40m.	+ 29°

Since it is impossible to observe the galactic centre by visual means owing to the absorption of light in interstellar clouds, the radio method may eventually give more accurate and detailed results than optical observations. The most intense regions of radio noise lie in some of the empty areas of the Milky Way, where the concentration of matter is probably highest though hidden from us by dark nebulae.

In addition to the general diffuse radiation coming from large areas of the sky, point sources of great intensity have been quite recently discovered. The first was observed in Cygnus, and has been found to be variable. Other sources, such as one in Cassiopeia, are steady; and the baffling thing about them is that nothing unusual can be found at the spots concerned! Radio-interfero-meter measurements have proved that they are certainly less than 8' of arc in diameter, and may be very much smaller. Perhaps a new and peculiar kind of star or astrophysical phenomenon has been discovered.

During the early stages of research in galactic radio noise, attempts were made to pick up signals from the Sun: but they were unsuccessful until the very sensitive radar receivers developed during the War were employed. It was then found that the Sun could sometimes interfere quite seriously with them, and the danger that the enemy might discover this and mount raids at periods of great solar activity was for a while taken very much to heart.

Solar radio observations have produced very unexpected results. At the high-frequency end of the radio-spectrum (10 to 1 cm) the Sun's radiation corresponds to that of a body at some 6,000 degrees K, in agreement with visual measurements. (Fig 1.) On longer wavelengths, however, the Sun's apparent "radio-temperature" is *at least* a million degrees. Occasionally the noise on the meter waves increases in intensity ten-thousandfold, and the Sun radiates as if its temperature was ten million degrees or more.

The explanation advanced to account for this is that the longer waves come from the corona, which may be at such high temperatures. Observations at eclipses—when a large amount of radiation is still received—support this. The meter waves could certainly not come from the lower regions of the Sun's atmosphere as they would be absorbed by it. The shorter and more penetrating waves come from these lower levels. Striking support for this theory has been given by observations of solar-noise "bursts" on different frequencies. When such a burst occurs, the high-frequency signal arrives first and the low frequency signals may be five minutes later. This suggests most vividly that some great disturbance is rising, layer by layer, through the Sun's outer shell, and that the more penetrating waves are giving us the first intimations of its advent. Radio observations may thus provide—if I may borrow a metaphor from the other end of the spectrum—an X-ray picture of the Sun which could not have been obtained in any other way.

It has also been shown that the increased level of solar radio noise which frequently occurs originates in sunspots, and it is possible that in galactic noise we may now obtain information about spots on the stars—a thought which would have seemed quite fantastic a few years ago!

All these observations were originally made by radio engineers attempting to solve communications problems of great practical importance. The astronomical dividends were, at first, only incidental, but equipment has now been built primarily for astronomical research. The first equatorially-mounted radio-telescope, of about 200-inches aperture, has now been built at Cornell University. Much larger parabolas have been constructed (there is a 200 feet diameter one at Manchester!) but these have been partially or completely fixed so that observations had to be taken by letting the sky drift through the narrow "field of vision"—a rather tedious procedure, reminding one of the Earl of Rosse and his giant reflector.

This brief survey should, I hope, be enough to show that a new technique of very great power is now available to astronomers. Clearly it will be necessary to carry out a long series of synchronized visual and radio observations of the Sun before its full power can be determined. What may ultimately be revealed by these new methods is to-day as unpredictable as were the results which came from the application of the spectroscope to astronomy: and they may be at least as important.

References.

Figs. 1 and 2 and most of the information in this paper are from:

"Radio Astronomy". C. R. Burrows. (by courtesy of *Electronics*, 1949, February.)

"Galactic Noise and the Plane of the Galaxy". Ruth J. Northcott and Ralph E. Williamson. (*Journal of the Royal Astronomical Society of Canada*, 1948, November.)

14 | *The Rocket and the Future of Astronomy*

By 1952 rockets had become respectable enough to be brought to the serious attention of the professional astronomers, and not merely the wild amateurs who had no scientific reputations to worry about. Greatly daring, the Royal Astronomical Society asked me to write a survey paper on the subject.

I would like to think that my essay had some impact, at least on the younger members of the RAS. (One of them, however, did complain that I used too many exclamation marks. Objection granted.)

As for the more senior members, I am not so sure. Just four years later, the newly appointed Astronomer Royal made his notorious comment, "Space travel is utter bilge." Unluckily for him, he had barely taken up his job when Sputnik 1 was launched.*

The one line drawing in the article—an endpaper from *The Exploration of Space*—may well have been the first presentation of the communications satellite to the scientific world.

*In all fairness, it should be recorded that the poor man was being interviewed at the end of an exhausting flight from Australia in what was virtually a converted wartime bomber, so he would have been quite justified in feeling that even air travel was utter bilge. I have always had a soft spot for Dr. Woolley since I encountered him galloping over the slopes of Mount Stromlo, in search of a sick cow. The future Astronomer Royal looked as if he had ridden straight out of a Western movie.

THE ROCKET AND THE FUTURE OF ASTRONOMY

Introduction

Recent developments in rocket engineering have made possible the direct exploration of the atmosphere at heights which would have seemed fantastic only a decade ago, and have focused attention on the prospects for interplanetary flight. This paper is an attempt to summarize present achievements in the field of rocketry, as far as they are of interest to astronomers, and to assess what may reasonably be expected in the future on the basis of existing knowledge. Such an assessment seems all the more necessary in view of the many exaggerated or, alternatively, over-pessimistic statements that have appeared on the subject in the past few years.

Fundamentals

For the purpose of this survey the basic facts of rocket propulsion can be stated very briefly without going into engineering details. The importance of the rocket arises from two facts :

(1) it is the only known means of providing propulsion in a vacuum, and

(2) it is, when working under optimum conditions, the simplest and most efficient method of converting chemical energy into motion.

Whereas the thrust produced by airscrews, turbo-jets and similar devices falls to zero outside the atmosphere, that of a rocket motor *increases* by 10 or 15 per cent. The problem of sending a vehicle into planetary space is, therefore, primarily one of devising a rocket which can carry enough fuel for the mission contemplated.

For efficient operation a rocket cannot be used to provide a steady, continuous thrust during the whole of a journey. It must burn its fuel as quickly as possible, imparting all its energy to a vehicle which then " coasts " for the rest of its trajectory. The reason for this is seldom appreciated, but can be explained very simply. If the fuel is used up as near the Earth as possible, little energy is wasted in lifting the propellant against gravity. For maximum efficiency, in fact, combustion should be instantaneous—which, though of course impracticable for rockets, is virtually what happens in a gun. A slow ascent would be hopelessly extravagant, and this is why all schemes of interplanetary flight envisage reaching " escape velocity " at the earliest possible moment and then travelling in free orbit. Only if a virtually unlimited source of power were available could one leave the Earth as slowly as one pleased.

Escape velocity from the Earth is 11·2 km/s (25 000 m.p.h.), so that the minimum requirement of astronautics is that a rocket must be able to reach this speed. To see if this is practicable, we must therefore examine the factors which determine a rocket's speed.

By far the most important is the jet or exhaust velocity. This, of course, depends upon the energy of the fuel and the efficiency of the combustion process. Some typical figures attained with various fuels in existing rockets are given below :

Black powder	0·6 km/s or	1 300 m.p.h.
Oxygen and petrol	2·5	5 600
Oxygen and hydrogen	3·6	8 100
Fluorine and hydrogen	3·8	8 500

It is believed that ultimately exhaust speeds of perhaps 4·5 km/s (10 000 m.p.h.) may be achieved. This appears to be about the absolute ceiling for

[Published in *Occasional Notes of the Royal Astronomical Society*, Vol. 2, no. 14, 1952, pp. 127–36]

chemical propellants, even when motors of the highest efficiency have been developed.

Given a fuel producing a certain exhaust speed, the second factor which determines the rocket's velocity is, of course, the actual amount of the propellant it can carry. It is a source of some surprise to many people to realize that a rocket can travel faster than its exhaust. A rocket which weighed 1 ton when empty, and could carry 1·72 tons of fuel, would be capable of equalling its exhaust speed. To double this figure, the same rocket would have to carry 6·4 tons of fuel—a very much more difficult proposition, but not an impossible one. This means that we may ultimately have rockets capable of reaching speeds of the order of 9 km/s (20 000 m.p.h.)—though it should be emphasized that the present record is only a quarter of this.

Even with more modest exhaust speeds, however, it is possible to obtain high rocket velocities by the use of the " step principle ", in which one rocket carries another as its payload and drops off when its fuel is exhausted. The second rocket, starting at a great height and a considerable initial velocity, then continues to increase its speed by using its own propellant material. The present velocity record of 2·3 km/s (5 100 m.p.h.) was achieved by a two-stage rocket.

The step principle, then, enables us to compensate to some extent for the inadequacy of our fuels. However, it is an expensive method and if more than a few stages are involved the masses required become impracticably large.

The reductions in the initial take-off mass of a rocket which are made possible by quite modest improvements in exhaust velocity are often very surprising. A striking example of this is given by Goddard in his classic 1919 paper, " A Method of Reaching Extreme Altitudes ". Using an efficient rocket motor of a type he had developed, Goddard showed that it would require a starting weight of about 10 pounds to carry 1 pound to a height of 200 miles. Using the old-fashioned ship's rockets, however, the required starting weight for this same payload would be *six times that of the Earth !*

Although this is rather an extreme example, it shows how sensitive rocket performance is to improvements in exhaust velocity, and demonstrates how projects which are totally impossible in one case may become quite practical in another.

With these basic ideas in mind, we can now consider some of the astronomical tasks to which the rocket may be applied.

High-altitude research

The atmosphere has long been one of the most serious—and apparently insuperable—obstacles to astronomical research. Its distorting influence sets a limit to usable telescopic power, and, what is perhaps even more important, it blocks almost all the ultra-violet rays from space. Installing observatories on the tops of mountains goes only a short way to solving the first problem, and does not begin to deal with the second. The only complete answer is to use instruments above the atmosphere.

The German V.2 rocket could carry a ton of instruments to a height of 180 km (110 miles), and although it was expensive to operate by civilian standards (each firing costs something like $250 000—ignoring the price of the rocket !), much valuable research work has been done with V.2s in the United States. Of particular interest to the astronomer is the securing of solar ultra-violet spectra from altitudes of up to 160 km (100 miles). A great deal of valuable experience has also been gained in the design of automatic instruments which can send their observations by radio to ground stations, thus making physical recovery unnecessary.

Much more efficient rockets than the V.2 are now available, which can do similar work at a fraction of the cost. The Martin " Viking " has reached heights of 215 km (135 miles), and will do considerably better when fully developed. The cheap and simple " Aerobee " has performed valuable soundings up to heights of 110 km (70 miles). At the time of writing, the greatest altitude reached by any rocket is 385 km (242 miles).

One disadvantage of all these flights is that the rocket spends only a few minutes " above the atmosphere "—to use a loose but convenient expression. A rocket which could stay up permanently, in a stable orbit, would obviously be much more valuable and would open up a great range of scientific possibilities. The satellite rocket is, therefore, generally agreed to be the next major step in astronautics, and it is instructive to see what it implies in terms of present-day practice and materials.

The Earth Satellite Vehicle

Orbital velocity at a height of 500 km (310 miles) is 7·6 km/s (17 000 m.p.h.). At this altitude air resistance is negligible, and once projected a body would stay up indefinitely.

Many studies of such satellite vehicles have been published. One of the most authoritative is that of Seifert, Mills and Summerfield in the *Journal of Applied Physics* (**15,** 255–272, 1947 May–June). They showed that a rocket fuelled by nitric acid and aniline (the propellants used in the " Aerobee ") could take a payload of 50 kg and achieve orbital velocity if its initial mass was 25 000 kg (25 tons). This is less than twice that of a V.2. A rocket burning oxygen and hydrogen would require a take-off mass of 4 400 kg (4·5 tons). The surprising smallness of this figure demonstrates, once again, the great importance of high exhaust velocity. However, although small oxy-hydrogen rockets have been tested, we have a long way to go before they are practical propositions.

Even taking the more pessimistic figure, it will be seen that there are no fundamental difficulties in the way of developing an Earth Satellite Vehicle (E.S.V.). Five years ago the authors of the above paper concluded : " The present state of rocket technology as embodied in the V.2 rocket is actually sufficiently advanced for the accomplishment of the task." All later investigations have confirmed this fact, and there is thus no excuse for the occasional statements by well-known astronomers that the satellite vehicle lies at the extreme limit of engineering feasibility.

Nor, in terms of the present research effort, would the E.S.V. be excessively expensive. At the moment the United States is spending over $1 000 000 000 a year on rockets and guided missiles, and a vast research institution largely devoted to problems of this sort is now being constructed in Tennessee at a cost of $1 575 000 000. These figures make the development costs of the E.S.V. (which would probably be in the region of $100 000 000) look very modest.

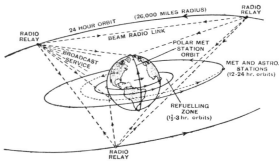

Possible orbits of space stations and artificial satellites.
This shows some of the services which could be provided by Earth Satellite Vehicles.

(Reproduced by courtesy of the Temple Press from " The Exploration of Space ".)

That the E.S.V. is being actively investigated in the United States is now well known, and at one time all three Services were engaged in separate design projects. These efforts have now been combined under the general supervision of a somewhat mysterious body known as the RAND Corporation, and the present status of the project is obscure. A number of extremely interesting papers, some of them discussed later, have emerged from the security curtain around Project RAND.

Although the bill for the first satellite will certainly be footed by the military (who are interested in it owing to its unique possibilities for reconnaissance and microwave relaying), it is to be hoped that the liberal policy of releasing scientific results already displayed by the American high-altitude research authorities will be continued in this sphere.

The uses of the E.S.V. for astronomical and scientific research are obviously very great, and many of them could be exploited even with present-day equipment. Examples are: continuous measurement of the solar ultra-violet and X-ray spectra; cosmic ray monitoring; ionospheric measurements of all kinds, and perhaps even high-definition observations of planetary surfaces, by the employment of very long-focus television cameras.

The full advantage of the E.S.V. as an astronomical observatory will not be realized until it can be manned, which leads us to the more speculative conception of the " Space Station ", discussed later. In *Occasional Notes* No. 13, Mr Sadler suggested that an artificial satellite would be of great value to navigators, owing to the parallax it would exhibit. However, the advent of such devices as SHORAN, " Gee ", and LORAN makes one doubtful if purely astronomical methods of position finding have much of a future anyway !

Escape missiles

For a rocket to escape from the Earth completely its velocity must be about 40 per cent higher than that needed in the orbiting case. To achieve this, higher take-off masses would be required, and in the case of the 100-pound payload mentioned above they would be 22 000 kg (22 tons) and 190 000 kg (190 tons) for the oxy-hydrogen and acid-aniline rockets respectively.

Such an " escape " rocket, aimed at the Moon, would reach it in about two days. The psychological effect of such an experiment would undoubtedly be tremendous, but even if the missile were landed intact by rocket braking it is difficult to think of any very useful experiments that could be carried out. The measurement of the Moon's magnetic field, as a test of Blackett's theory of magnetism, is one interesting proposal put forward by Chapman.

It would be relatively easy to arrange for such a missile to go past the Moon so that observations could be made of its hidden side. Although the results of such an experiment are hardly likely to revolutionize astronomy, one cannot help thinking that even the cosmologists would put aside their spectrograms of extragalactic nebulae for a few minutes to come and look at the photographs !

It is a surprising fact that only a small increase of speed over escape velocity would take a rocket from the Earth to the orbits of Mars or Venus. The actual figures (calculated from a point just above the atmosphere) are given below for the velocities required :

Earth to Moon	11·1 km/s	or 24 800 m.p.h.
Escape from Earth	11·2	25 000
Earth to Venus	11·5	25 700
Earth to Mars	11·6	25 900
Escape from solar system	16·4	36 700

The last figures give the speed the rocket would have to attain in order to escape from the gravitational fields of both the Earth and the Sun. It is assumed in each case that the maximum use is made of the Earth's existing orbital velocity of some 29·8 km/s (67 000 m.p.h.). All the bodies in the solar system could therefore be reached by rockets capable of attaining velocities between 11 and 16 km/s—though the transit times to the outer planets would be many years.

Such rockets would, in the absence of gravitational perturbations, eventually return to the Earth's orbit. Alternatively, they might become satellites of other planets by the use of a very small amount of braking. The automatic surveying of the nearer planets, by " reconnaissance rockets " carrying television equipment, is therefore certainly within the bounds of engineering possibilities.

Spaceships

Although a great deal can be done—and indeed has already been done— by instrument-carrying rockets, these possibilities are quite overshadowed by the idea of "spaceships" or manned rocket vehicles, capable of taking human beings to other planets and bringing them safely home to Earth. Such vehicles would, obviously, have to carry payloads of several tons out of the Earth's gravitational field, across the solar field, and through the field of the planet being visited. It is relatively simple to construct a kind of " velocity budget " for any given trip, and the figures below are for the most economical route to Venus :

Escape from Earth and transfer to voyage orbit	11·5 km/s or	25 700 m.p.h.
Transfer from voyage orbit to Venus orbit and landing on Venus	10·7	23 900
Total	22·2	49 600

The total figure is what is known as the " characteristic velocity " for the mission, and enables one to calculate how much fuel must be carried, since the rocket must be capable of making such a velocity change, though in two instalments—at the beginning and end of its journey.

For a round trip under the same conditions the figures would have to be doubled, giving a total of nearly 100 000 m.p.h. However, studies of aerodynamic braking now make it highly probable that the landings on Earth and Venus could be done *without* any large use of rocket fuel, in which case this figure would be reduced by 30 000 or 40 000 m.p.h.

It is easy to prove that, using the most powerful chemical fuels that exist, and assuming that motors can be developed to the theoretical limits of their efficiency, no spaceship could be designed to carry out such a mission. Even the far simpler undertaking of a lunar return voyage would probably be out of the question.

Nevertheless, interplanetary flight can be shown to be possible, even with chemical fuels, though it would be an undertaking of such magnitude that even a prosperous World State could only afford rather infrequent expeditions ! The key to space-travel, it is now universally agreed, lies in use of " orbital refuelling ", and by this technique the employment of single, enormous vehicles is rendered unnecessary.

The argument is as follows. Once a spaceship has achieved orbital velocity above the atmosphere, it is effectively " weightless " and, of course, its occupants would have no sense of motion. If another ship entered an approximately similar orbit, the relative velocities of the two vehicles would be very small and, by the use of low-powered auxiliary jets, they could make physical contact. Fuel could then be transferred from one vessel, acting as a " tanker ", until the other's supplies had been replenished. A relatively small increase in speed would then enable this ship to leave its orbit around the Earth and travel on an interplanetary mission. Probably a large number of " tankers " would be required for the complete operation, but the masses involved at any one time would not be unmanageably large.

This kind of "orbital technique" has a second advantage which greatly improves the economics of space flight. Spaceships operating from orbit to orbit, unlike those which have to fight their way upwards against the Earth's gravitational field, could be very lightly built and would need little structural strength. They would require no streamlining, and perhaps not even a hull. Their motors could also be of very low thrust, since in space an acceleration of $0.001\ g$ for 1 000 minutes is just as effective as $1\ g$ for 1 minute.

Dr Wernher von Braun, probably the world's leading rocket engineer, has made a detailed analysis of a rather ambitious Martian expedition on such a basis. He assumed the use of nitric acid and hydrazine (N_2H_4) as fuels : this combination is not as powerful as many possible mixtures, but avoids the use of liquefied gases. Von Braun calculates that to land an expedition of 50 men on Mars with supplies for a year would involve the combustion of 36 600 tons of fuel for the actual voyage, and no less than 5 320 000 tons for the " supply operation " whereby the ships were supplied with fuel in an orbit around the Earth. The largest vehicles used on the expedition would be the short-range supply vessels, which would have a take-off mass of 6 400 tons.

One hesitates to call this project quite impracticable, and certainly von Braun (who after all was largely responsible for the second greatest engineering achievement of the war—the V.2 rocket) does not consider it impossible. As he remarks, *à propos* of the fuel figures : " The Berlin Airlift consumed one-tenth of this amount in high-octane gasoline—just because of a little misunderstanding between diplomats ! "

A more modest expedition, employing only a dozen or so men and utilizing more powerful fuels, might require less than 1 000 000 tons of propellants and rockets of up to 1 000 tons in mass. A lunar expedition might need something of the order of 10 000 tons of propellants, used in a series of rockets weighing a few hundred tons. These figures—certainly the last ones—are not unreasonable, but they are certainly not very encouraging. They demonstrate that interplanetary flight, with chemical fuels, is a " marginal " engineering possibility—an undertaking so difficult that it will not be attempted very often, if at all.

For space travel to be really practicable something a good deal better than any chemical propellant is needed. Fortunately it exists, in theory at least, and there seems every reason to believe that it may be realized in practice.

Atomic energy: the ion rocket

Nuclear reactions liberate about a million times the energy of chemical reactions. An exploding atom bomb releases enough energy to take a mass of a thousand tons from the Earth to the Moon and back again. If an " atomic rocket " with an efficiency of even a few per cent could be devised, the problem of space flight would be solved.

We are as yet a long way from achieving this, but at least one method of using atomic energy appears quite feasible and would enormously improve the economics of space travel. This is the so-called " ion rocket ", discussed in some detail by Lyman Spitzer in one of the most important papers delivered to the Second Congress on Astronautics at London in 1951 (*Journal of the British Interplanetary Society*, **10**, 249–57, 1951 November). By *electrically* accelerating charged particles, very high " exhaust velocities " could be attained at modest voltages (for example, with nitrogen ions, 730 volts would give an exhaust velocity of 100 km/s (225 000 m.p.h.). The " ion rocket " could produce only very low thrusts and hence extremely small accelerations, but it would be ideal for operating between the orbits of the planets, e.g. after starting from a satellite orbit around the Earth. Spitzer shows that, using this principle, a 10-ton ship carrying only 3 tons of nitrogen as propellant could reach Mars in a few months. The power would be generated by a uranium pile operating an electrical generator, and the crew would be protected from radiation by the simple, though startling, expedient of having the power plant 100 km (60 miles) away from the crew chamber ! The necessary towing wires would weigh only 600 pounds and would obviate the need for tons of shielding.

One very attractive feature of the " ion-rocket " is that propellant material could be obtained from the atmosphere of any planet. The " nuclear fuel " used would only be about 2 kg (4 pounds) for a year of continuous operation ! As a result of his study Spitzer concludes that " there is every reason to believe that an interplanetary spaceship could be built with essentially present techniques ".

High-powered, chemically fuelled rockets would still be needed to make contact with the planetary surfaces, but the overall fuel requirements for an expedition to Mars would be reduced from millions to thousands of tons. At a later stage it may be possible to use nuclear energy for the entire journey but at the moment no certain way is known of doing this. Most of those who have studied the problem, however, believe that it is only a matter of time.

Space medicine

Space flight introduces physiological as well as engineering problems. To deal with them, the U.S. Air Force has already set up a Department of Space Medicine at its School of Aviation Medicine, and it recently arranged a very extensive symposium on the subject at San Antonio, Texas. This interest is not at all premature, since, as far as the human body is concerned, the first flights into space have already begun. Although the performance of such rocket vehicles as the Douglas " Skyrocket " have not yet been revealed, it is known that men have flown in them at speeds very far in excess of 1 000 m.p.h. and at heights of over 15 miles—in other words, above 98 per cent of the atmosphere. The pilots of such vehicles will even have encountered the phenomenon of "weightlessness" for appreciable periods, when they have exhausted their fuel supply and are falling back into the lower atmosphere.

All the leading medical authorities who have studied the problem believe that flight in space will not introduce any extreme physiological conditions. The only biological hazard which cannot be assessed at present is that of the heavily ionizing component of the primary cosmic rays.

Similar problems are also involved in designing protective equipment which will enable men to explore the surfaces of the planets. These are obviously capable of solution, even by existing techniques, and have been thoroughly discussed in the literature of the subject (e.g. J. B. S. Haldane, " Biological Problems of Space Flight ", *J.B.I.S.*, **10,** 154–8, 1951 July).

The Space Station

The conception of the satellite vehicle has been extended to more ambitious structures—" Space Stations ". These would be constructed from materials ferried up into an orbit, and would act as laboratories, observatories, and so on. Even in its early stages the space station could make very great contributions to astronomy. Some of these have been discussed by Lyman Spitzer in a declassified " Project RAND " paper entitled " Astronomical Advantages of an Extra-Terrestrial Observatory ".

As a long-term project, the construction of *really* large astronomical instruments might be possible, since all gravitational forces would be virtually absent and the very lightest methods of construction could be employed. There would, indeed, be no obvious limits to the size of optical or radio telescopes in space, where their performances would be incomparably better than on the Earth's surface. The satellite observatory, Spitzer concludes, can " revolutionize astronomical techniques and open up completely new vistas of research ".

Observatories on the Moon and planets

Once it becomes technically feasible to reach the planets and their satellites, the next stage will be the establishment of permanent bases. Exactly what this will imply in terms of engineering it is, of course, impossible to foresee today. For obvious reasons, it may never be possible to land on Jupiter, Saturn, Uranus and Neptune, but all the other planetary bodies in the solar system should be accessible once the necessary techniques have been mastered. In many respects the Moon will be an ideal " proving ground " for this purpose.·

It also seems an ideal site for an observatory, and R. S. Richardson has discussed this idea in " Astronomical Observations from the Moon " (*Astronomical Society of the Pacific*, Leaflet 219, 1947 May). Although lunar " seeing " would be incomparably better than on Earth, there would still be a trace of zodiacal light. To eliminate this completely we might have to go out to the orbit of Jupiter !

It is a paradoxical fact that interplanetary flight may produce the greatest astronomical consequences in the realms of stellar and extragalactic studies by liberating our instruments from the atmosphere. The direct exploration of the planetary surfaces, interesting and exciting though it seems today, may ultimately be of much less scientific importance by comparison.

Astronomical problems of space flight

Astronautics involves many interesting problems in theoretical and practical astronomy, several of which have already formed the subject of stimulating papers. Navigation in space has been discussed by Herrick, Atkinson and Porter. The optimum type of interplanetary orbit has been investigated mathematically by Herrick and Lawden. Richardson and Porter have considered specific voyages. The largely but not entirely fictitious danger of meteors to space flight has been the subject of papers by Grimminger, Whipple and Ovenden, while Spitzer has studied the stability of a satellite near the Earth. The most startling excursions into astronautics have undoubtedly been made by Zwicky, who remarked in his 1948 Halley lecture (*The Observatory*, **68**, 121–43, 1948 August) that one of the ultimate results of this work, coupled with the efficient use of nuclear energy, may be " plans for making the planetary bodies habitable by changing them intrinsically and by changing their positions relative to the Sun ". One likes to hope that before we embark on such projects the wishes of the local inhabitants, if any, may be fully consulted !

This, perhaps, is as far as imagination dare go at the present time, yet, to quote Zwicky again : " These thoughts are today perhaps nearer to scientific analysis and mastery than were Jules Verne's dreams in his time."

Summary

The conclusions concerning which there is now no serious doubt are as follows :

(1) With existing techniques it will be possible, in the relatively near future, to send small, automatic rockets into stable orbits round the Earth.

(2) Slight improvements in performance would enable such rockets to reach the Moon and planets.

(3) At a somewhat later date, manned rocket vehicles will be able to achieve circular velocity and descend to the Earth by " atmospheric braking ", finally landing as gliders.

The following conclusions are more speculative, but are accepted by the great majority of engineers and astronomers who have studied the subject :

(4) Using " orbital techniques ", true interplanetary voyages will be possible. With chemical fuels they may be prohibitively expensive, but since the use of nuclear energy for inter-orbit flight seems highly promising, this objection may soon be overcome. The first expeditions will merely survey the nearer planets from short ranges, without attempting to land. Later, special vehicles, using wings or rocket braking, will be used to make a landing.

(5) The " economical " development of interplanetary travel appears possible along the following lines of development :

(*a*) production of an efficient atomic drive, and

(*b*) avoidance of the need to carry material for the round trip by obtaining propellant mass from sources of low gravitational potential (e.g. the Moon, the asteroids, the smaller satellites).

The importance of atomic propulsion lies not only in the energies available, but also in the fact that simple and common substances such as nitrogen, water or methane may be used for the inert propellant material.

———————

It is probably not inaccurate to say that the main problems of space-flight are already solved in theory, just as the problems of heavier-than-air flight had been solved by the end of the 19th century. How soon the practical realization will follow the theoretical studies is another matter, but it must be emphasized that much described in this paper is already firmly based on an impressive foundation of engineering achievements.

Astronomy is now in a state of revolution, thanks to recent developments in electronics. But the present upheaval is nothing compared with what may be expected from rocket research before the end of this century. This fact is now realized by an increasing number of astronomers, as the references quoted in this paper demonstrate.

Astronomy is the oldest of the sciences, yet it is still in its infancy. Not until we have achieved the freedom of space—which now lies almost within our grasp—will it truly come of age.

References

1. *Rockets, Missiles and Space Travel*, Willy Ley (Chapman & Hall, London; Viking Press, N.Y.).
2. *Interplanetary Flight*, Arthur C. Clarke (Temple Press, London; Harper Bros., N.Y.).
3. *The Exploration of Space*, Arthur C. Clarke (Temple Press, London; Harper Bros., N.Y.).
4. 200 *Miles Up*, J. Gordon Vaeth (Ronald Press, N.Y.).
5. *Das Marsprojekt*, Werner von Braun (Umschau–Verlag, Frankfurt).
6. *Raumfahrtforschung*, edited by H. Gartmann (Verlag Oldenbourg, Munich).

VII | *Introduction to Astronautics*

15 | *Principles of Rocket Flight*

Having successfully graduated from King's College in 1948, I was entitled to a year of postgraduate studies, and as mentioned in the last section, decided to devote my time to astronomy. Luckily, before terminal boredom set in, the Dean called me to his office and said that he'd heard of a job that would suit me perfectly. I applied, and got it; and he was right on target.

Since 1900 the Institution of Electrical Engineers has published one of the principal abstracting journals in the field of science—*Physics Abstracts*. Its tiny staff, led by Dr. Bernard Crowther, was now struggling to cope with years of wartime arrears, and needed reinforcements. I was hired as Assistant Editor.

My job was to go through mountains of journals (we had cupboards-full of German and Japanese publications that had not yet been opened), and to see that everything of value was abstracted, so that it would be readily available to the world's scientific community. To assist me in this fascinating and responsible job, I had a small army of abstractors who among them could cope with any branch of physics (and mathematics and astronomy) in any language. Some of my employees were professional scientists who were happy to do the job for virtually nothing, so that they could keep up with the literature. Others, poor souls, were refugees or retired persons who probably relied on our modest fees for their bread and butter.

There were no office copying machines in those days, so I had to tear up the journals and send the bits to the appropriate abstractor. (Where some obscure language was involved, the whole issue might have gone to one person, irrespective of his speciality. This was not as bad as it sounds because most scientific papers are preceded by the author's (nowadays, usually authors') own abstract, which merely has to be translated.)

All too often, the abstract I got back had itself to be retranslated into English, which was not the native tongue of many of my widely recruited experts. (Their most frequent mode of communication was what I called Anglo-German.) Having done this, I was then faced with a still more difficult job—indexing the resulting mass of documents.

I don't know (and don't think I want to know) how my successors at *Physics Abstracts* cope today, but even in my time the job was, by definition, impossible. How *can* you index a new scientific discovery, so that years in the future anyone can look it up? The name for it won't have been invented yet. . . .

Anyway, I did my best with thousands of file cards, through the years 1948–50. During that period, I probably had a bird's-eye view of research in physics unmatched by anyone else on Earth—since *every* important journal, in *every* language, passed across my desk. And the abstracts were edited there, on the way to the printer.

Occasionally, I wrote the abstracts myself, when the subject was of particular interest. (You will not be surprised to learn that the heading *ASTRONAUTICS* made its appearance during my regime.) And although an abstract should be as impersonal as a railway timetable, there was at least one occasion when I felt compelled to make an interjection. Some hapless scientist (I won't reveal his nationality—I have too many good friends who share it) published a paper in one of his country's leading physics journals "proving" that a rocket could never travel faster than the speed of sound *in the material of which it was constructed*. As, in all metals, this is considerably less than the velocity of escape, space travel was, in principle, impossible.

I couldn't resist a footnote, hinting that there was something wrong, somewhere; and I have often wondered about the future career of the author.

The mountainous arrears of scientific journals—complete wartime runs from ex-enemy countries, as well as an increasing avalanche of new material as the physicists got back to their labs—presented me with the sort of personal challenge I enjoyed. I worked like a demon until the bulging cupboards were all empty, though I am sure I would have done a better job if I hadn't been so determined to get up to date. For deficiencies in editing and (especially) indexing in the 1949–50 volumes of *Physics Abstracts*, you will know who is to blame. But I am proud of the fact that I appear as a distinct second-order differential coefficient on the curve "Thousands of *Physics*

Abstracts since 1900'' in Derek J. de Solla Price's *Science Since Babylon*.

In many ways, my job at the Institution of Electrical Engineers was ideally suited to me. The work was fascinating, my colleagues were intelligent and affable, and the location was superb—on the Embankment, within easy walking distance of Westminster, the Strand and Fleet Street. By a strange coincidence, it was also very close to the two other establishments which had played such an important role in my life—being practically next door to King's College, and not far from Audit House, headquarters of my first employer, H.M. Auditor General.

I might have spent the rest of my life quite happily at the IEE, surveying the advance of physics from my Olympian height, but my spare-time income from writing (and also radio talks) was now rising steadily. When my two-year trial period was up and Dr. Crowther wanted to put me on his permanent staff, it was with genuine regret that I declined. That was more than thirty years ago, and I have never been on a payroll since.

Perhaps the deciding factor was my first book commission. This, as will be explained later, rose directly out of two articles "The Principles of Rocket Flight" written for the leading British aviation magazine *The Aeroplane*, while I was still at college. As far as I know they have never been reprinted—except in Czech. . . .

Principles of Rocket Flight

Part I—The Laws of Rocket Motion

SCIENTIFIC HISTORY has seen few technical advances more dramatic than those which, in little more than five years, have transformed the rocket from a firework into a machine which is beginning to dominate military and political thought. This contraction of several decades of peace-time research into a few years has resulted in a curious state of affairs. Because of its speculative nature, almost all the literature of rocket flight has been published by small societies, such as the Verein fur Raumschiffhart, the American Rocket Society and the British Interplanetary Society, and so is not generally available. It is, therefore, not surprising that the most profound misconceptions exist concerning rockets and their mode of operation.

The object of these articles is to give as briefly as possible the basic laws of rocket motion, so that newcomers to the field can have a clear picture of the factors involved. These laws are relatively simple, though they deal with conceptions more familiar to the astronomer and the ballistician than the aeronautical engineer.

The rocket is a machine which can only operate efficiently in the near-vacuum 20 or more miles overhead, and the fact that numerous rocket devices (assisted take-off units, rocket artillery, the Me 163) are used inside the atmosphere must not be allowed to obscure this fundamental fact. All atmospheric applications of the rocket are of very low efficiency—only a few per cent. in some cases—and rely entirely on the ability of the rocket to provide enormous amounts of power for short periods of time.

We are not concerned with devices of this nature, important though they are, but with the ultimately more significant applications of the rocket which have been discussed for half a century and which are now beginning to materialize. The great heights to which V.2s have already risen (well over 100 miles) show the possibilities of the meteorological sounding rocket, while the enormous velocities attained promise incredibly swift transport for mail and light freight.

The essential difference between a rocket-propelled machine and an aircraft is that in the case of the former there is no continuous application of power. The rocket motors operate for only a fraction of the total duration of flight, and for most of the time the machine is "coasting" along its trajectory like a shell. The performance of a rocket is thus completely determined by the velocity it achieves after the combustion of its fuel.

The problem, therefore, divides itself naturally into two sections. First we have to discover the way in which the rocket's velocity depends on its construction, fuel and other relevant factors. This is largely a matter of engineering and chemistry. Then we must consider the rocket as a projectile and derive the orbit or trajectory along which it travels. This involves ballistics and, eventually, celestial mechanics, one of the most exact of all sciences.

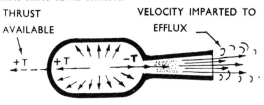

THRUST   **VELOCITY IMPARTED TO**

AVAILABLE   **EFFLUX**

FIG. 1

The Rocket Motor

Nowadays everyone knows that a rocket operates at maximum efficiency in a vacuum, though many people still find it difficult to picture the manner in which the thrust is applied. The rocket, they feel, must have "something to push against." This is quite true, and it actually "pushes against" its own exhaust gases. If the rocket ejected solid material instead of gas, this would be obvious, but the tendency to regard gases as massless seems to confuse many people who should know better.

The exploding fuel in the combustion chamber (Fig. 1) applies thrust in all directions. Laterally, the thrust has no effect, being taken up by the walls. Towards the rear, the thrust may be regarded as accelerating the "plug" of burnt gases farther down the nozzle, just as the charge in a cartridge accelerates the shot. This rearward force is balanced by that in the forward direction, accelerating the rocket as a whole.

In a vacuum, this process operates at greater efficiency and there is a slight increase in thrust, as Goddard showed experimentally nearly 30 years ago.

If the efflux velocity is very high compared with that of the body being propelled, most of the kinetic energy is carried away by the exhaust and the propulsive efficiency is low. It reaches a maximum when the two velocities are equal, and this is the main reason why rocket reaction cannot be applied economically to slow-moving vehicles (including aircraft!)

Rocket-assisted take-off of aircraft is in the category of "inefficient but effective devices" justified by results which can be obtained in no other way.

Mass Ratio and Exhaust Velocity

It is easy to show that the final velocity of a rocket, in the absence of external forces, depends on two factors alone. They are: (1) the velocity of the exhaust and (2) the mass ratio of the rocket. This is defined as the loaded weight of the

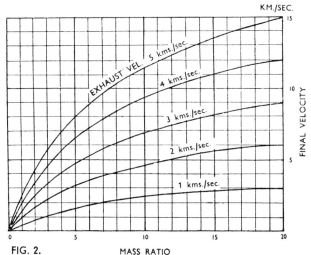

FIG. 2.   MASS RATIO

machine divided by its final weight when the fuel is burnt. Thus a four-ton rocket, carrying three tons of fuel, would have a mass ratio of four.

If the exhaust velocity is v km. sec., and the mass-ratio is R, then the final velocity of the rocket in km./sec. is given by the well-known equation:—

$$V = v \log_e R \quad \text{.............. (1)}$$

Probable values of v and R, and hence V, will be discussed in detail later. For the moment it might be mentioned that for ordinary fuels v lies between one and three km./sec., while R varies very considerably with the type of rocket. In the case of V.2 (initial mass about 12 tons, final mass about $3\frac{1}{2}$ tons) it was 3.4—a rather low figure owing to the pumping equipment and the ancillary controlling gear. Probably a figure of 10 can ultimately be reached by careful design. Solid-fuel rockets can have even higher ratios.

The prime object of efficient rocket design is to achieve the greatest possible exhaust velocity and to reduce dead-weight to give the highest value of R. Fig. 2 shows graphically how the final velocity of the rocket depends on these factors.

These curves demonstrate very clearly the enormous importance of high exhaust velocity. To take a specific example, consider the case of a rocket which is required to reach a velocity

[Published in *The Aeroplane* for January 3, 1949, pp. 14–6, and January 10, 1947, pp. 48–50]

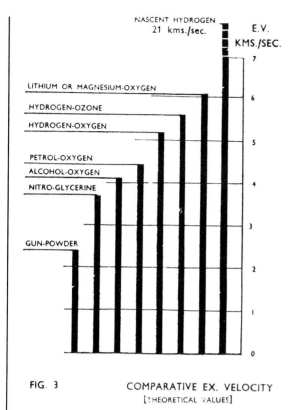

FIG. 3　　COMPARATIVE EX. VELOCITY
[THEORETICAL VALUES]

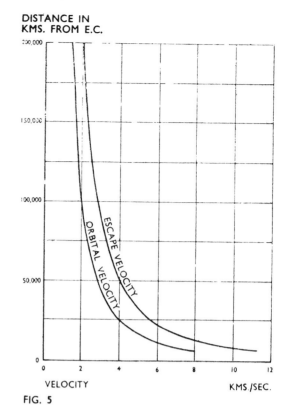

FIG. 5

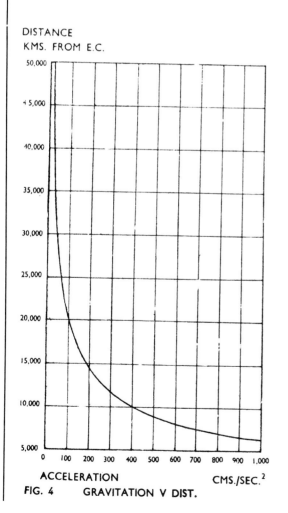

FIG. 4　　GRAVITATION V DIST.

of 4 km./sec. Burning a fuel with an exhaust velocity of 1 km./sec., it would require a mass-ratio of 55—a quite impossible figure for a simple rocket, as will be realized by considering the engineering difficulties in making a 55-ton (all-up weight) machine carry 54 tons of fuel! If, however, the exhaust velocity were 4 km./sec., the ratio would be reduced to less than three (actually 2.72), which is smaller than the value for V.2.

It is, therefore, not surprising that performance was poor as long as the low-energy powder fuels were used, and that only the advent of liquid fuels of the alcohol-oxygen type made the high-altitude, long-range rocket possible.

Rocket Fuels

Until a generation ago, all rockets were of the "dry" type, burning solid fuel such as black powder. These gave effective exhaust velocities of less than 1 km./sec. Liquid fuels, first experimentally investigated by Professor Goddard in America and later by the Verein für Räumschiffhart (" Society for Space Travel ") in Germany, have energies of a much higher order. Fig. 3 shows the theoretical exhaust velocities of various combinations. The top three listed are highly speculative, and it will be seen that the normal fuels just pass the 4 km./sec. line.

How much of this velocity can be attained in practice depends on the efficiency of the rocket motor, and as there are no moving parts this can be very high indeed. A figure of 3.5 km./sec. has been reached by Sanger, using Diesel oil under considerable pressure. There is, however, some doubt as to how far this value was the result of the very high injection pressures used.

At the present time, the main limitation to further increase in exhaust velocity is metallurgical rather than chemical—present combustion chambers cannot withstand the temperatures involved. This is, of course, a field in which a great deal of development can and will take place.

As will be seen later, exhaust velocities of the 3 km./sec. class will suffice for the World-wide ranges and the attainment of altitudes of thousands of miles. They are even adequate to take a rocket into interplanetary space, but are too low to permit of return voyages to and from other Worlds.

The Earth's Gravitational Field

Before proceeding any farther, it is necessary to consider in some detail the gravitational laws which control the motion of the rocket, both when it is on its powered trajectory and later when it is coasting freely with its motors shut off.

For ordinary purposes, gravity is regarded as a constant force, perpendicular to the surface of the Earth. The rocket can, however, reach regions where "g" is very small, and it can attain velocities which, even close to the Earth, are sufficient to overcome gravity completely.

The Earth's gravitational field obeys Newton's inverse square law. If g is the acceleration of gravity at sea level (981 cm./sec.[2] or 32 ft./sec.2), r is the radius of the Earth and x the distance *from the Earth's centre*, then the gravity at x is given by

$$g_x = \frac{g\,r^2}{x^2} \quad \ldots \ldots \quad (2)$$

Fig. 4 shows how g decreases with increasing distance from the Earth. It follows from this that the work done in lifting a body vertically through a given distance is much less at a great altitude, diminishing according to the same law as Fig. 4. If we measure the area beneath the curve, it will give the *total* work done in lifting a body from the surface of the Earth to a point where gravity is zero (i.e., infinity).

The calculation gives a rather interesting result. The work done in lifting a body to infinity is the same as that that would be done in lifting it through one radius of the Earth *if gravity remained constant*. Thus,

W = gr   .   .   .   (3)

This gives us an easy way of visualizing and remembering the energies needed. Thus, to take one ton completely away from the Earth would require 4,000 mile-tons of work, since the Earth's radius is about 4,000 miles.

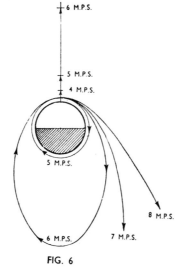

FIG. 6

The "energy of release" may be imparted to the body in a single impulse or by an acceleration prolonged over a considerable period of time. The first case represents that of a shell fired from a gun, the second that of the rocket.

Escape Velocity

If a body is given a velocity of 11.2 km./sec. (7 m.p.s.), its kinetic energy will equal the energy of release. It will, therefore, recede from the Earth indefinitely, always slowing down but always having some residual velocity. Any attempt to escape from the Earth involves giving the body the equivalent (at least) of this critical impulse.

It will be apparent that the velocity of escape itself diminishes with increasing distance, and the actual variation is shown in Fig. 5.

Orbital Velocity

If there were no air resistance, it would be possible for a body in horizontal motion to travel at such a velocity that the centrifugal force acting on it balanced gravity. The body would, therefore, never fall to the surface, but would remain in a circular orbit indefinitely. This, of course, is the principle of all planetary motion.

The "orbital velocity" at the Earth's surface is 8 km./sec. (5 m.p.s.), and although air resistance would quickly destroy any body which moved at such a speed at low altitudes, a stable orbit is a practical proposition outside the atmosphere, i.e., at any altitude over a few hundred kilometres. Like escape velocity, orbital velocity decreases with distance (see Fig. 5). The two velocities at any point are related by the simple equation

Escape velocity = $\sqrt{2}$ Orbital velocity . . (4)

A body in the closest possible orbit would make one complete revolution of the Earth every 90 minutes, and it is interesting to note that there is one orbit, with a radius of 42,000 km., which has a period of exactly 24 hours. A body in this orbit, if above the Equator, would remain stationary for ever over the same spot on the Earth's surface. The Moon (distance 385,000 km.) requires a velocity of only 1 km./sec. to maintain itself in its orbit, as may be seen by producing the chart.

We are now in a position to consider what happens to a body if it is projected away from the Earth at various speeds, always assuming that the operation takes place at such an altitude that air resistance can be ignored. Projected vertically, it would rise to a height which depends on the initial velocity. It would always fall back again if this speed were less than 11 km./sec. (or 7 m.p.s.), but if this figure were reached it would never return to Earth but would recede into space indefinitely.

The case for *horizontal* projection is slightly different. At velocities up to 8 km./sec. (5 m.p.s.) the body would fall back to Earth at steadily increasing ranges. When 8 km./sec. was reached, it would not fall back, nor yet escape. It would revolve in a circular orbit, and if this velocity were exceeded the circle would become an ellipse. At the critical speed of 11 km./sec. the ellipse would open out into a parabola and, as before, the body would escape completely. (Fig. 6.)

We have now discussed (very briefly and with some lack of precision) the main factors determining the motion of a rocket in space. In the next article we shall look at some of them in more detail, and will see what results may be expected from practical cases.

Part II—Rocket Flight in Space

WE HAVE SEEN in Part I that with ordinary fuels and present-day designs it will be possible to build rockets capable of reaching speeds in vacuum of several kilometres a second, and we will now examine what this means in terms of, for example, altitudes attained. Fig. 6 gave a rough estimate, but Fig. 7 shows accurately the heights reached by a body projected at any speed up to 11 km./sec.

This curve shows very clearly one most important fact. At modest speeds the heights attained (although considerable by ordinary standards) are still relatively small. However, as the velocity of the rocket passes 4-5 km./sec. (about twice the speed of V.2) the curve begins to rise very rapidly, reaching infinity at 11.2 km./sec. Spectacular increases in rocket performance will, therefore, be obtained once we have passed through the present speed range.

It is extremely instructive to combine Figs. 7 and 2 to produce curves (Fig. 8), showing the way in which the height a rocket would attain depends on its mass ratio and exhaust velocity.

This demonstrates very clearly the crucial importance of high exhaust velocity. As the lowest curve shows, with a 1 km./sec. fuel no conceivable rocket could ever reach any considerable altitude.

Although, as we will see in the next section, air resistance and what is known as "gravitational loss" would profoundly modify these results, they are approximately true for the case of a rocket launched from a very high mountain with an initial acceleration of several times due to gravity.

Gravitational Loss

If a rocket is fired vertically, its final velocity will be less than that indicated in Equation 1, owing to the fact that gravity will be retarding it during its period of powered flight. If the time of burning is t seconds, and there is no variation of gravity, the final velocity will, therefore, be—

$$V = v \log_e R - gt \quad \ldots \ldots \quad (5)$$

The gt term represents the "gravitational loss" of the rocket. It may clearly be reduced by reducing t, which implies the use of a high acceleration.

"g" loss may be very serious for a low-acceleration rocket. A rocket travelling at only 1g would lose half its calculated final velocity for this reason, and its mass-ratio would have to be squared to make good the loss.

There would be no g loss at an infinite acceleration, but in practice the acceleration which can be used is limited by the thrust of the motors, by the stresses which can be withstood by the machine and the crew (if any) and by air resistance. It is interesting to note that one high-altitude rocket (the U.S. "Wac Corporal") used accelerations of up to 30g in the initial "boosted" portion of its flight.

Air Resistance

If the rocket is projected vertically to a considerable distance beyond the atmosphere, air resistance is a factor that can only affect it during the initial portion of its flight, when it is travelling at minimum velocity. Nevertheless, it can result in a

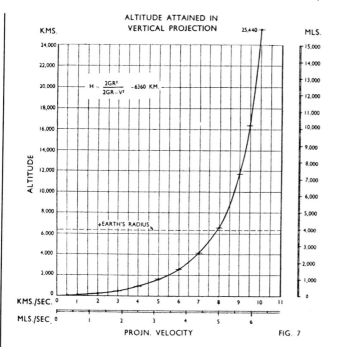

ALTITUDE ATTAINED IN VERTICAL PROJECTION

$$H = \frac{2GR^2}{2GR - V^2} - 6360 \text{ KM.}$$

FIG. 7

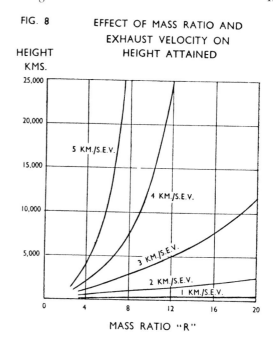

FIG. 8

EFFECT OF MASS RATIO AND EXHAUST VELOCITY ON HEIGHT ATTAINED

prohibitive reduction in performance, particularly in the case of small rockets. In the case of large machines the frontal and surface areas are proportionally less in relation to the mass, by operation of the square-cube law.

For the first 20 km. above the Earth's surface, the density of the air falls off rapidly with increasing height; very approximately, it is halved every 6 km.

At greater heights the exact figures for density are a matter of conjecture, although measured values should be obtained in the near future. However, it is known that V.2 experienced no appreciable resistance in the upper portion of its trajectory. At 100 km. the density is probably much less than one-millionth of that at sea level.

The presence of the atmosphere makes it imperative that a rocket should never travel at a considerable speed at low altitudes. A body may become red-hot through friction in the lower atmosphere when travelling at only 2 km./sec., but it would require the enormous velocity of 50 km./sec. to produce incandescence at a height of 100 km., as observations on meteors have shown.

These considerations make it very probable that ultra high-altitude rockets and true spaceships would be launched from mountain peaks. There are many possible launching sites which are effectively half-way through the atmosphere.

Single-stage Rockets

To compute accurately the performance of a specific rocket is a lengthy affair, involving a detailed flight analysis of the trajectory. However, the laws given above enable possible maximum performances to be roughly estimated.

A rocket with an exhaust velocity of $3\frac{1}{2}$ km./sec. and a mass ratio of 7—figures which should soon be realized—would, by Equation 1, attain a final velocity of about 7 km./sec. If it employed an average acceleration of 4g, the gravitational loss would reduce this figure to about $5\frac{1}{2}$ km./sec. The velocity lost by air resistance would depend largely on the height of the launching site. Taking a somewhat pessimistic estimate, the rocket would be left with a velocity of 4 km./sec. at a height of about 200 km. when power was cut off. With this initial velocity it would be able to rise another 1,000 km. (600 miles) before falling back to Earth.

It will thus be possible to use rockets of simple design to reach altitudes far beyond the limits of the atmosphere, either with automatic instruments or with human passengers. It is understood that the U.S. Army is designing a sounding rocket with a 500-mile ceiling, and such machines should be appearing in the next few years.

Although developments in fuel and design will produce great improvements over the figures given above, construction of a rocket to reach interplanetary space and to leave the Earth completely, requires an advance in technique over the elementary, one-stage rocket. The reason for this is shown in Fig. 10, which

gives the relationship between exhaust velocity and mass ratio for a rocket which can just escape from the Earth (making no allowance for air and gravitational losses).

This is perhaps the most striking demonstration of the importance of exhaust velocity, and it will be seen that for any fuel now known, a mass ratio of at least 20-30 is required. In practice the figure would have to be at least 50—a quite impossible value for a rocket of normal design.

The Step-rocket

Engineering considerations limit the mass ratio of a single-stage rocket, and hence its ultimate velocity. By making the rocket's payload another self-contained rocket, this limitation can be circumvented. This is the principle of the "step-rocket." Each step starts with the velocity given to it by the preceding

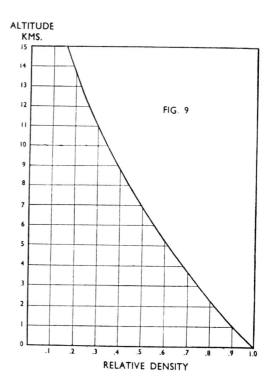

ALTITUDE KMS.

FIG. 9

RELATIVE DENSITY

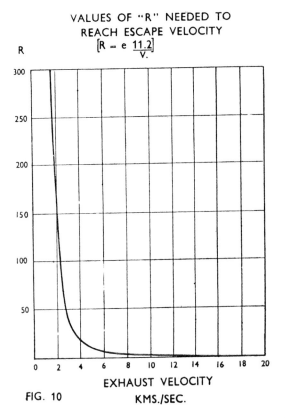

VALUES OF "R" NEEDED TO
REACH ESCAPE VELOCITY
$$R = e\ \frac{11.2}{V_e}$$

EXHAUST VELOCITY

FIG. 10   KMS./SEC.

one, and by having a sufficient number of steps any final velocity may (in theory) be realized. If a rocket were designed to give a final velocity of 5½ km./sec., a two-step version could escape from the Earth and so enter interplanetary space. This step-principle was the basis of the German transatlantic project A.9, which would have been a winged V.2 with an 80-ton "booster" to start it with an initial velocity of several thousand kilometres an hour.

The Cellular Rocket

The cellular rocket, evolved by the British Interplanetary Society, is the step rocket taken to its logical conclusion. This envisages a machine consisting of some hundreds of self-contained rocket units, capable of being jettisoned when completely discharged. In this way the mass of the machine would progressively decrease, and effective mass-ratios of several hundred could be achieved. Such a design would be necessary to permit of interplanetary voyages with any fuels at present in sight. (The highly speculative subject of atomic energy will be discussed in a later section.)

Conditions in Space

In this brief and necessarily limited survey we have concentrated on the wider aspects of rocket development, ignoring the more immediate and restricted applications which will be covered by many specialist papers in the near future. It may, therefore, be as well to end by a consideration of the new problems and conditions engineers will face when flight in vacuum becomes a practical possibility.

Maintaining life in a vacuum is a technical problem which has been largely solved by high-altitude research, although in some ways it bears a closer similarity to submarine practice than to "pressurization." Maintaining a rocket at the correct temperature, however, involves certain new factors concerning which there is a good deal of popular confusion.

Space cannot have a "temperature." Matter in interplanetary space will assume a temperature which depends upon the rate of incident radiation, and the stable temperature for a body in space is that temperature at which the radiation from all its surface equals the heat received, plus any developed internally. Thus the shape, attitude and conducting properties of the surface, among other things, are all major factors affecting the final temperature and the rate at which it is established. In the Earth's shadow a small body would get very cold, but in direct sunlight it would assume a temperature of up to 100 degrees C. Excess heat can be reflected by silvering the surface

of the rocket, and in this way a balance may be reached at any required temperature.

Meteors

An entirely incorrect impression is current about the danger of meteoric impact. For one thing, it is not generally realized that most meteors are very tiny particles indeed. The great majority of those visible to the naked eye are far smaller than peas; those which show telescopically are almost microscopic grains. By far the greater number of meteors striking the Earth lie in this second class. Although something like a thousand million a day reach the Earth, a simple comparison of the relative areas of Earth and any conceivable rocket shows how negligible the danger will be.

Radiations

A possibly more serious hazard lies in the radiations, particularly "cosmic rays," which are known to exist in space. One of the first aims of rocket research will be to learn more about these radiations, which are believed to be connected in some way with the fundamental structure of matter. Men have already, in very high altitude flights, travelled through regions where cosmic ray intensity was much greater than at sea-level. At still greater heights the radiation falls in intensity, owing to the absence of secondary particles produced in the atmosphere. The whole subject is very complex, but a great deal more will be learned about it from automatic rocket ascents in the near future.

Conclusion

The technology of rocket flight in space will ultimately be at least as extensive as is that of aviation to-day. These articles have only been able to touch the fringe of the new science of astronautics, which is now where flying was in the late 19th century. Whether it will progress as rapidly as flying depends on factors which cannot be foreseen to-day. One of the most important of these is, of course, progress in atomic research.

Nuclear reactions liberate energies incomparably in excess of those needed for voyages to the remotest planets. Calculation shows that even the 0.1 per cent. efficient uranium reaction is a million times as powerful as any chemical combination. Unfortunately the atomic bomb releases energy at temperatures of some thousands of millions of degrees, while the uranium pile operates at only a hundred degrees.

The application of nuclear energy to aircraft or rocket propulsion is therefore a problem of very great difficulty, but atomic research is in its infancy and it would be a rash man who would make any negative prophecy. It is quite certain that a great research effort will be devoted to this subject (the Fairchild Corporation is already working on it under a U.S. contract) and a practical solution may arrive in the not-too-distant future.

However, making no allowance for any atomic dividends, the pattern, if not the time-scale, of future rocket research is fairly clear. The present exploration of the ionosphere by automatic machines of the V.2 type will continue on an increasing scale, until it becomes permissible to talk of "distance" rather than "altitude." Multi-step rockets will be developed at a later stage, and these will ultimately be able to make circuits of the moon with automatically recording instruments. At some indefinite date the true "spaceship" will arrive and will take men into interplanetary space.

Although prophets are apt to be confounded by the speed of events, these later developments will probably not materialize until the last quarter of the century. But the earlier ones are projects of the immediate future, and a period of intensely interesting research lies ahead. It is hoped that these notes will help in an understanding of what may reasonably be expected in the next decade.

The coming generation of engineers has in its hand one of the most powerful machines yet created by man. It may help to bring about a culture of a richness and variety which will make our present age seem prehistoric by comparison, and our mental horizons as bounded as those of an African bushman. Or, combined with the atomic bomb, it may provide the ultimate weapon for the destruction of civilization. But it is here, and the manner of its employment is for us to choose.

Acknowledgments

I wish to thank my colleagues in the B.I.S. for their assistance in the preparation of these articles. They must not be held responsible for any opinions expressed. Particular thanks are due to Mr. R. A. Smith for the preparation of the drawings.

16 | *A Universal Escape-Velocity Mass-Ratio Chart*

I was now getting more and more interested in rocketry, partly under the influence of my good friend the late A.V. Cleaver, who was then in charge of rocket development at the de Haviland Company. One result was a brief paper giving in a very compact form the effects of "gravitational loss" on a vehicle escaping from the Earth.

A UNIVERSAL ESCAPE-VELOCITY MASS-RATIO CHART

In a recent issue of the *Bulletin* (Vol. 2, No. 2; Feb., 1947) equations were derived showing how the final velocity of a rocket is affected by its acceleration, the "optimum" value calculated from the familiar equation $V = v \log_e R$ only being reached at an infinite acceleration. This implies, as was shown, that the mass-ratio needed for escape must be increased to some higher value to allow for this "gravitational loss."

These results may be expressed graphically in the following very simple manner. Writing the theoretical mass-ratio for infinite acceleration as R_0 we have

$$R_0 = e^{\frac{V}{v}} \quad \ldots\ldots\ldots\ldots\ldots \text{ Eq. 1}$$

where V is escape velocity and v is the exhaust velocity for the rocket under consideration. In the case of the Earth V is 11·2 km./sec. and plotting this function we obtain the left-hand curve on the graph. It will be seen at once how impossible of attainment are the mass-ratios needed for escape with low-energy fuels, and how quickly they fall as exhaust velocity is increased beyond about 4 km./sec. (The reduction is even more striking when the curve is plotted on a linear scale.)

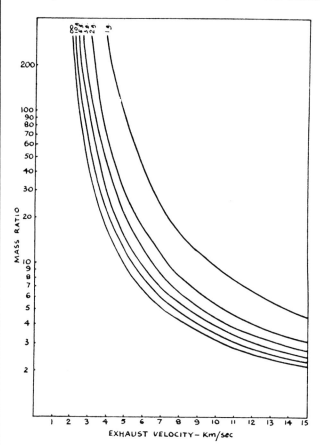

Let us now consider the practical case, in which the rocket has an acceleration (assumed uniform) of n gravities. We will assume that the Earth's field is constant, which is a reasonable approximation for accelerations of over three gravities, and in any case has the effect of making the results too pessimistic. The time of burning of the rocket is therefore V/ng seconds, and thus the new mass-ratio R needed is given by

[Published in the *Bulletin of the British Interplanetary Society* for May 1947, Vol. 2, no. 4, pp. 72–3]

$$V = v \log_e R_n - \frac{V}{ng} \cdot g$$

Hence $\qquad R_n = e^{\frac{V}{v} \cdot \frac{n+1}{n}} \quad$ or $\quad R_n = (R_0)^{\frac{n+1}{n}} \quad \ldots\ldots\ldots\ldots$ Eq. 2

This simple result shows that, for example, at an effective acceleration of $1g$ the mass-ratio of the rocket would have to be *squared* to overcome gravitational loss.

Curves have been plotted for the cases $n = 1, 2, 3, 5$ and 10, and from these it is possible to read off at once the mass-ratio needed for any given exhaust velocity. Above $n = 10$ the approach to the limiting curve becomes very slow, and there is no great advantage in employing excessively high accelerations even if they were possible.

17 | *The Dynamics of Space-Flight*

My college career had now given me the basic tools needed to tackle elementary problems in space flight, so I wrote a paper for the BIS setting out the general principles involved. Combined with the two earlier papers on rocketry, it would have made a mini-textbook on astronautics. I am not sure if I was aware of it at the time, but that was exactly where I was heading.

THE DYNAMICS OF SPACE-FLIGHT

By Arthur C. Clarke, B.Sc.

1.—Introduction

The number of books on astronautics is now very considerable, but they fall rather sharply into two categories—the "popular" or semi-technical, and the highly mathematical. This paper is an attempt to fill the gap between these extremes, and to give a reasonably accurate quantitative treatment of many of the problems of astronautics without advanced mathematics. Indeed, it is hoped that many of the conclusions reached can be understood without much trouble by those with no mathematical training at all.

The subject divides itself naturally into three sections: first, the motion of a body in the Earth's gravitational field; then the problem of the lunar voyage; and finally, true interplanetary journeys. The cases are of increasing difficulty and complexity and will therefore be dealt with in this order.

It may be as well to point out that this discussion is perfectly general and does not presuppose any particular form of propulsion—chemical rocket, atomic rocket, or even rockets at all. To travel from one body in space to another involves the expenditure of a definite amount of energy: from this point of view it does not matter in the least by what technical means the journey is made. It is true that the rocket is the only conceivable form of interplanetary locomotion at the moment: but even if the anti-gravity screen beloved of early science-fiction writers appears, it will still have to obey the same fundamental laws.

These laws are extremely simple and have been well understood since their formulation by Newton nearly 300 years ago. It is, indeed, a curious thought that there is probably nothing in this paper which would be unfamiliar to Newton—whereas such relatively far less spectacular aspects of our subject as aerodynamics or thermodynamics would be almost incomprehensible to him.

Astronautics is a branch of celestial mechanics, the science dealing with the movement of heavenly bodies. Spaceships will obey the same laws, and will hence move along the same sort of paths, as planets and comets—except during those very short periods of time when they are under power. It is a fortunate fact that, with accelerations which the human body can withstand comfortably, a spaceship need operate its motors for only about 10 minutes to attain velocities which would take it anywhere in the Solar System—even on journeys that might last for decades. It follows, therefore, that for practically the whole duration of any voyage a spaceship would be "inert," like any heavenly body, entirely under the control of the gravitational forces in the surrounding space.

2.—Gravitational Fields

The gravitational field with which we are most familiar, and from which all our journeys must commence, is the Earth's, which at sea-level produces an acceleration on a falling body of 9·81 metres per second per second (32·2 feet per sec. per sec.) Table I shows how the value of g varies for the most important bodies in the Solar System, and it will be seen that there are only two planets on which human beings would feel heavier than they do on Earth. To bring the meaning of these figures home more vividly, the second column shows how long it would take to fall 4·9 metres from rest on each of these bodies—the distance one falls in the first second on Earth.

The gravitational field of a body falls off with distance according to Newton's inverse square law—if one doubles the distance from the centre, "g" is reduced to a quarter, and so on. Thus the fields of the planets are effective only over very small distances, astronomically speaking. Fig. 1 shows the variation of

[Published in the *Journal of the British Interplanetary Society*, March 1949, Vol. 8, no. 2, XXVII, pp. 71–84]

TABLE I

Body	Gravity E = 1	Time to fall 4·9 m. (sec.)	Escape velocity (km./sec.)	Circular velocity (km./sec.)
Sun	28	0·2	618	437
Mercury	0·26	2·0	3·5	2·5
Venus	0·90	1·1	10·4	7·3
Earth	1	1	11·2	7·9
Moon	0·16	2·5	2·3	1·6
Mars	0·38	1·6	5·0	3·6
Phobos	0·001*	30*	0·01*	0·01*
Jupiter	2·65	0·6	60	42·5
Ganymede ..	0·2*	2*	3*	2*
Saturn	1·14	0·9	36	25
Titan	0·2*	2*	3*	2*
Uranus	0·96	1·0	22	15·5
Neptune	1·0	1·0	23	16

* Approximate figures.

the Earth's field with distance. Despite the fact that beyond 100,000 kilometres it is too small to be presented accurately on the graph, it never reaches zero however far away one goes. Even at 385,000 kilometres it is sufficient to keep the not inconsiderable mass of the Moon chained to its orbit!

When a body is lifted against the Earth's gravitational field, the work that has to be done equals the product of the vertical distance and the force. But since the force is steadily decreasing, it follows that the work done over equal distances is also decreasing, according to the same inverse-square law. The *total* work that has to be done in lifting a body from the Earth's surface to a point where gravity is negligible (to infinity, as the mathematician would put it) is therefore proportional to the total area beneath the "g" curve in Fig. 1. This can be calculated very easily, and leads to the important and surprisingly simple result that for unit mass:—

$$E = gR$$

where R is the radius of the Earth.

This means, for example, that to lift one ton completely away from the Earth (R = 4,000 miles) we must do 4,000 mile-tons of work. *The task is*

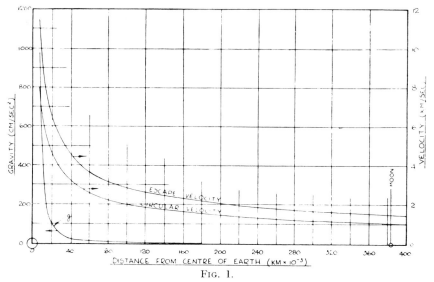

Fig. 1.

Variation of gravity, and escape and circular velocities, with distance from Earth's centre.

therefore exactly equivalent to that of climbing a mountain 4,000 miles high, assuming that gravity remained constant. Perhaps this brings home more vividly than anything else the order of magnitude of the energies involved.

The formula $E = gR$ applies to all other bodies, if g and R stand for the appropriate surface gravities and radii. In this way we can calculate that to escape from the Moon is equivalent to climbing vertically 180 miles under one terrestrial gravity, a height not much greater than that attained by V.2.

The Earth's gravitational field, therefore, may be regarded as producing a sort of valley or pit 4,000 miles (6,360 kilometeres) deep out of which we have to climb if we wish to travel to other worlds. The walls of the pit are very steep near the beginning, but rapidly flatten out with increasing distance (Fig. 2). At the Moon's distance the gravitational slope is very gentle: it is never *perfectly* flat, but beyond about a million kilometres it is so nearly level that scarcely any more work need be done in moving away from the Earth. As far as energy considerations are concerned, we have reached "infinity," though by astronomical standards we are still very near the Earth.

If we happen to be going towards the Moon, we presently come across its private gravitational pit, only 278 kilometres (180 miles) deep, and with much more gently sloping sides. Fig. 2 shows very clearly how relatively easy it is to leave the Moon, and how important it may be as a base for expeditions to other planets. Though so close, astronomically speaking, it is really nine-tenths of the way to infinity.

There are two ways of climbing out of a valley. The usual method is to proceed up the slope at a low but more or less constant speed, exerting a fairly steady effort all the time. The second method, not unfamiliar to cyclists, is to build up such a speed at the bottom of the hill that one can then relax and rely on one's momentum to carry one to the top without any further effort—trading velocity for height.

Both methods are, in theory, possible for a spaceship leaving the Earth. If a rocket, for example, had unlimited power supplies, it could climb to the stars at a steady 100 miles an hour. But this slow, steady departure would require an enormous expenditure of energy, since most of the machine's effort would be wasted merely maintaining its position. (The extreme case of this is the rocket just balanced on its exhaust, which burns the whole of its fuel getting nowhere.) We are therefore forced to consider only the case in which a sufficient initial velocity is built up, in a relatively short distance, to enable the rocket to make the rest of the journey on momentum alone.

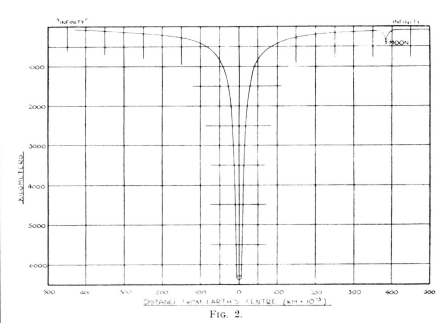

FIG. 2.

Potential Energy Diagram of Earth-Moon System.

The velocity needed to enable us to "coast" up our 4,000-mile-high hill is almost exactly 25,000 miles an hour (11·2 km./sec.). This is the famous "velocity of escape," and its physical meaning is nothing subtler than this. A body projected vertically from the Earth at 11·2 kilometres (or 7 miles) a second would travel outwards, always slowing down, but would never fall back. At a lower speed, it would come to rest before reaching the top of the "hill," and would come falling down the slope again. It would return to Earth with exactly its initial speed, as would any body projected up a frictionless slope with a velocity insufficient for it to reach the top.

3.—Escape and Circular Velocities

Every planet has its characteristic escape velocity, usually quoted for the surface of the body. Escape velocity falls off with increasing height: as might be expected, the velocity needed to reach the top of the "gravitational slope" is reduced if one starts some way from the bottom. The rate of decrease is rather slow, depending inversely on the square *root* of the distance. (See Appendix.)

Related to escape velocity is the conception of circular velocity. This is the velocity a body needs, not to escape from a planet, but to circle it like a moon. At the Earth's surface this velocity is about 18,000 miles an hour (7·9 km./sec.). If a body reached this speed in horizontal flight just outside the atmosphere the outward centrifugal force would exactly balance gravity. It would circle the Earth once every 90 minutes or so. At greater heights the velocity required is naturally less, the variation with distance being the same as for escape velocity. In fact, at any point the escape velocity is equal to $\sqrt{2} \times$ circular velocity.

Fig. 1 shows the variation of the Earth's escape and circular velocities with distance: it will be seen that they fall off very much more slowly than does "g". Fig. 3 shows the value of circular velocity for points close to the Earth, and also the period of revolution of a body in a circular orbit. These orbits will probably be the first to be of practical importance in astronautics.

Table I lists the escape and circular velocities for the chief bodies in the Solar System. They range from 60 km./sec. for Jupiter down to about 10 metres/sec. for Phobos, the inner moon of Mars. It would be possible to jump completely away from a body a little smaller than this: Phobos' "gravitational pit" is only about five *metres* deep, as against the Earth's 6,360 kilometres!

We are now in a position to discuss the requirements for a voyage from the Earth to the Moon. Looking at Fig. 2 again, we see that the velocity needed to

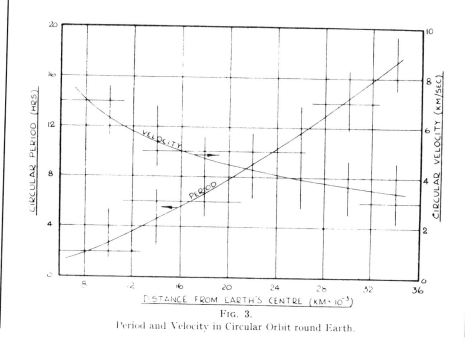

Fig. 3.
Period and Velocity in Circular Orbit round Earth.

reach the Moon from the Earth is a little less than that needed to reach "infinity." The difference, however, is only about a tenth of a kilometre a second, so we will assume that the full velocity of escape, 11·2 kilometres a second, is required.

A spaceship given this velocity in the direction of the Moon would slowly lose speed until it came almost to rest about 40,000 kilometres from the Moon. Then, as it began to enter our satellite's "gravitational pit" it would begin to accelerate again. If unchecked, it would reach the Moon at a little less than that body's velocity of escape, 2·3 kilometres a second. The ship's motors must therefore be used to neutralize this speed, and hence the *absolute minimum* velocity requirement for the journey is 11·2 + 2·3 or 13·5 kilometres a second (30,000 miles an hour). The ship would, of course, never actually reach this speed: but it must be potentially capable of doing so.

This figure is a theoretical minimum which must be exceeded in practice owing to (*a*) air resistance at take-off, (*b*) "gravitational losses" due to the retarding effect of the Earth's field and (*c*) margins for navigational corrections, which might be considerable at the lunar end of the voyage. These additional figures are rather indefinite and depend a good deal on particular cases. In general, they should not exceed 20 per cent., making the total "velocity budget" for the one-way lunar voyage about 16 kilometres a second (36,000 miles an hour).

The air resistance loss, though it is the one most often mentioned, is in fact, the least important. A rocket leaving Earth is travelling relatively slowly in the atmosphere, and on a large ship the velocity loss due to frictional drag would be only a fraction of a kilometre a second—a negligible quantity compared with the requirements for the rest of the voyage.

The return journey is the same as the outward one, but with this difference, that the Earth's atmosphere may be used to produce a certain amount of frictional braking at the end of the voyage. Ignoring this, the requirement for the round trip would be 2 × 16 or 32 kilometres a second (72,000 miles an hour). Allowing for atmospheric braking, it would be about 30 kilometres a second (67,000 miles an hour), or perhaps a little less. Once again it should be emphasized that the maximum velocity the ship would ever actually reach would be less than a third of this.

We have been able to use this relatively simple treatment in the case of the Earth–Moon voyage because both bodies are at the same distance from the Sun, and so the Sun's gravitational field acts on them equally and may, therefore, be ignored. If we wish to consider true interplanetary journeys, however, we can no longer do this. Not only must our spaceship escape from one planet and lower itself safely on to another, but it must also do work either moving outwards against the Sun's gravitational field, or decelerating itself after falling down the solar field. It is therefore necessary to consider how this field varies across the orbits of the planets.

4.—The Sun's Gravitational Field

The Sun's gravitational field obeys exactly the same laws as the Earth's: the only difference is that it is far more intense and is effective over a far greater volume of space. Escape velocity at the surface of the Earth is 11·2 kilometres a second: at the surface of the Sun it is no less than 618 kilometres a second. Thus the energies needed to leave the two bodies are of an altogether different order of magnitude. The Earth's 6,360-kilometre-deep "gravitational pit" seemed quite impressive: but to escape from the Sun is equivalent to climbing, under one gravity, out of a pit 20,000,000 kilometres (12,000,000 miles) deep!

Luckily for astronautics, this "pit" is so very narrow that even Mercury, the innermost planet, is far up on the shallow, higher slopes. All the planets, in fact, are within a quarter of a million kilometres of the top, and as a result the velocities needed to go from one orbit to another are in most cases less than those needed to escape from the planets themselves. This is certainly very fortunate. One could easily imagine Solar Systems with very massive suns in which it might be quite simple to escape from a planet and go to its satellite, whereas the journey from one planet to another might be almost impossible.

We will now construct an "energy diagram" of the Solar System on much the same lines as we have already done for the Earth and Moon. This time, however, we will measure the depth of the "gravitational pit" in terms of the velocity needed to escape from it at any point, since it is this in which we are primarily interested. To escape from the Sun requires a velocity of 618 kilometres a second, which gives the maximum depth of the pit. To escape from the orbit of the innermost planet, Mercury, requires only a tenth of this—68 kilometres a second. But Mercury's orbital speed is already 48 kilometres a second: hence the additional velocity needed is 20 kilometres a second. This additional or excess velocity, which we will call "transfer velocity," is much less for the outer planets. In the Earth's case it requires only an extra 12·3 kilometres a second above orbital speed to reach infinity.

The left-hand side of Fig. 4 shows these transfer velocities for points out to the orbit of Jupiter. If the planets *had no gravitational fields of their own*, these would be the velocities needed by a spaceship to leave them and to escape completely from the Solar System.

But, of course, the planets have their own gravitational fields, each with its characteristic escape velocity. Thus we can, to a good degree of approximation, represent the true state of affairs by attaching to the main curve subsidiary "icicles" whose depths, in kilometres a second, are the escape velocities of the planets concerned.

This type of diagram was first constructed, as far as we know, by Dr. Robert S. Richardson, though we believe he employed energy units instead of velocities as ordinates. Physicists have, of course, used such figures for a long time to represent the potential barriers around atomic nuclei.

The resulting picture is not much like one's ordinary idea of the Solar System: but it is much more useful for astronauts. It shows, for example, the surprising fact that a journey to the outer planets could start more easily from Mercury than from Venus! It also demonstrates very vividly the difficulty of getting away from Jupiter, should one be unfortunate enough to be born there. Mercury is far further away from the Sun, dynamically speaking, than is the surface of Jupiter!

To sum up, Fig. 4 indicates that the velocities needed to travel from one orbit to the next are, in general, less than those needed to escape from the

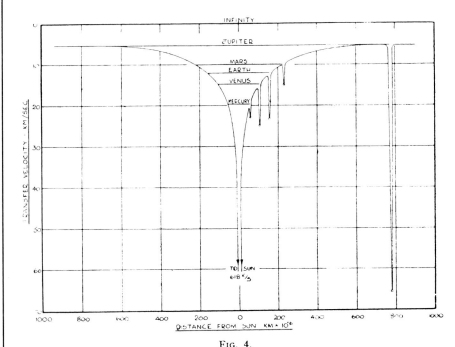

FIG. 4.

Energy Diagram of Solar System, in terms of Required
Transfer Velocities.

planet of origin. The diagram even gives a rough idea of the *total* velocity needed for an interplanetary journey, from surface to surface, but more accurate results require a fuller treatment which we will briefly discuss in the next section.*

5.—Orbits and Trajectories

So far, our treatment has been somewhat abstract: we have not considered the actual shapes of the paths that spaceships must follow, but only their initial velocities of projection. To fix ideas, we will first discuss possible orbits in the Earth's field.

We have already seen that a body travelling horizontally just outside the atmosphere at 7·9 kilometres a second would maintain itself in a circular orbit, never falling to Earth. At any lesser speed, it would return to the planet, though it might travel half-way round the world before doing so. But what of speeds *greater* than 7·9 kilometres a second?

Fig. 5 shows what happens in these cases. As the speed of projection increases, the orbit elongates into an ellipse of greater and greater eccentricity. As the velocity of escape—11·2 kilometres a second—is approached, the ellipse becomes larger very rapidly indeed. At exactly 11·2 kilometres a second it opens out, as it were, into a parabola, and the body never returns.

* A warning should be given here. Fig. 4 only gives the velocities needed to travel from one orbit to *infinity*. It cannot be used directly to find the speeds needed to get from one orbit to *another orbit*, though it gives a rough idea of their magnitudes.

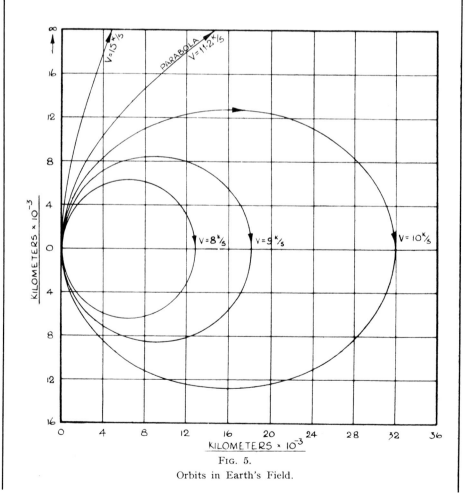

FIG. 5.

Orbits in Earth's Field.

It should therefore be noted that a spaceship will escape from Earth at 11·2 kilometres a second whether its direction of motion is horizontal or vertical or at any intermediate angle.

When the velocity exceeds 11·2 kilometres a second, the orbit is an hyperbola which becomes more and more nearly a straight line as the velocity approaches infinity.

These orbits are of fundamental importance because they arise whenever a body moves in a gravitational field, whether it be that of the Earth or the Sun. Planets, comets and asteroids give all possible types of closed orbit from almost perfect circles to very elongated ellipses. It has often been suggested that some meteors and comets may travel on hyperbolic paths, so that they pass through our system only once: but it is difficult to prove this, since (as will be seen from Fig. 5) all the paths are very similar at the nearest point to the central force.

From the astronautical point of view the elliptical paths are the most important, since they can be used to link one circular orbit to another. Fig. 6 (a) shows such an orbit touching the paths of, say, two "space-stations" S₁ and S₂ circling the Earth.

The body in the elliptical orbit will touch the space-station orbits at A and B: but at A it will be travelling *faster* than S₁ while at B it will be travelling *more slowly* than S₂. Small velocity increments would therefore be needed at A and B to change from one type of orbit to another.

If one is in a circular orbit, and *increases* the speed slightly, the orbit becomes elliptical, lying outside the original circle—as happens at A. If one *decreases* the speed, the orbit becomes an interior ellipse, as at B.

Exactly the same argument applies for journeys between planets. Fig. 6 (b) shows the actual velocities involved in a journey from Earth to Venus (or vice versa). It will be seen that the transfer velocities where the orbits touch are quite small. They are within the range of present-day rockets: a V.2 starting from space in the Earth's orbit could reach Venus quite easily with full payload!

(At this point we recall an instructive mistake made by the author of a space-travel story many years ago. In this tale an interplanetary journey was made by sending a rocket to an asteroid which happened to be passing close to the Earth and which, owing to its elliptical orbit, gave its passengers a "free lift" to their destination. Unfortunately, of course, the presence of the asteroid would have made no difference at all. Once the spaceship had matched the asteroid's velocity—which it would have to do to make a landing—it would have travelled on exactly the same elliptic orbit whether the asteroid was there or not. So the expedition would have gained nothing but a few acres of probably rather uninspiring scenery.)

This type of orbit, which just grazes two planetary orbits, is by no means the only possible one. It will, however, be almost intuitively obvious that it

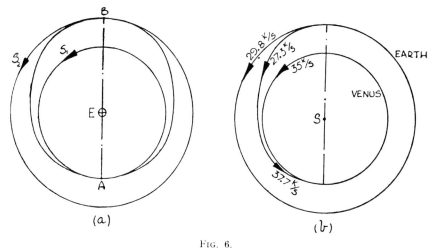

Fig. 6.
Tangential Ellipses.

requires the minimum energy. In the case of the Venus journey, we obtain a total "velocity budget" as below:—

	km./sec.
Escape from Earth	11·2
Earth orbit to voyage orbit	2·5
Voyage orbit to Venus orbit	2·7
Landing on Venus	10·4
	26·8

Gravitational losses and navigational corrections would bring this figure up to at least 30 kilometres a second. The journey would last about 146 days, apart from the actual landing-time at Venus.

For Mars the requirements are as follows, assuming mean distance between the planets. (As the orbit of Mars is somewhat eccentric, the figures vary slightly.)

	km./sec.
Escape from Earth	11·2
Earth orbit to voyage orbit	2·9
Voyage orbit to Mars orbit	2·7
Landing on Mars	5·0
	21·8

This would be at least 25 kilometres a second in practice—considerably less than for the voyage to Venus. But the journey would last longer—237 days.

These times of transit, though long, are not impossibly so. They could be reduced indefinitely by travelling in more eccentric orbits, or even along hyperbolic paths. Such orbits, however, would cut across the paths of the planets at steep angles and so would require very high transfer velocities. The fuel requirements for such journeys would thus be multiplied by very large factors indeed, making them out of the question for the first and perhaps even the second generation of atomic spaceships.

Orbits of this type would be necessary for journeys to the outer planets, which would last many decades if the tangential paths were employed.

6.—Summary

We may now summarize our main results in Table II, which shows the theoretical velocities needed for various typical journeys, as well as estimates of what these values may be in practice. In some cases the latter figures may turn out to be unduly pessimistic, since they make no allowance for atmospheric braking. Some authorities consider that a landing on Earth (and presumably on Venus) could be made almost entirely by air-braking, with very little use of the rockets. We hope that this is the case, but have felt it safer to ignore the possibility.

7.—Conclusion

Our survey has now gone as far as is possible without employing mathematics of great complexity and extreme ugliness. Most of the problems in astronautics can only be discussed by numerical, step-by-step calculations, and no exact general solutions are possible. The conclusions we have reached must therefore be regarded as first approximations to the truth, but in most cases they are very good approximations indeed—correct, that is, to a few per cent. As such, they are quite sufficient to give a good idea of the general nature of the problem, which we now hand on to those engineers who are brave—or rash— enough to tackle it.

TABLE II

Mission		Theoretical velocity*	Approximate actual value.†	
		km./sec.	km./sec.	m.p.h.
One-way journeys.	Orbit round Earth ..	8	10	22,000
	Escape from Earth ..	11·2	13	29,000
	Earth to Moon	13·5	16	36,000
	Earth to Mars	22	25	56,000
	Earth to Venus	27	31	70,000
Return journeys.	Earth–Moon–Earth (no landing). ..	22·4	25	56,000
	Lunar return trip (with landing). ..	27	32	72,000
	Earth–Mars–Earth (no landing). ..	28	32	72,000
	Mars return trip (with landing). ..	44	50	110,000
	Earth–Venus–Earth (no landing). ..	28	32	72,000
	Venus return trip (with landing). ..	54	62	140,000

* Ignoring air resistance and gravitational losses.   † Including allowance for losses.

Appendix

For convenience in reference, some of the more important results in interplanetary dynamics are summarized below.

Earth's Gravitational Field

If g is surface gravity, r is distance from Earth's centre, R is radius of Earth, then gravity g_1 at any point r is, by inverse square law,

$$g_1 = g\text{R}^2/r^2 \qquad \dots\dots\dots\dots\dots\dots\dots\dots\text{I}$$

Hence work done in moving unit mass to infinity from the Earth's surface is

$$\int_{\text{R}}^{\infty} \frac{g\text{R}^2}{r^2}\,dr = g\text{R} \qquad \dots\dots\dots\dots\dots\dots\dots\text{II}$$

This is the result used in Section 2 and is true for all bodies if g and R are given their appropriate values.

At the velocity of escape, the kinetic energy of the projected body must equal gR, i.e. $\frac{1}{2} v_\text{R}^2 = g\text{R}$

Hence
$$v_\text{R} = \sqrt{2g\text{R}} \qquad \dots\dots\dots\dots\dots\dots\text{III}$$

Similarly the velocity of escape at any point r is given by

$$v_r = \sqrt{\frac{2g\text{R}^2}{r}} \qquad \dots\dots\dots\dots\dots\dots\text{IV}$$

Circular velocity is given by the condition that at r, the outward centrifugal force due to the body's motion must equal the inward gravitational force.

Hence
$$\frac{v^2}{r} = \frac{g\text{R}^2}{r^2}$$

or
$$v = \sqrt{\frac{g\text{R}^2}{r}} \qquad \dots\dots\dots\dots\dots\dots\text{V}$$

$$= \sqrt{g\text{R}} \text{ at Earth's surface.}$$

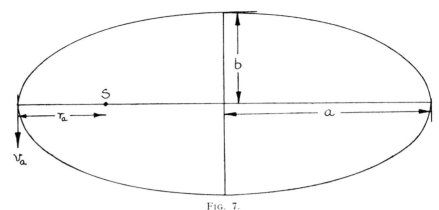

Fɪɢ. 7.

Ellipse: leading dimensions.

Hence escape velocity at any point equals $\sqrt{2}$ times circular velocity at that point.

The height obtained by a body projected vertically from the Earth's surface (ignoring air resistance) is given by

$$H = \frac{2g\mathrm{R}^2}{2g\mathrm{R} - v^2} - \mathrm{R} \dots\dots\dots\dots\dots\dots\mathrm{VI}$$

This becomes infinite as $v \to \sqrt{2g\mathrm{R}} = 11 \cdot 2 \,\mathrm{km./sec.}$

Orbits

The velocity at any point in an orbit under a central force is given by:—

$$v^2 = \mu\left(\frac{2}{r} \pm \frac{1}{a}\right) \dots\dots\dots\dots\dots \mathrm{VII}$$

the minus sign being taken in the elliptic case, the plus in the hyperbolic case. r is the distance from the centre of force, a the semi-major axis, and μ is a gravitational constant $= g\mathrm{R}^2 (= 4 \times 10^5 \,\mathrm{km.^3/sec.^2}$, very nearly, for the Earth).

In the parabolic case this reduces to

$$v^2 = \frac{2\mu}{r} \dots\dots\dots\dots\dots\dots\mathrm{VIII}$$

If the perigree or perihelion velocities and distances v_a, r_a are known, we may then calculate a from equation VII, which becomes

$$a = \frac{\mu}{(2\mu/r_a) - v_a{}^2} \dots\dots\dots\dots\dots\mathrm{IX}$$

The semi-minor axis b is given by:—

$$b = \frac{v_a r_a}{\sqrt{(2\mu/r_a) - v_a{}^2}} \dots\dots\dots\dots\dots\mathrm{X}$$

Equations IX and X enable us to calculate the orbits in Fig. 5, while from equation VII we can calculate the v_a needed to travel from one circular orbit to another. In this case the major axis $2a$ will clearly be the sum of the radii of the two circular orbits.

18 | *Interplanetary Flight*

The two articles on the principles of rocket flight in *The Aeroplane* had come to the attention of Jim Reynolds, a senior editor at Temple Press (*The Aeroplane*'s publishers), and he suggested that I work them up into a volume for a series he was launching, "Technical Trends." To consider space travel a technical trend in 1949 was daring indeed; the other titles in the series were *Modern Aircraft Design, The Industrial Gas Turbine, Mechanized Agriculture, Modern Railway Motive Power.* . . .

When it appeared in May 1950, *Interplanetary Flight* was not only surprisingly successful, but was quickly followed by an American edition (Harpers, 1951).* That gave me the necessary encouragement to step off the IEE escalator onto the freelance writer one, which seemed to be ascending more rapidly. I do not recall any particular trauma; it was as easy as that.

Though quite a few popular books and a few highly specialised treatises on rocket theory had now appeared, *Interplanetary Flight* was the first work in the English language to give the basic theory of space travel in any technical detail. As it was intended for the interested layman as well as the engineer, I put all the mathematics into an appendix, which at one time James Newman was considering for inclusion in his classic four-volume work

---

*My editor at Harpers, George Jones, had a particular interest in rockets; as a U.S. Air Force colonel, he helped to plan the famous RAF Bomber Command attack on Peenemunde, the home of the V2. In 1953, when I mentioned to him that I was visiting Huntsville, Alabama, he said, "Tell Wernher I once did my best to kill him." On receiving this information, Dr. von Braun laughed, reached into his desk, pulled out a collection of "morning after" photos of the bomb damage. "Tell George he did a pretty good job," he said wryly.

The World of Mathematics. Though I don't think it would have fitted very well, I'm sorry it was not used.

Interplanetary Flight has long been out of print because most of its forecasts are now history. But the appendix remains totally undated, and can still serve as a sort of mathematical Abstract of Astronautics, so I would like to reprint it here—-even though it necessarily duplicates some of the material in the previous papers.

I would also like to reprint, for different reasons, an extract from the concluding chapter of the book, when (probably to the surprise of most readers) I departed from technology and took the wider view.

This, then, is the Solar System; and at first sight it may not appear a very attractive place, although it is certainly an interesting one with plenty of variety. The planets, as far as we know today, are all too hot or too cold, or have other disadvantages of a still more fundamental nature, to make them habitable by human beings. Certainly there can be no question of colonizing them in the relatively easy way that the unknown lands of our own world were opened up in the past. Against this, we must not forget that we now possess far greater technical powers to match the challenge of hostile environments. Professor Fritz Zwicky, one of the world's leading astrophysicists, has suggested that eventually the use of atomic engineering will enable us to shape the other planets to suit our needs—and even, if necessary, to alter their orbits.

It is more than probable, however, that the most important material uses of the planets will be in directions totally unexpected today. This has often been the case in the history of exploration on our own Earth. In his vain search for gold, Columbus certainly never dreamed of the far greater treasure that would one day gush from the oil-wells of the New World; and the first men to survey the barren wastes of the Canadian Arctic—which to many must have seemed as unrewarding as the deserts of the Moon—could never have guessed of the faintly-radioactive metal that lay guarding its secrets beneath their feet.

No one can ever foresee what role a new land may play in history; and we are considering now not merely new countries, or even continents—but worlds.

No investment pays better dividends to humanity than scientific research, though it sometimes has to wait a century or two for the profits. Some of the scientific repercussions of space flight have already been mentioned, and could be multiplied indefinitely. It is not merely the physical sciences which will benefit: consider, for example, the possibilities of medical research opened up by "free-fall" or low-gravity conditions. Who can say how much our lives are shortened by the heart's continual battle against gravity? On the Moon, sufferers from cardiac trouble might live normal lives—and normal lives might be greatly prolonged. This is only a random example of the way astronautics might conceivably affect mankind vitally and directly.

But the important consequences of space flight, and the main reasons for its accomplishment, are intangible, and to understand them we must look not to the future but to the past. Although man has occupied the greater part of the habitable globe for thousands of years, until only five centuries ago he lived—psychologically—not in one world but in many. Each of the great cultures in the belt from

[First published in *Interplanetary Flight* (London: Temple Press, 1950, and New York: Harper & Bros., 1951) pp. 140–59]

Britain to Japan was insulated from its neighbours by geography or deliberate choice: each was convinced that it alone represented the flower of civilization, and that all else was barbarism.

The "Unification of the world", to use Toynbee's somewhat optimistic phrase, became possible only when the sailing ship and the arts of navigation were developed sufficiently to replace the difficult overland routes by the easier sea-passages. The result was the great age of exploration whose physical climax was the discovery of the Americas, and whose supreme intellectual achievement was the liberation of the human spirit. Perhaps no better symbol of the questing mind of Renaissance man could be found than the lonely ship sailing steadfastly towards new horizons, until east and west had merged at last and the circumnavigation of the globe had been achieved.

First by land, then by sea, man grew to know his planet; but its final conquest was to lie in a third element, and by means beyond the imagination of almost all men who had ever lived before the twentieth century. The swiftness with which mankind has lifted its commerce and its wars into the air has surpassed the wildest fantasy. Now indeed we have fulfilled the poet's dream and can "ride secure the cruel sky". Through this mastery the last unknown lands have been opened up: over the road along which Alexander burnt out his life, the businessmen and civil servants now pass in comfort in a matter of hours.

The victory has been complete, yet in the winning it has turned to ashes. Every age but ours has had its El Dorado, its Happy Isles, or its North-West Passage to lure the adventurous into the unknown. A lifetime ago men could still dream of what might lie at the poles—but soon the North Pole will be the cross-roads of the world. We may try to console ourselves with the thought that even if Earth has no new horizons, there are no bounds to the endless frontier of science. Yet it may be doubted if this is enough, for only very sophisticated minds are satisfied with purely intellectual adventures.

The importance of exploration does not lie merely in the opportunities it gives to the adolescent (but not to be despised) desires for excitement and variety. It is no mere accident that the age of Columbus was also the age of Leonardo, or that Sir Walter Raleigh was a contemporary of Shakespeare and Galileo. "In human records", wrote the anthropologist J. D. Unwin, "there is no trace of any display of productive energy which has not been preceded by a display of expansive energy". And today, all possibility of expansion on Earth itself has practically ceased.

The thought is a sombre one. Even if it survives the hazards of war, our culture is proceding under a momentum which must be exhausted in the foreseeable future. Fabre once described how he linked the two ends of a chain of marching caterpillars so that they circled endlessly in a closed loop. Even if we avoid all other disasters, this would appear a fitting symbol of humanity's eventual fate when the impetus of the last few centuries has reached its peak and died away. For a closed culture, though it may endure for centuries, is inherently unstable. It may decay quietly and crumble into ruin, or it may be disrupted violently by internal conflicts. Space travel is a necessary, though not in itself a sufficient, way of escape from this predicament.

It is now four hundred years since Copernicus destroyed mediæval cosmology and dethroned the Earth from the centre of creation. Shattering though the repercussions of that fall were in the fields of science and philosophy, they scarcely touched the ordinary man. To him this planet is still the whole of the universe: he knows that other worlds exist, but the knowledge does not affect his life and therefore has little real meaning to him.

All this will be changed before the twentieth century draws to its end. Into a few decades may be compressed more profound alterations in our world picture than occurred during the whole of the Renaissance and the age of discovery that followed. To our grandchildren the Moon may become what the Americas were four hundred years ago—a world of unknown danger, promise and opportunity. No longer will Mars and Venus be merely the names of wandering lights seldom glimpsed by the dwellers in cities. They will be more familar than ever they were to those eastern watchers who first marked their movements, for they will be the new frontiers of the human mind.

Those new frontiers are urgently needed. The crossing of space—even the mere belief in its possibility—may do much to reduce the tensions of our age by turning men's minds outwards and away from their tribal conflicts. It may well be that only by acquiring this new sense of boundless frontiers will the world break free from the ancient cycle of war and peace. One wonders how even the most stubborn of nationalisms will survive when men have seen the Earth as a pale crescent dwindling against the stars, until at last they look for it in vain.

No doubt there are many who, while agreeing that these things are possible, will shrink from them in horror, hoping that they will never come to pass. They remember Pascal's terror of the silent spaces between the stars, and are overwhelmed by the nightmare immensities which Victorian astronomers were so fond of evoking. Such an outlook is somewhat naive, for the meaningless millions of miles between the Sun and its outermost planets are no more, and no less, impressive than the vertiginous gulf lying between the electron and the atomic nucleus. Mere distance is nothing: only the time that is needed to span it has any meaning. A spaceship which can reach the Moon at all would require less time for the journey than a stage-coach once took to travel the length of England. When the atomic drive is reasonably efficient, the nearer planets would be only a few weeks from Earth, and so will seem scarcely more remote than are the antipodes today.

It is fascinating, however premature, to try and imagine the pattern of events when the Solar System is opened up to mankind. In the footsteps of the first explorers will follow the scientists and engineers, shaping strange environments with technologies as yet unborn. Later will come the colonists, laying the foundations of cultures which in time may surpass those of the mother world. The torch of civilisation has dropped from failing fingers too often before for us to imagine that it will never be handed on again.

We must not let our pride in our achievements blind us to the lessons of history. Over the first cities of mankind, the desert sands now lie centuries deep. Could the builders of Ur and Babylon—once the wonders of the world—have pictured London or New York? Nor can we imagine the citadels that our descendants may build beneath the blinding sun of Mercury, or under the stars of the cold Plutonian wastes. And beyond the planets, though ages still ahead of us in time, lies the unknown and infinite promise of the stars.

There will, it is true, be danger in space, as there has always been on the oceans or in the air. Some of these dangers we may guess: others we shall not know until we meet them. Nature is no friend of man's, and the most that he can hope for is her neutrality. But if he meets destruction, it will be at his own hands and according to a familiar pattern.

The dream of flight was one of the noblest, and one of the most disinterested, of all man's aspirations. Yet it led in the end to that silver Superfortress driving in passionless beauty through August skies towards the city whose name it was to sear into the conscience of the world. Already there has been half-serious talk in the United States concerning the use of the Moon for military bases and launching sites. The crossing of space may thus bring, not a new Renaissance, but the final catastrophe which haunts our generation.

That is the danger, the dark thundercloud that threatens the promise of the dawn. The rocket has already been the instrument of evil, and may be so again. But there is no way back into the past: the choice, as Wells once said, is the Universe—or nothing. Though men and civilisations may yearn for rest, for the Elysian dream of the Lotos Eaters, that is a desire that merges imperceptibly into death. The challenge of the great spaces between the worlds is a stupendous one; but if we fail to meet it, the story of our race will be drawing to its close. Humanity will have turned its back upon the still untrodden heights and will be descending again the long slope that stretches, across a thousand million years of time, down to the shores of the primeval sea.

MATHEMATICAL APPENDIX

Chapter II

If g is the value of gravity at the Earth's surface, and R = Earth's radius, then at a radial distance r, gravity is given by Newton's inverse square law as

$$g_r = g\frac{R^2}{r^2} \qquad \dots \qquad \dots \qquad \text{(II.1)}$$

Thus the work E in moving unit mass from R to infinity is given by

$$E = \int_R^\infty g\frac{R^2}{r^2}\,dr = gR \qquad \dots \qquad \text{(II.2)}$$

Similarly the work in moving unit mass from an external point r to infinity is

$$E_r = \int_r^\infty g\frac{R^2}{r^2}\,dr = \frac{gR^2}{r} \qquad \dots \qquad \text{(II.3)}$$

To project a body from the Earth's surface to infinity it must, by Equation II.2, be given a kinetic energy of gR per unit mass. Hence the escape velocity V is given by

$$\tfrac{1}{2}V^2 = gR$$

$$\text{or } V = \sqrt{2gR} \qquad \dots \qquad \dots \qquad \text{(II.4)}$$

Similarly, from Equation II.3, the escape velocity V_r at a distance r is given by

$$\tfrac{1}{2}V_r^2 = \frac{gR^2}{r}$$

$$\text{or } V_r = \sqrt{\frac{2gR^2}{r}} \qquad \dots \qquad \text{(II.5)}$$

Hence V_r varies inversely as the square *root* of the distance from the Earth's centre.

The distance from the Earth attained by projection at less than escape velocity can be readily calculated by energy considerations. If the body comes to rest at a radial distance r, then the work done against gravity equals the initial kinetic energy, or

$$\int_R^r g\frac{R^2}{r^2}\,dr = \tfrac{1}{2}V^2$$

$$\therefore V^2 = 2gR^2\left[\frac{1}{R} - \frac{1}{r}\right] \qquad \dots \qquad \text{(II.6)}$$

$$\text{Hence } r = \frac{2gR^2}{2gR - V^2} \qquad \dots \qquad \text{(II.7)}$$

or the altitude from the Earth's surface is given by

$$h = \frac{2gR^2}{2gR - V^2} - R \dots \text{(II.7a)}$$

which becomes infinite when $V^2 = 2gR$, as in Equation II.4.

For a body to be maintained in a circular orbit radius r, the outward centrifugal force must equal the inwards gravitational attraction, **and hence**

$$\frac{V_r^2}{r} = \frac{gR^2}{r^2}$$

Hence $V_r = \sqrt{\dfrac{gR^2}{r}}$ ... (II.8)

Near the Earth's surface this becomes

$$V = \sqrt{gR} \quad \text{...} \quad \text{(II.8a)}$$

Comparison with Equations II.4 and II.5 shows that at any point the escape velocity is $\sqrt{2}$ times the circular velocity at that point.

The time of revolution in a circular orbit radius r is given immediately from II.8, being equal to

$$\frac{2\pi r}{V_r} = \frac{2\pi r^{\frac{3}{2}}}{\sqrt{gR^2}} \quad \text{...} \quad \text{(II.9)}$$

which is Kepler's Third Law of planetary motion for the special case of a circular orbit.

The equations of motion in conic section orbits will not be derived here, as they may be found in any dynamics text-book. (e.g. Lamb's or Ramsay's "Dynamics"). Only the more important results will be collected for convenience of reference.

If the centre of force is at S, the velocity V at any point distance r from S is given, for an elliptic orbit, by:—

$$V^2 = \mu \left(\frac{2}{r} - \frac{1}{a} \right) \quad \text{...} \quad \text{...} \quad \text{(II.10)}$$

where μ is a constant for any gravitational field, equal to gR^2, and a is the semi-major axis.

At A (see Figure 15), where $r_a = a(1+e)$, e being the eccentricity, this equation becomes

$$V_a^2 = \frac{\mu}{a} \cdot \frac{1-e}{1+e} \quad \text{...} \quad \text{...} \quad \text{(II.11)}$$

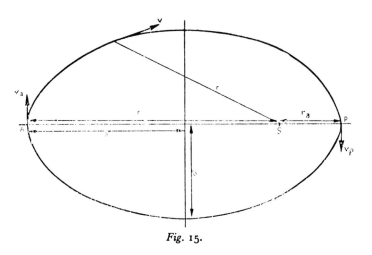

Fig. 15.

At P, where $r_p = a(1-e)$

$$V_p^2 = \frac{\mu}{a} \cdot \frac{1+e}{1-e} \quad \dots \quad \dots \quad (\text{II.12})$$

Hence $\dfrac{V_p}{V_a} = \dfrac{1+e}{1-e} \quad \dots \quad (\text{II.13})$

Hence also the important result (which may be obtained directly from conservation of momentum) that

$$V_p r_p = V_a r_a \quad \dots \quad (\text{II.14})$$

The axes of the ellipse may be expressed in terms of μ, V_p and r_p as follows:

$$\left.\begin{aligned} a &= \frac{\mu}{(2\mu/r_p) - V_p^2} \\[2mm] b &= \sqrt{\frac{V_p r_p}{(2\mu/r_p) - V_p^2}} \end{aligned}\right\} \quad \dots \ (\text{II.15})$$

For hyperbolic orbits, Equation II.10 becomes

$$V^2 = \mu\left(\frac{2}{r} + \frac{1}{a}\right)$$

and for parabolic orbits

$$V^2 = 2\mu/r$$

Chapter III

If the instantaneous mass of the rocket is m, its exhaust velocity c, and the rate of mass-flow dm/dt, then the thrust developed is c.dm/dt. Hence the equation of motion is:

$$m\frac{dV}{dt} = -c\,\frac{dm}{dt} \quad \dots \ (\text{III.1})$$

which on integration over the time of burning gives

$$V = c\,\log_e \frac{M_o}{M_t} = c\,\log_e R \quad \dots \ (\text{III.2})$$

*　　　*　　　*　　　*

Let the rocket propellants, after combustion, attain a temperature $T°$ absolute and a pressure p_1. T is determined by the nature of the propellants—their available chemical energy, the mixture ratio at which they are used, and the specific heat of their gaseous products. It is affected only slightly by p_1, through the mechanism of the reverse dissociation reactions.

The nozzle now accepts the gases flowing into it from the combustion chamber and expands them down to a lower exit pressure p_2, thereby converting their internal pressure and temperature energy as fully as possible into kinetic energy of the emergent jet. The application of the classic Bernoulli relation for adiabatic flow of a compressible fluid shows that for an ideal gas of molecular weight M, expansion under these circumstances gives an exhaust velocity c according to this equation:—

$$c = \sqrt{\frac{2\gamma}{\gamma-1} \cdot \frac{GT}{M}\left\{1 - \left(\frac{p_2}{p_1}\right)^{\frac{\gamma-1}{\gamma}}\right\}} \quad \dots \quad \dots \quad (\text{III.3})$$

where G is the universal gas constant and γ the ratio of the specific heats of the gas.

For any given gas mixture, γ is a constant (and does not vary much for most of the different mixtures of practical interest); the expansion ratio p_2/p_1, is also fixed for a motor operating under given conditions. Hence we can write the approximate relation:—

$$c \simeq k \sqrt{\frac{T}{M}} \qquad \dots \qquad (III.4)$$

where k is a constant for the particular case under consideration, and will in fact not vary greatly for any type of rocket motor. For motors operating in vacuum, $k = 0.25$ will give c correct to about ± 10 per cent. in most practical cases, when the units are km/sec and degrees K.

Chapter IV

If the acceleration (assumed constant) of the rocket is ng, the time t to reach the final velocity V is V/ng. But, if air resistance is neglected,

$$V = c \log_e R - gt$$
$$= c \log_e R - \frac{V}{n}$$
$$\therefore V \frac{n+1}{n} = c \log_e R$$

Hence the mass-ratio R_n required at any acceleration ng is

$$R_n = e^{\frac{V}{c}\frac{n+1}{n}} \qquad \dots \qquad \dots \qquad (IV.2)$$

Chapter V

The duration of a journey from the neighbourhood of the Earth to that of the Moon (neglecting the effect of the Moon's field) may be calculated as follows for the three cases of rectilinear motion that arise.

(1) **INITIAL VELOCITY JUST SUFFICIENT TO REACH THE MOON** (Elliptic Case).

Since the velocity at the Moon's distance (S) is zero, the velocity at any intermediate point r is given, by Equation II.6, by

$$v^2 = 2gR^2\left[\frac{1}{r} - \frac{1}{S}\right] = k^2\left[\frac{1}{r} - \frac{1}{S}\right] \quad \text{say}$$

$$\text{Hence } v = \frac{dr}{dt} = k\left[\frac{1}{r} - \frac{1}{S}\right]^{\frac{1}{2}}$$

This may be readily solved by the substitution $r = S \cos^2\theta$ which gives, after some reduction,

$$kt = -2S^{\frac{3}{2}}\int_{\theta_0}^{\theta} \cos^2\theta \, d\theta$$

Substituting the limits, we obtain

$$t = \frac{S^{\frac{3}{2}}}{k}\left[\theta_0 + \cos\theta_0 \sin\theta_0\right] \quad \dots \quad (V.1)$$

where $\cos^2\theta_0 = R/S$

(2) BODY PROJECTED AT PARABOLIC VELOCITY.

In this case, since $v = 0$ when $r = \infty$, the equation of motion reduces to

$$\frac{dr}{dt} = k\left(\frac{1}{r}\right)^{\frac{1}{2}}$$

whence $t = \dfrac{2}{3k}\left[S^{\frac{3}{2}} - R^{\frac{3}{2}} \right]$ ... ... (V.2)

At the distance of the Moon, S is so much larger than R that this can be written

$$t = \frac{2}{3k} S^{\frac{3}{2}}$$

(3) BODY PROJECTED AT MORE THAN ESCAPE VELOCITY
(Hyperbolic Case).

If the initial velocity is $v_0 \,(> \sqrt{2gR})$ then at any point r the velocity v is given, from energy considerations, by the equation

$$\tfrac{1}{2} v_0^2 - gR = \tfrac{1}{2}v^2 - \frac{gR^2}{r}$$

or $v^2 = v_0^2 - 2gR + \dfrac{2gR^2}{r}$

This may be simplified by introducing the constant S_1, defined by $v_0^2 - 2gR = \dfrac{2gR^2}{S_1}$, whence

$$v^2 = \left(\frac{dr}{dt}\right)^2 = k^2\left[\frac{1}{r} + \frac{1}{S_1}\right]$$

This equation may be solved by the substitution $r = S_1 \sinh^2\theta$ which gives, after reduction,

$$kt = 2 S_1^{\frac{3}{2}} \int_{\theta_0}^{\theta} \sinh^2\theta\, d\theta$$

Hence $t = \dfrac{S_1^{\frac{3}{2}}}{k}\left[\theta_0 - \cosh\theta_0 \sinh\theta_0 - \theta + \cosh\theta \sinh\theta \right]$...(V.3)

where $\sinh^2\theta_0 = R/S_1$ and $\sinh^2\theta = S/S_1$

For large values of v_0 this can be shown to reduce to

$$t = \frac{S}{\sqrt{v_0^2 - 2gR}} \qquad \ldots \qquad (V.4)$$

a result which is immediately obvious, since the denominator is simply the "velocity at infinity" which the body approaches asymptotically. This equation gives results no more than 5 per cent. too large for velocities of projection over 20 km/sec. At higher velocities it will be still more accurate.

All the above equations may, of course, be used for vertical ascent in any gravitational field if the constants are suitably adjusted. They may thus be used to find the time of radial travel between one planetary orbit and another.

Chapter VII

Consider a rocket mass M, exhaust velocity c, rate of fuel consumption per second m, acceleration ng.

Then thrust $= Mng = mc$

Now the rate at which kinetic energy is being put into the jet must be

$$P = \tfrac{1}{2}mc^2$$

Hence $P = \tfrac{1}{2}Mngc$ ...   (VII.1)

or the "specific exhaust power" per unit mass of ship is

$$p = \tfrac{1}{2}ngc \quad\quad ... \quad\quad ... \quad\quad (VII.2)$$

If c is in km/sec., $p = 4900 \, nc$ kilowatts/tonne or $6600 \, nc$ H.P./ton.

Chapter IX

TEMPERATURE OF A BODY IN SPACE

Consider a sphere in space: let its radius be r, and the amount of heat intersected per second per cm² of area perpendicular to the Sun be s. Assume that it is perfectly absorbing and that its temperature T is uniform over the whole surface. (This condition would be nearly fulfilled for a black-painted body which was slowly rotating or had good conductivity).

Then the energy exchange relation for thermal equilibrium is

$$\pi r^2 s = 4\pi r^2 \sigma T^4 \quad (\sigma = \text{Stefan's constant})$$

Hence $T = \left[\dfrac{s}{4\sigma}\right]^{\tfrac{1}{4}}$ ...   (IX.1)

Now $\sigma = 5.67 \times 10^{-5}$ erg.cm.$^{-2}$ sec.$^{-1}$ deg.$^{-4}$ and at the Earth's distance from the Sun $s = 1.35 \times 10^6$ c.g.s. units. Hence $T = 277°K = 4°C$. ($39°F$.).

If the body did not radiate appreciably from the "night side" (e.g. if that was silvered and only the sunward side blackened) then

$$T = \left[\dfrac{s}{2\sigma}\right]^{\tfrac{1}{4}} \quad\quad ... \quad\quad ... \quad\quad (IX.2)$$

This gives values of $329°K$ ($132°F$.) for a body at the Earth's orbit. Intermediate temperatures could be obtained by suitable coating material. It must not be forgotten, moreover, that a considerable amount of heat would be generated by the crew's bodies and the ship's auxiliary mechanisms, so that—at any rate in the neighbourhood of the Earth—the problem is that of discarding excess heat rather than the reverse.

Temperatures elsewhere in the Solar System may be easily obtained from these equations by adjusting the value of s according to the inverse square law. They range from $445°K$ at Mercury to $44°K$ at Pluto. ($340°F$ and $-380°F$, respectively). These figures, of course, bear little relation to the actual surface temperatures of the planets, which are greatly affected by rotation, atmosphere, etc.

*   *   *   *

RADIO RANGES IN SPACE

Let the transmitted power be P_t watts, the received power be P_r watts, the areas of the transmitter and receiver arrays be A_t and A_r square metres, the range be d metres, the wavelength be λ metres. Let the gain of the transmitting array (i.e. the number of times it multiplies the power received at any point over that produced by an omni-directional source) be G_t.

Then by the inverse square law the power density at the receiver is.

$$\frac{G_t P_t}{4\pi d^2}\;\text{watts/metre}^2$$

Therefore the received power is given by

$$P_r = \frac{G_t P_t A_r}{4\pi d^2}\;\text{watts}$$

It can be shown that the gain of a circular array is given approximately by $G = 4\pi A/\lambda^2$. Substituting for G_t thus gives:—

$$P_r = \frac{A_t A_r P_t}{d^2 \lambda^2}$$

$$\text{or } P_t = \frac{d^2 \lambda^2}{A_t A_r} P_r \qquad \dots \qquad (\text{IX.3})$$

It may be assumed that the effective areas of the transmitting and receiving arrays are approximately equal to their physical areas. Given the minimum acceptable receiver power P_r required for any type of service, Equation IX.3 thus enables one to estimate the power needed by the transmitter at a given distance.

VIII | Electronics and Space Flight

19 | Electronics and Space-Flight

The enormous technical developments that had taken place during the war had, in principle, solved most of the basic problems of space travel. This was obvious in the case of propulsion; the V2 rocket had merely to be refined and scaled up, as indeed happened. Less spectacular, but equally essential, was the need for guidance and communications systems that could operate across unheard-of distances. The electronics revolution—especially the development of radar—had made these possible, and with the end of the wartime censorship one could talk freely about devices which, a few years ago, had been top-secret. (I can recall being issued with a revolver when I had to take a broken klystron tube back to RAF Stores, presumably to fight off any parachutists who might try to grab it from me.)

"Electronics and Space-Flight" was read to the British Interplanetary Society on November 8, 1947—just ten years before Sputnik 1 opened the Space Age. It was an attempt to tell my fellow would-be astronauts what I had learned during the war, and is now an interesting reminder of how far we have gone—astronomically and technologically—during the last third of a century. Everything discussed in the lecture has since happened—though often with far superior techniques than those I was able to discuss. The radio valve (vacuum tube) would be challenged by the transistor within a decade; the laser would open up unimagined new horizons. They have amply confirmed my concluding sentence, "We can be sure that by the time these matters are of practical importance, even simpler and better solutions will be available."

ELECTRONICS AND SPACE-FLIGHT

By Arthur C. Clarke

A paper read before the British Interplanetary Society in London on 8th November, 1947

I. Introduction

Flight beyond the atmosphere—whether by guided automatic rockets or by manned "spaceships"—involves the solution of problems in almost every field of engineering, and the rocket designer will be merely one of the specialists who will contribute to its achievement.   Scarcely less important will be the electronic engineer, who will be required to solve major problems in communications, control, position-finding and telemetering.   This paper is an attempt to discuss some of these without, however, going too deeply into circuit detail or mathematics.

Strictly speaking, "electronics" is concerned only with the movement of electrons in various types of circuit, but the word is now often—if not generally—used in the much wider sense of covering all applications of radio.   In this discussion I shall extend it to embrace the entire electromagnetic spectrum, and will in fact spend comparatively little time dealing with physical circuits alone.

Combinations of valves, photoelectric cells, cathode ray tubes and other electronic devices, as is well known, can be set up to perform an enormous range of operations from splitting atoms to cooking hamburgers, from guarding jewellers' windows to guiding aircraft through fog.   In fact, it is probably true to say that electronic circuits can be devised to carry out or control all activities except those termed "creative."   Circuits with memories, circuits with powers of discrimination and selection, circuits capable of making judgments in very complex situations, have all been produced in recent years and many were employed during the War.   Given a specific problem, the electronic engineer can almost always produce an answer.   Sometimes it is the only answer: e.g., no-one is ever likely to invent a steam-driven television set made entirely from gearwheels and levers.   Sometimes there are alternative solutions: for example, there is still a lot to be said for the acoustical gramophone.   Occasionally, what the electronic engineer takes fifty valves and a sackful of resistances and condensers to do, someone else can perform with three cogwheels and a piece of string.   Even here, however, the electronic engineer frequently has the last laugh, because his equipment is extremely flexible and may often be used for several other purposes as well.   Also—string wears out much more quickly than a well-designed and well-built circuit, so a complex electronic device may *sometimes* be preferred to a simple mechanical one.   (It is however very difficult to decide when!)

I would like to stress this point.   Reliability will be of paramount importance in spaceflight, as it is in aeronautics to-day, and for even more urgent reasons.   The fact that when anything goes wrong with an aeroplane it falls back to Earth again, is a great though usually overlooked advantage.   It does at least give the occupants a sporting chance of reaching safety—and much more than that, if they have parachutes.   But a disabled spaceship would be liable to recede to infinity together with its unfortunate crew.

Electronic circuits have now been built to operate when making 600 revolutions a second, while being fired from a gun at 20,000 gravities.   This acceleration is nearly a thousand times that at the surface of the Sun, and five or ten thousand times that ever likely to be used by a manned rocket.   These remarkable achievements have been made possible by the development of very small and hence very strong valves, and by the use of circuits which are solid—indeed compressed—masses of wiring and insulation, so that no breaks or mechanical faults can occur.   When these techniques are fully developed, it will be possible to employ, if the need arises, circuits of any degree of complexity with the assurance that no failures will occur.   A modern battleship may have ten or twenty thousand radio valves functioning when it goes into action.   A

[Published in the *Journal of the British Interplanetary Society*, Vol. 7, no. 2 (XXI), March 1948, pp. 49–69]

spaceship, which has to carry out more complicated functions though not so many of them, may well require circuits containing two or three thousand valves. Even to-day, the V.2's fired from New Mexico take up something like a hundred valves with them in their telemetering and control circuits.

I propose to divide this discussion into two parts, the first dealing with the "circuitry" which might be needed inside space-rockets (manned or unmanned), while the second and larger will consider the various external radio, radar and optical devices which would be employed for communication, navigation or other purposes.

II. Internal Circuits

II.1. *Power Supplies*. Small rockets would employ storage batteries for their source of electrical power, and would use motor-generators or valve inverters when alternating current was required. For spaceships, the 1,000 cycle/second alternating current circuits developed for aircraft use would seem very suitable, since rectification and transformation can be carried out with small, light components. I do not know how high the mains frequency can be pushed with profit, but somewhere at the bottom of the radio range so much radiation leakage will be occurring that the process will have to stop. At a guess, 5 kilocycles/second, or a hundred times the present British grid frequency would seem to be a reasonable "ceiling" for a spaceship's mains. This would make possible the elimination of electrolytic condensers—perhaps the cause of more trouble than any other component—and would make possible very light and compact power units indeed.

II.2. *Instrumentation*. A spaceship would need at least as much instrumentation as a modern airliner. Fuel gauges, pressure and temperature measuring devices and many other instruments would be required. The fact that the motors would only be operating for ten minutes at the most during the whole of a voyage would, however, eliminate many of the dials and gauges that make the engineer's position in a large bomber so impressive. But the arrival of an atomic drive, with its need for safety controls and radiation detectors, would more than redress the balance. Few of these instruments would need continual attention; they would be coupled to automatic warning devices which would give notice of any fault or breakdown. There would, for instance, be an air-warning indicator which would attract the crew's attention in no uncertain manner if the pressure or composition of the air supply deviated from the safe limits. Since all these devices are quite orthodox and, in some form or other, in common use to-day, I will not discuss them in any further detail.

As automatic rockets are developed for the exploration of the upper atmosphere and beyond, a whole range of measuring instruments will be devised to control radio transmissions so that their readings can be recorded at ground stations. Pirani vacuum gauges have already been used for this purpose in V.2 rockets, and we will return to this important subject later.

II.3. *Computers*. The navigation of spaceships will involve mathematical calculations of a very difficult kind, as anyone may see by glancing into a book such as *Ballistics of the Future* or one of the early German treatises on the subject. All the preliminary computations, it is true, will have been carried out months before the start of a voyage, but emergencies may make it necessary to change an orbit once a ship is in space. Moreover, the time will undoubtedly come when spaceships will cease to travel like trams on carefully predetermined cotangential paths from orbit to orbit, but will have enough energy reserves to make interesting detours should the need arise. They will therefore require computing machinery which can at least deal with the simpler types of manoeuvre.

A good example of this is the famous operation of transferring equipment or personnel from one rocket to another in space. It would be quite easy to do—once the velocities of the machines had been matched. But to achieve this the pilot must first solve an intricate dynamical problem and must then derive a suitable approach orbit in three dimensions. In many cases one might be able to tell at a glance that the manoeuvre was either possible or impossible, but not even Gauss, perhaps the greatest computer who ever lived, could say just *how* it would have to be carried out.

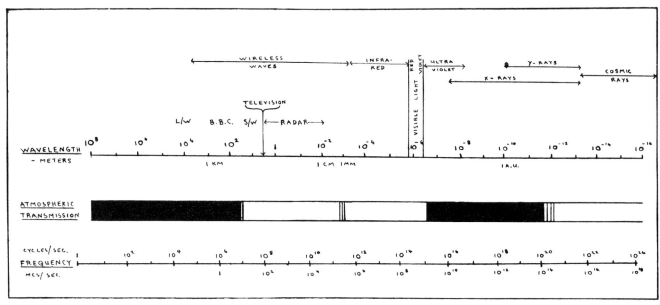

Fig. 1.   The Electromagnetic Spectrum

We see, therefore, that what at first sight seem to be routine manoeuvres may demand very heavy mathematics, and no doubt in the future there will be a great development of calculating machines to deal specifically with such problems.   The fire control and prediction equipment now used on battleships and heavy bombers contains many of the features needed for this purpose. Extreme accuracy would not be required in most cases, since the problem could be continually re-solved as range shortened, and additional course corrections could be applied at any time.   The main requirement would be speed: one would wish to know an answer to an accuracy of say one per cent. within a few seconds.   Electronic computers are ideally suited for this sort of work, and the basic units can be quickly set up to deal with many different types of problem.[1]

The final stage in the approach by rocket power alone to an airless planet gives perhaps the simplest example of such a problem.   This is a manoeuvre which could be carried out intuitively by a skilled pilot, but the expenditure of fuel would probably be heavy as he would almost certainly tend to overbrake. An automatic landing computer would be given the ship's altitude and velocity (we will see later how this could be done) and from these it would calculate the final velocity and the time of impact if no braking was employed.   It would then have to compute the amount of fuel needed to neutralise this velocity, and the last moment to which firing could safely be delayed.   The answer would probably be applied directly to the controls so that the landing—except perhaps for the last few meters—would be automatic.   Such a computer would have to solve a few simple algebraic equations of the first and second degrees and would be much less complicated than, for example, the gun-laying equipment in a superfortress.   This is far too specialised a subject to go into here, but in general it may be said that all ordinary mathematical operations can be carried out by systems of coupled potentiometers and specially designed amplifiers.[2,3]

II.4.   *Trainers.*   For completeness, we should mention one subsidiary but very important class of equipment which will never go into a spaceship and which, indeed, might even be dismantled before any voyage began.   Just now I used the optimistic phrase "a skilled pilot" and it might well be asked where one obtains such a paragon, particularly in the early stages of the art.

In order to train the crew, it will be necessary to build what are known as "flight simulators" which can reproduce artificially the conditions liable to be met on any given journey.   Equipment of this sort was used extensively during the War for training bomber crews and radar operators.   Physically, it would consist of a fairly exact replica of the spaceship's cabin, with all its meters, indicators and controls.   The meters would be fed information of the same kind as that which they would receive on an actual voyage, and the crew would have to react accordingly by working the appropriate controls. When it is tired of aircraft, no doubt the Link Corporation will enter this interesting field.

Such trainers are never exactly like the real thing, but they can be exceedingly useful in allowing operators to make their initial mistakes without disastrous consequences. Unfortunately—and on this subject I speak with great feeling—a really comprehensive trainer is liable to become much more complicated than the equipment it is teaching people to operate. If our spaceship circuits contain a modest thousand valves, then there will probably be at least five thousand in the trainer on which the crew will practice.

III. **The Electromagnetic Spectrum**

The greater part of this discussion will be concerned with radio and optical waves and their uses. The whole range of electro-magnetic waves covers about 24 octaves—14 below visible light and 9 above. Figure I shows the complete spectrum as known at present, from one cycle a second up to a million million million million. In empty space, waves of all frequencies are transmitted equally well, but our atmosphere is opaque to a large portion of the spectrum. I have tried to indicate this by the band in the centre of the figure.

At low frequencies, radio waves are reflected back to Earth by the ionosphere, but about five octaves—say from ten megacycles a second up to about a million megacycles a second—will pass through it and out into space. This enormous band, wide enough to carry hundreds of millions of speech channels, or millions of television ones, can therefore be used for Earth-to-ship or Earth-to-planet communication.

Down among the millimeter waves there are occasional bands of absorption which I have roughly indicated. Even here, however, there are enormously wide "windows" through which one can squeeze thousands of channels.

Still shorter in wavelength, and higher in frequency, we have the infra-red and finally the visible waves. Our Californian colleagues would probably say that the atmosphere is quite transparent to these, but in this climate we must make certain reservations.

We see, therefore, that the atmosphere will pass an enormously wide band of waves, all of which may be modulated to transmit intelligence. In terms of frequency, which is what decides the number of available channels, the atmosphere will pass a band a thousand million times as wide as the familiar medium wave band on our domestic sets. This will be pleasant to know when the time comes to build interplanetary radio-telephone exchanges!

Just above the visible spectrum in the ultra-violet the atmosphere becomes rather suddenly opaque—and I mean this quite literally. Even a few inches of air will completely block waves in the far ultra-violet—hence the considerable efforts that have been made lately to put spectroscopes in V.2 rockets.

As the frequency is raised and we pass into the X-ray and Gamma-ray region the energy of the radiations becomes steadily greater until they are capable of blasting a way right through the atmosphere. The air loses its opacity in the way that a sheet of tin-foil which is opaque to raindrops is quite transparent to rifle-bullets. However, we have only just learned how to generate these very-high-energy radiations, and it seems very unlikely that we shall ever want to use them for such purposes as communication. They have rather obvious disadvantages from the point of view of the receiving station.

To sum up, we see that for Earth-to-space contacts we can use a band of frequencies from about ten megacycles a second out to around a thousand million megacycles a second, apart from a few narrow and variable gaps. For space-to-space contacts, there are no such restrictions and the band may be extended if necessary two octaves on either side. It is, however, very unlikely that the low-frequency end of the spectrum will be employed, since waves more than a meter long require large aerial systems for transmission and reception. The centimeter waves, which can now be generated at high power levels and are very easily beamed, appear to be ideal for most astronautical purposes. As our techniques improve, the millimeter and infra-red waves will become available, but lightbeam or photophone systems have already reached a high state of development and could probably be used even to-day for communication over astronomical distances.

Whatever purpose electromagnetic waves are used for, certain requirements have to be fulfilled. We need a means of generating the waves at a sufficiently high power level, and then of modulating them by speech, vision or in any other manner required. In the radio range the generator would be some type of valve, probably a magnetron: in the optical range, it might be a gas-discharge tube, some types of which can produce thousand million candlepower flashes.

The waves must next be beamed from some radiating device such as a parabolic reflector or a radio-lens—and this at once introduces considerable complications. To save power we will be forced to use narrow beams, and these must therefore be aimed accurately and kept in position despite all movements of the bodies concerned. If one of them is a space-rocket, this may mean gyro-stabilised arrays like those which battleships use to keep their radar aerials steady despite pitching and rolling. However, stabilisation of the entire spaceship would be preferable—if not essential—since otherwise the vessel would be continuously rotating about all three axes and any circuit could only be maintained intermittently.

In Fig. 2 I have tried to indicate the basic elements in any type of radio or optical link between two such stations. The transmitter I have just discussed: the "aiming mechanism" for the beam will, we assume, be controlled electrically from a knowledge of the receiving station's position.

At the second station, we need some kind of receiving array which again must be kept aligned on the transmitter. This can be done relatively easily by using the actual signal to control the aiming mechanism through a servo-system —that is, a device which can convert electrical impulses into mechanical movements. If the aerial moved away from the beam, the servo-system would automatically bring it back into alignment. This technique was used in radar sets which automatically followed or "tracked" aircraft across the sky.[4]

The received signal would then be amplified and detected and the output converted into speech, vision or used in any of the other ways discussed later.

In the case of a ship using a radar system, then the same array would be employed both for receiving and transmitting, and there would be only the one aiming mechanism.

III.1. *Communication Circuits—General Considerations.* Reliable communication systems will, of course, be of the utmost importance in astronautics. At

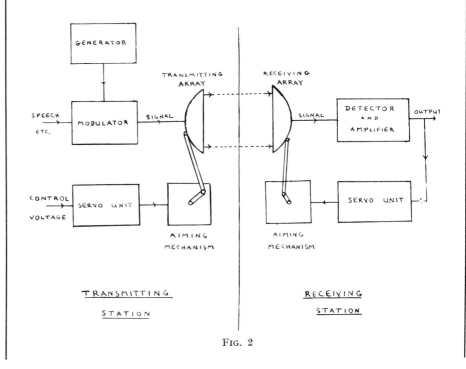

Fig. 2

first, we will only be concerned with Earth-to-ship circuits, but later the more complex problem of ship-to-ship communication will arise.

It is simple to set down the mathematical equations involved in interplanetary radio circuits, since they are a straightforward application of the law of inverse squares. We will assume that the transmitting and receiving arrays are parabolic mirrors, or the equivalent, of areas A_T and A_R square meters respectively. Then if the power of the transmitter is P_T watts, the power picked up by the receiver P_R watts, the wavelength λ meters, the distance between transmitter and receiver d meters, we have the relationship (see Appendix I):—

$$P_T = \frac{\lambda^2 d^2}{A_T \, A_R} \, P_R \text{ watts} \dots \dots \dots \text{Eq. 1.}$$

It is, however, not at all easy to pin down the quantities on the right-hand side. P_R will be the minimum signal which will work a sensitive receiver, and it varies enormously with the type of service being considered. If we only wish to *detect* a transmitter, without being able to read its messages, then special techniques might enable us to manage with as little as 10^{-20} watts. This is about a tenth of the (average) power picked up by the receiver which first made radar contact with the Moon.[5]

If we wish to transmit morse, then 10^{-15} watts might be sufficient. For speech, 10^{-12} watts, and for television, 10^{-9} watts are perhaps reasonable figures, since we can fairly assume that there will be no interference on the highly directional, free-space circuits we are considering. Different circuit techniques and standards of quality would cause great variations in these estimates, which should be taken as no more than helpful signposts.

The minimum usable signal depends on the noise in the receiver, which in turn is proportional to the band-width, and hence to the rate at which intelligence is transmitted. By reducing band-width, extreme sensitivity is possible, and if one is content to pass a few morse characters a minute, one could operate at levels around 10^{-15} watts.

The *absolute* limit of detectable signal strength is probably set by the fact that the Universe itself is somewhat noisy and a very sensitive receiver picks up "cosmic static" from interstellar space, which swamps weak signals. This natural interference varies over the sky and is concentrated in the plane of the Milky Way, being possibly caused by ionised gas-clouds in the galactic system.[6]

The important variables within our control are the wavelength λ and the areas of the arrays. At the present 10 cms. is a very convenient wavelength, and one at which we can generate large amounts of power. I will use it in these calculations, though I have no doubt that by the time this discussion is of much practical interest, 10 cms. will be regarded as quite a long wavelength.

within present ranges, except for the case of Jupiter—though I should not be surprised to hear that someone has a 40,000 watt c/w magnetron even now. The thick line running across the table gives the approximate limit of power available at this frequency to-day.

We see, therefore, that there will be no difficulty in signaling to ships, despite the small arrays they can carry, even when they are well beyond Mars. However, at such great distances the spaceship might have to carry a somewhat larger array—say 5 square metres—before its weaker transmitter could signal back to Earth.

III.1.2. *Planet to Planet Circuits.* If we can use 100 square metre arrays at either end of the circuit, as would be possible once a base had been set up on the surface of a planet, the powers needed fall very sharply. I have shown this in Column (*b*) of Table 1. We see that it would now be possible to talk to Mars— while one could send morse right out to the satellites of Jupiter.

In all these calculations we have assumed that the array at the Earth end of the circuit has an effective area of 100 square metres. It would be perfectly practicable—though it would involve considerable engineering—to make a 1,000 square metre array. This would reduce the power shown in Table 1 by a factor of ten. Such an array might be a parabolic mirror about 120 feet in

TABLE I

TRANSMITTER POWER—WATTS

	Distance Kms.	Time Lag (One way)	Speech (a)	Speech (b)	Telegraphy (a)	Telegraphy (b)	Beacon (a)	Beacon (c)
Moon	400,000	1·3 s.	16	0·16	0·016	≪0·1	≪0·001	≪0·1
	1,000,000	3·3 s.	100	1	0·1	≪0·1	<0·001	≪0·1
	10,000,000	33 s.	10,000	100	10	0·1	0·001	<0·1
Venus	42,000,000	2 m. 20 s.	180,000	1,800	180	1·8	0·002	1·8
Mars	78,000,000	4 m. 20 s.	600,000	6,000	600	6	0·006	6
	100,000,000	5 m. 30 s.	10^6	10,000	1,000	10	·01	10
Jupiter	630,000,000	35 m.	40×10^6	400,000	40,000	400	0·4	400

$\lambda = 10$ cms.
(a) $A_T \times A_R = 100$ metres⁴
(b) $A_T \times A_R = 10,000$ metres⁴
(c) $A_R = 100$ metres² : transmitter isotropic

diameter, but it seems more likely that it would be a metal lens of the type recently developed by the Bell Telephone Laboratories.[7] It would, of course, have to be equatorially mounted like a telescope to counteract the Earth's rotation.

Although we have referred to telephonic circuits in this discussion, there would not be much point in using actual speech over such distances in view of the time lags (several minutes between the inner planets) which would make conversations out of the question. Broadcast programmes would be possible, but

A_T and A_R are rather more controversial. Very large radar arrays—some of over 50 square metres—were used during the War, and at Manchester a fixed parabola of over 300 square metres area is now being built. There is no definite limit to the size of array that might be constructed if it was worth while, but clearly a spaceship could only carry quite a small aerial system. Since A_T and A_R in Equation 1 are interchangeable, it does not matter which end has the bigger array as long as both transmitters have the same power. This reciprocity is fortunate, for altogether apart from weight considerations it would be highly desirable to have the larger aerial on the Earth. The larger the aerial, the narrower the beam it produces and the more accurately it must be aimed and guided. The small array which the spaceship could carry would not need such great precision of aiming as its beam would be fairly broad. (**Appendix II**).

We will now consider the three cases that arise: Earth-to-ship, planet-to-planet, and finally ship-to-ship circuits.

III.1.1. *Earth to ship Circuits.* Let us assume that the array on the Earth has an effective area of 100 square metres, which is quite a modest figure since it means a system with a diameter of about 40 feet. We will also be conservative and assume that the spaceship's array is only a square metre in area. There is in fact no reason why it should not be considerably larger than this, since it could be unfolded in space once the ship had left atmosphere. Thus we can hope to avoid the sanguinary battles which used to take place between the aerodynamicists and the designers of radar scanners during the War.

Substituting these figures in Equation 1 we obtain:—

$$P_T = \frac{10^{-2}}{10^2} d^2 P_R = 10^{-4} d^2 P_R \text{ watts}$$

If our spaceship is in the neighbourhood of the Moon ($d \leqslant 4 \times 10^8$ metres) we see that for telephony communication we need a transmitter power of

$$10^{-4} \times 16 \times 10^{16} \times 10^{-12} = 16 \text{ watts,}$$

while for a television programme 16 Kw. might be needed.

Now 16 watts is the sort of power level used in ordinary amateur operation, so we see that there will be no difficulty at all in obtaining two-way telephony from the Moon. It would be quite easy to transmit television signals *to* the ship if one wanted to: but to get pictures back with the transmitter a rocket could carry we would probably have to use larger arrays. It would be quite practicable to erect a portable aerial system on the Moon that would enable television signals to be sent back to Earth. Still photographs, of course, could be sent over the telephony circuit with suitable equipment.

Now let us be a little more ambitious and consider *real* interplanetary communication. Table 1 shows the powers needed, in watts, to send speech and slow speed morse over various distances out to the orbit of Jupiter. In Column (*a*) we have assumed, as before, that we have a 100 square metre array on Earth and a one square metre array on the ship.

The powers needed for telephony are considerable: at the moment we can generate about 10,000 watts at 10 cms. on continuous wave operation, and we need 180,000 even to reach Venus. But the powers required for morse are well any high quality circuits would be much more profitably used for multichannel teleprinter operation.

There is no way around this difficulty. It will never be possible for anyone on one planet to hold a conversation—in the normal sense of the word—with someone on another. Even in the case of the Moon, the two and a half second lag would be slightly annoying.

III.1.3. *Ship to Ship Circuits.* A rough calculation shows, that, on the basis of Equation 1, two ships with square metre arrays could exchange messages at ranges of a million kilometers with powers of a few watts, and could talk to each other quite easily when 100,000 kilometres apart. However, it seems very likely that for ship-to-ship communication the optical frequencies, including visible light, would be used. These waves can be focussed and generated with great ease, and extremely sensitive detectors are now available in the form of electron-multiplier tubes and other devices. The transmitter would consist of some type of searchlight, modulated at speech or radio frequency, while the receiver would be a parabolic mirror—or a Schmidt camera—with a photocell at its focus. The sensitivity of such devices is enormous. Dumont has recently sent television programmes along a light-beam in broad daylight, using only the spot on a cathode ray tube as the source of transmitter power! In the infra-red region, bolometers have now been developed which can detect 10^{-16} watts at a fairly high rate of signalling[8] and for very-long-distance circuits optical waves may be more suitable, and may require much lower powers, than radio.

I should again like to emphasise that changes in operating frequency, improvements in technique, and so on, might make these figures appear extremely conservative. They are no more than an indication of what could be done in the present or the near future. When spaceships are actually built, say in the last quarter of this century, many of these ideas will seem as old-fashioned as a 1920 radio set.

III.2. *Beacons.* For many purposes, it would be very valuable merely to be able to detect a rocket's transmitter: it would at least be an indication that the machine was still functioning. I suggested that perhaps 10^{-20} watts might be a detectable signal, if a bandwidth of a few cycles/second was employed. (This would be a very considerable achievement at 3,000 megacycles a second, but it should be ultimately attainable.) In Table 1, under the heading "Beacon," I have shown the transmitter powers required to produce this signal. In Column (*a*), as before, the use of a one metre square aerial at the transmitter has been assumed.

The figures are fantastically small—only half a watt out to the orbit of Jupiter! If we assume that, instead of using an array which at this frequency has a "gain" of about 1,000, we let the transmitter broadcast in all directions, then we get the figures in the final column. These are the powers for an omnidirectional radio beacon which could be picked up in the whole volume of space around it, and not merely along a narrow cone. Even these powers are still very small indeed, and indicate that automatic rockets carrying light, simple transmitters could be tracked from Earth over astronomical distances.

It is probable that these figures may be optimistic by a few orders of magnitude, since at such extremely low power levels cosmic static might be serious Also, quantum difficulties may arise owing to the limited number of photons which the receiver would intercept.

III.3. *Doppler and Displacement Effects.*   When we are exchanging messages with stations travelling at high speeds, two effects occur which do not arise in terrestrial circuits.   In the first case, one station may have moved appreciably before the message from the other has reached it.   Just as an A.A. gunner has to aim ahead of his target, so a transmitter array should be aimed ahead of a ship travelling across the line of sight.   Fortunately this correction is quite negligible at the speeds which we are likely to be concerned with for a century or so.   A spaceship would have to be travelling tangentially at the colossal speed of 500 kilometres a second (over a million m.p.h.) before a beam displacement of even a tenth of a degree occurred.

The second effect is much more important.   As is well known, the apparent frequency of a signal is changed if the source or the receiver is in motion.   If the relative velocity along the line of sight is v, the velocity of light is c, and the signal frequency is f, then the frequency change df is very nearly $f.v/c$.[9]   Thus, at 10 cms., or 3,000 megacycles a second, for a velocity of even 1 kilometre a second we would have a frequency shift of 10,000 cycles a second—quite enough to move the signal clear out of the receiver's pass-band unless it was retuned.   This same effect took place when the Americans made radar contact with the Moon.   Their receiver had a band-width of only 57 cycles/sec., and the Moon's velocity produced shifts of up to 300 cycles/sec.

Thus if we wish to communicate with another station, we must not only know its frequency and its position, but also its velocity so that we can slightly detune our receiver by the necessary amount.   In most cases a short search would quickly locate the transmitter, and the Doppler effect is only likely to be a nuisance in the case of the very narrow band transmissions discussed in the last Section.   For navigational purposes, as we shall see, it can be very useful indeed.

III.4. *Types of Transmission.*   As we have already seen, interplanetary speech circuits would be rather a luxury and for most purposes telegraphic channels would be quite sufficient.   By employing the usual scanning devices, it would be possible to send photographs over these circuits.   There is however quite another type of transmission which will be extensively used in astronautics.   This is the sending of mathematical information in the form of pulse trains.   It is even possible—though the system would have obvious disadvantages—that by means of such links the computers in spaceships may be coupled directly to much larger ground installations.   During the War a considerable effort went into developing circuits which could handle, for instance, grid references and various numerical quantities.

IV. Navigational Aids

The use of radio aids for long-range navigation by manned spaceships appears somewhat pointless, since the surrounding astronomical bodies are always visible and their angular positions can be measured with extreme accuracy by quite simple equipment.   However, in the case of the first journeys to the Moon it might be useful if stations on the Earth could follow the ship accurately in position, and radio any course corrections that might be necessary. This would be quite easy if the rocket carried a small "responder beacon" triggered by the radars on Earth.   The repetition frequency, of course, would have to be very low to give time for the signals to return.   In this way the range of the ship could be found to within a few kilometres or less.

Radio position-finding devices would be essential for guiding unmanned rockets, since it seems virtually impossible to make an instrument which can automatically take astronomical fixes.   This may sound a sweeping statement, but if anyone doubts it I suggest that they try to design a machine which can pick out the brighter planets on the celestial sphere and then measure their angular displacements relative to the stars.

Radar aids would be chiefly of value when making the final approach to a planet.   A low-powered radar set would give instantaneous and accurate range indications—to within a metre or so—and by using the Doppler effect the velocity of approach could be measured at the same time. With a carrier frequency of 3,000 megacycles a second, a rate of approach of one metre a second would cause a frequency shift of 20 cycles a second, which would be quite measurable. This information could, if required, be passed automatically to the landing computer as well as shown visually to the anxious pilot.

There would be very little point in equiping a spaceship with long-range radar, even if it was possible. Although as I have shown elsewhere[10] radar systems could bridge interplanetary distances, this requires very powerful transmitters and very large arrays. Since one is fighting an inverse square law in both directions, as it were, the power needed for a radar system increases with the *fourth* power of the distance, and soon becomes exorbitantly great.

V. Radar Surveying

There is, however, one specialised application of direct radar which is of much interest and importance. One of the most remarkable inventions of the War was the device known as H_2S which enabled bombers to "see" the ground through fog or cloud, and extremely realistic pictures may now be obtained with the most recent forms of this equipment. Demarcations between land and water stand out exceptionally well, and mountains, lakes, roads, cities, etc., can also be seen.

We may expect therefore that before any attempt is made to land on Venus, a complete radar survey will be carried out from a ship orbiting the planet at a height of a few hundred kilometres. Such a survey would give an accurate map of all land areas—if any—and would even enable approximate contour lines to be drawn. If Venus is as murky as some writers have suggested, this would be in fact about the only way of mapping her! It would be such an important achievement that it might well be the prime object of the first expedition.

If we ever hope to learn much about those partly gaseous worlds Jupiter and Saturn, it may be by radar surveys from the innermost moons. It is not likely, however, that we could do more than penetrate the outer layers of those turbulent atmospheres.

VI. Meteor Detection

I now intend to devote some time to the problem of meteor detection, not because it is important to spaceships—it isn't—but because so much has been written on the subject that it seems high time the matter was investigated quantitatively.

It is shown in the Appendix that for a radar system, with the notation already used,

$$P_r = \frac{4\pi\lambda^2 d^4}{\sigma A^2} P_R \quad \ldots \ldots \text{ Equation II.}$$

The only new symbol is σ, the "effective reflecting area" of the target, which depends not only on the target's physical size, but also upon its composition and attitude relative to the incident beam, and upon λ. For a radar system operating at $\lambda = 10$ cms., and capable of accurate range measurement, the minimum workable signal P_R is about 10^{-12} watts. If we again take our array area as one square metre, let us see how much power is needed to detect a meteor at the modest range of a hundred kilometres. Substituting the numerical values, we have:—

$$P_r = \frac{4\pi \times 10^{-2} \times 10^{20} \times 10^{-12}}{\sigma}$$

$$\approx \frac{10^7}{\sigma} \text{watts.} \quad \ldots \ldots \text{ Equation IIa.}$$

Now for spherical bodies which are large compared with λ, and which are perfect conductors, the "echoing area" σ is the same as the area of cross-section.

Thus to detect a metre square meteor a hundred kilometres away we should need a peak power of 10^7 watts, or 10 megawatts.

10 Mw. is a very great deal of power indeed—13,000 h.p.—but we now have magnetron valves which can develop a quarter of this. It would certainly be possible to make such a transmitter, once some rather difficult waveguide problems had been overcome, and it *might* weigh as little (!) as half-a-ton, though this seems optimistic.

But a body a yard across is not a meteor at all—it is a young asteroid. Only very large meteors, in fact, have a radius of even one centimetre. The usual radius is about a millimetre or less, and this at once introduces difficulties of a fundamental nature.

If a body is smaller than the wavelength of the radiation falling upon it, its reflecting power is very low indeed. Lord Rayleigh, who had a remarkable habit of discovering mathematically things which became enormously important half a century later, showed that the reflecting power of a small body falls according to the inverse fourth power of the wavelength of the incident radiation, Fig. **3** shows the operation of this law for a perfectly conducting, spherical body.[11]

From this we see that for a one millimetre radius meteor, at 10 centimetres wavelength, the reflecting area is only about a ten thousandth of its visual area. Substituting in Equation IIa we thus obtain the interesting result:—

$$P_{\tau} = \frac{10^7}{\pi \times 10^{-6} \times 10^{-4}} \approx 3 \times 10^{16} \text{ watts.}$$

or, if you prefer, 40,000,000,000,000 h.p., which is, I believe, something like the output of an atomic bomb.

Obviously, we have to change our wavelength to something comparable with the meteor's dimensions. Let us look a good way into the future and assume that we can generate and handle one millimetre waves as readily as we can now deal with ten centimetre ones. We then have, with the same conditions as before:—

$$P_{\tau} = \frac{10^3}{\sigma} \text{ watts.}$$

At this wavelength, we can now take σ as being the visual area of the meteor, so that

$$P_{\tau} = \frac{10^3}{\pi \times 10^{-6}} \approx 3 \times 10^8 \text{ watts.}$$

So we have, with a prodigious research effort, reduced our peak power requirements to 400,000 h.p.—from the atomic bomb to Battersea Power Station. This figure, however, would have to be increased to considerably more than a million h.p. since meteors are very far from being perfect reflectors or perfect spheres.

Clearly, therefore, there is no possibility whatsoever of using ordinary radar for the detection of meteors—at least with the small arrays a spaceship could carry. Quite apart from this, such an achievement would, by itself, still be completely useless.

Of all the meteors which will enter the hundred kilometre sphere around the spaceship, only about one in a hundred million will pass through the volume of the ship itself. It will reach the ship probably no more than five seconds after detection: in that time we have to plot its course so accurately that we can tell—from a hundred kilometres away—that it is going to hit a target of only a few square metres. I believe that this feat alone would be totally impossible, but having performed it, and decided that unlike its hundred million colleagues *this* meteor is going to hit us, we then have to make the ship "sidestep" smartly by firing its motors. Surprisingly enough, this last feat would be quite possible (though highly disconcerting to the crew) as it would require accelerations of only a tenth of a gravity.

Lest anyone feel slightly encouraged at this point, I hasten to drive another nail into the meteor detector's coffin. For our 300 megawatts (at one millimetre wavelength!) we have located the meteors inside an extremely narrow beam—one, in fact, only a tenth of a degree wide. To obtain complete coverage all around the ship, we must "scan" the array at a quite impossible speed. The fast meteors are the dangerous ones, and they can reach us in two seconds flat from a hundred kilometres away. Our 1/10 degree wide beam must therefore "look" at a different part of the sky not less than ten million times a second, which is of course mechanically and electrically impossible.

I hope that this disposes of radar-type "meteor detectors" for spaceships. It is probably fair to say that to run them would need so much power that they would volatilise any meteor which approached—so the detecting part of the equipment would be superfluous! In the far future, this feat may become possible.

I have spent some time on this subject because it would be of considerable interest to the astronomers if we could detect meteors in space. Once they have entered the atmosphere, of course, the tremendous ionisation produced enables us to obtain echoes very easily.

Finally, let us remember that even a one millimetre radius meteor would still be a very rare specimen indeed. According to the most recently published tables,[12] a rather large spaceship travelling at 10 kilometres a second would be liable to collide with such a body once every million years—unless it was rash enough to venture into the middle of one of the heaviest showers known. In that case, it might be punctured, though probably no more than this, after waiting only ten thousand years!

VII. Telemetering and Remote Control

We now come to the subject which is of the most concern and interest to rocket engineers at the present time—that of controlling rockets from a distance, and, equally, important, of knowing what they are doing when beyond direct observation.

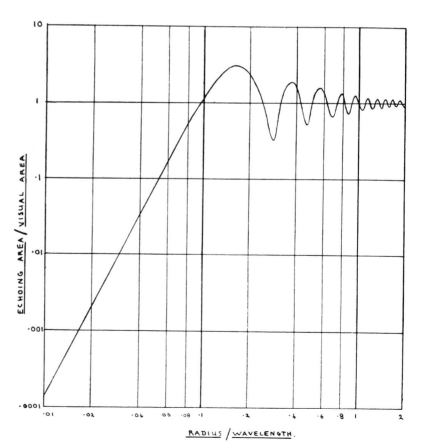

Fig. III. Law of reflection for perfectly conducting sphere.

It has been possible for a long time to transmit simple orders by radio—for example, to turn switches on or off, or to make controls move in distinct "steps." To obtain smooth and continuous control at a distance is much more difficult and demands rather complex equipment. A recent American paper[13] described a system for the remote control of ⅛th scale model flying boats, in which there were seven independent control circuits, five of them capable of continuous variation. The aircraft equipment weighed only 21 pounds, and the ground control station consisted of a normal pilot's seat with the usual control column, rudder pedals and throttle levers.

Some of these control systems operate by the transmission of continuous waves, while others employ pulse trains, but it is unnecessary to go into circuit detail here. Many different types of equipment have been described in the technical literature, but the most recent and interesting ones are probably still secret.

To control a rocket in space, when it is quite invisible, is very much more difficult than to fly an aircraft by radio. The most important difference between the two cases is that whereas the aeroplane has—or should have-a measure of inherent stability and will thus maintain a horizontal position when the controls are centralised, the rocket may assume any attitude it pleases once it is in space. It is therefore no good having a means of control unless we also know the orientation of the rocket's axis. This may mean that the machine may have to carry some form of directional radiator whose signals will enable us to deduce the rocket's instantaneous attitude. Perhaps the most promising system would be to equip the machine with a set of photoelectric cells which would control radio signals in accordance with the rocket's angle with respect to the sun. Three such cells would suffice to define the machine's orientation uniquely.

The design of an aerial system for a small rocket is not at all easy. It is sometimes suggested that the body of the machine would serve for this purpose, but unfortunately it would then pick up or transmit practically no signals when pointed away from the Earth, which is about the most important position. Another difficulty is the fact that a rocket blast may act as an excellent absorber of radio waves, making it impossible to send or receive signals. This would not be serious in astronautical applications where the motors would only be firing for very short intervals of time.

At the moment we can say that it would be feasible to transmit control signals to a rocket as far away as the Moon, but considerable research will have to be carried out before we will be in a position to know what effect our orders had produced.

This problem leads us naturally to the question of "telemetering" or sending instrument and other readings by radio. This is a technique which has become of great importance in recent years and is now used extensively in radio sondes, experimental aircraft (manned and unmanned) and in ionospheric rocket research.

It is not difficult to design instruments which produce their readings in the form of electrical voltages, and these in turn may be employed to modulate radio waves so that records may be obtained at a ground station. A recent paper[14] described the system now employed in the V.2 rockets being fired at White Sands, New Mexico. Twenty-three separate channels are employed and the technique used is one derived from radar. For each channel, a train of microsecond-wide pulses is sent out, and as the instrument readings increase the spacing between the pulses increases.

The pulse sequence is repeated after the twenty-three sets of readings have been broadcast. On reaching the receiver, the separate trains are disentangled and automatically converted into meter readings which can be filmed. The radio-frequency used is 1,000 mc/sec., and the pulse spacing varies from 50 microseconds at zero instrument voltage to 200 microseconds at full-scale reading.

It is very probable that pulse systems of this sort will be used exclusively for long-range telemetering. They have the great advantage that power consumption is much lower than for continuous wave operation. It would be

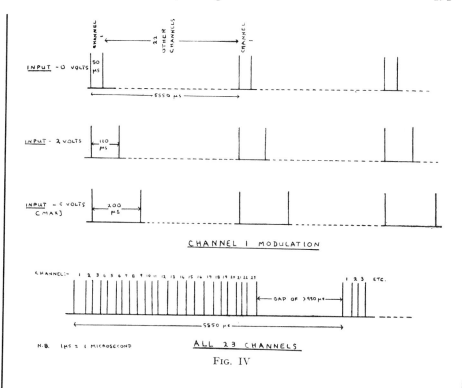

N.B. 1 µS = 1 MICROSECOND

ALL 23 CHANNELS

Fig. IV

possible to radio instrument readings from the Moon, and it is understood that Westinghouse believes that such a transmitter could be made to withstand the shock of unretarded impact. This seems highly optimistic, for if the rocket was stopped in a few metres its deceleration would be a hundred thousand gravities. However, even the Moon's atmosphere might have some retarding effect at 2·5 kilometres a second, and it is conceivable that a safe landing could be made—that is, a landing under no more than 10,000 gravities!

A less difficult feat, and a much more useful one, would be the telemetering of instrument readings from orbital rockets circling the Earth at heights of a few hundred kilometres. It would require only a few watts of power to do this, even with omni-directional transmission from the rocket. Batteries might provide this power for considerable periods, but it should be possible to develop thermoelectric devices which, utilising the very great temperature range obtainable in space, would operate the equipment indefinitely.

This will probably be one of the first achievements of astronautics, and will provide information of the utmost importance. To give but one example, variable frequency transmissions from instruments beyond the ionosphere would be of great value to the radiophysicist.

VIII. Conclusions

This discussion has been concerned with the ultimate possibilities of electronics applied to space-flight, as well as with its more immediate uses. Many of the devices mentioned may not materialise for a very long time, not only because of the usual development time-lag, but simply because the first space-ships will be quite unable to afford the resultant weight penalty. Even atomic ships will, in the early stages, require perhaps a hundred tons of "working fluid" for every ton of payload. Any electronic aid must, therefore, either be essential or must be capable of saving at least a hundred times its own weight of fuel before its inclusion in the spaceship can be considered.

The general picture, however, is reassuring. Even to-day we know, in principle, how to solve the problems of communication and navigation over astronomical distances. We can be sure that by the time these matters are of practical importance, even simpler and better solutions will be available.

Signal and Radar Ranges

Signal Range

Let transmitted power be P_T watts, received power be P_R watts, area of transmitter array be A_T square metres, of receiver array A_R square metres, range be d metres, wavelength be λ metres. Let array gain (defined as solid angle of point source compared with solid angle of beam) be G_T for transmitter.

Then power density at receiver is

$$\frac{G_T P_T}{4\pi d^2} \text{ watts/sq. metre.}$$

$\therefore$ received power is given by

$$P_R = \frac{G_T P_T A_R}{4\pi d^2}$$

Now the gain of a circular array is given approximately by $G = 4\pi A/\lambda^2$ [11]. Substituting for G_T gives:—

$$P_R = \frac{A_T A_R P_T}{d^2 \lambda^2}$$

or,
$$P_T = \frac{d^2 \lambda^2}{A_T A_R} P_R \qquad \ldots\ldots\ldots\ldots\text{Equation I.}$$

Radar Range

The "receiver" is now the reflecting target, which we will assume has an effective reflecting area σ square metres. The total power re-radiated is thus:

$$\frac{G_T P_T}{4\pi d^2} \sigma \text{ watts.}$$

Therefore the reflected power received back at the transmitter is given by:—

$$P_R = \frac{G_T P_T \sigma}{4\pi d^2} \frac{A_R}{4\pi d^2}$$

$$= \frac{4\pi A_T P_T \sigma}{\lambda^2 4\pi d^2} \frac{A_R}{4\pi d^2}$$

$$= \frac{A_T A_R \sigma}{4\pi \lambda^2 d^4} P_T$$

Since the same array will be used both for receiving and transmitting, we may write $A_T = A_R = A$

Hence
$$P_R = \frac{\sigma A^2 P_T}{4\pi \lambda^2 d^4}$$

or
$$P_T = \frac{4\pi \lambda^2 d^4}{\sigma A^2} P_R \text{ watts.} \qquad \ldots\ldots\text{Equation II.}$$

Note that P_T, P_R are now *peak* powers, whereas in the previous section they were *average* ones.

Beam Widths

For a circular array, diameter D metres, area A square metres, wavelength radiated λ metres, the beam width b between "half-power points" is given by:—

$$b = \lambda/D = \lambda\sqrt{\pi}/2\sqrt{A} \text{ radians}$$

$$\approx 50\lambda/\sqrt{A} \text{ degrees.}$$

The following table is calculated on this basis:—

A sq. metres \ λ—cms.	10	1	0·1	
1	5·0	0·5	0·05	
10	1·6	0·16	0·016	Beam Width
100	0·5	0·05	0·005	— Degrees.
1000	0·16	0·02	0·002	

Note, however, that the very small beam widths would not be attainable in practice owing to the precision required in constructing the array (better than $\lambda/32$), difficulties of feed, etc. The narrowest radio beam so far produced is 0·1 degrees wide.[7]

Throughout this paper it has been assumed that A is the physical area of the (circular) array. This is not true with all types of radiator, but it is a fair approximation.

REFERENCES

(1) Ragazzini, Randall and Russell. "Analysis of Problems in Dynamics oy Electronic Circuits," *Proc. I.R.E.*, May, 1947.
(2) Mynall. "Electrical Analogue Computing," *Electronic Engineering*, June, 1947, *et seq.*
(3) Murray. *Theory of Mathematical Machines.* (Columbia U.P., 1947.)
(4) Coales, Calpine and Watson. "Naval Fire-Control Radar," *J.I.E.E.*, Pt. IIIa, No. 2, March–May, 1946.
(5) Mofenson. "Radar Echoes from the Moon," *Electronics*, April, 1946.
(6) Reber. "Cosmic Static," *Astrophysical Journal*, Nov., 1944.
(7) Kock. "Metal Lens Antennas," *P.I.R.E.*, Nov., 1946.
(8) Andrews, Milton, de Sorbo. "A fast superconducting bolometer," *J. Opt. Soc. Amer.*, Sept., 1946.
(9) Griffiths. "Doppler Effect in Propagation," *Wireless Eng.*, June, 1947.
(10) Clarke. "Astronomical Radar," *Wireless World*, Oct., 1946.
(11) Norton and Omberg. "Maximum Range of a Radar Set," *P.I.R.E.*, Jan., 1947.
(12) Ovenden. "The Nature and Distribution of Meteoric Matter," *Journal of the B.I.S.*, Sept., 1947.
(13) Welge. "Radio Control of Model Flying Boats," *P.I.R.E.*, May, 1947.
(14) Heeren and others. "Telemetering from V.2 Rockets," *Electronics*, March and April, 1947.

20 | *Electromagnetic Launching as a Major Contribution to Space-Flight*

In 1950 I once again put together a lot of other people's ideas and, just as in the case of communications satellites, made them add up to something new. But "Electromagnetic Launching," unlike "Extra-Terrestrial Relays," is an idea whose time has not yet come, except on paper.

The moon-based launch system described here has been the basis for many space-industrialisation and colonisation schemes, notably those promoted by Dr. Gerard O'Neill and his collegues (see his book, *The High Frontier*). They have gone into many of the engineering details and made some fascinating tests with models of what they prefer to call a "mass-driver"—a nice name, until one tries to think of a propulsion system to which it *can't* be applied. . . .

ELECTROMAGNETIC LAUNCHING AS A MAJOR CONTRIBUTION TO SPACE-FLIGHT

The idea of using some form of ground-based launching system for spaceships, such as a very long electromagnetic accelerator, has often been suggested in the literature.[1] There are two fundamental objections to such a device which make it very improbable that it will ever be used in practice to provide much of the escape energy from Earth, though it may well be used to get winged spaceships airborne. In the first place, a body moving at anything like escape velocity in the lower atmosphere would be rapidly destroyed by friction (note that the extreme nose of a V.2 became red-hot at about 2,000 m.p.h., and as escape velocity is 25,000 m.p.h. the heating would be at least 100 times as great). This could be only partly reduced even if the launcher was built on the highest mountain.

A second equally serious objection is raised by the impossibility of using very high accelerations for manned spaceships. Even if we assume that 10 g. could be tolerated by a properly protected crew, the launcher would have to be no less than 600 kilometres in length, and proportionately longer if lower accelerations were used. It is, therefore, obvious that an accelerating device of any practicable length could provide only a very small part of the total velocity needed to escape from Earth, and that at such vast expense and inconvenience that the whole job would be better done by rockets.

This is particularly unfortunate, for an electromagnetic launcher or catapult would have great advantages, the most important of which arise from the fact that the energy of take-off would be provided by fixed and not mobile power-plants. Such a system is fundamentally more efficient than any arrangement using rockets, where the greater part of the fuel is required merely to accelerate more fuel, and therefore, in a sense, does no useful work at all. Electrical energy, on the other hand, possesses no mass and so it requires no extra power to apply it to a body in motion.

The great reductions in mass-ratio which would be made possible by orbital refuelling have often been pointed out,[2] and clearly this technique would become even more attractive if fuel could be projected into free orbits by means not involving rocket propulsion. It is also widely recognised that interplanetary travel will not be practicable on the large scale until propellants can be obtained on the Moon, with its very low gravitational potential. The idea therefore suggests itself rather forcibly, that, unless other developments make it unnecessary, a possible long-term solution to the space-flight problem may be found in the use of electromagnetic accelerators on the Moon, launching the fuel mined there into suitable orbits round our satellite.

The Moon's low escape velocity (2·3 km./sec. as against 11·2 km./sec. for the Earth, with a consequent reduction of kinetic energy per unit mass to 1/20), and its virtual absence of atmosphere, make it an ideal site for an accelerator. If we are considering only the projection of fuel supplies, and not manned spaceships, then large accelerations can be employed, and the launching track need be only a few kilometres long. At 100 g, for instance, escape velocity would be reached in a distance of less than 3 km., and a gently rising track of this length must be regarded as a reasonable engineering proposition. (It could even be horizontal if it was constructed on a plateau or open plain with no mountains in the line of sight.) The operation and technical characteristics of such a system will now be investigated.

General Principles

Circular velocity near the Moon's surface is 1·65 km./sec., but a body projected at a slight upward angle at this speed would return to the Moon again. The fact that any orbit must be symmetrical about some line through the centre of the Moon shows that it is impossible to fire a body from the surface

[Published in the *Journal of the British Interplanetary Society*, Vol. 9, no. 6 (XXXVII), November 1950, pp. 261–7]

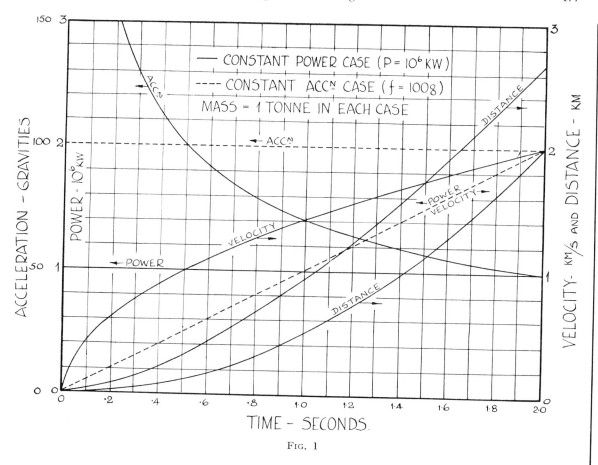

Fig. 1

into an orbit that does not either go to infinity, or else return to the surface again. However, if the initial speed is a little greater than circular velocity, the use of a very small amount of rocket power when the missile is at its greatest distance would convert the orbit into a stable, circular one. A suitable projection speed would be about 2 km./sec., which will be used as the basis of the following calculations.

If a constant acceleration of $100\,g$ were used, this speed would be attained after 2 seconds and in a distance of 2 km. $100\,g$ is quite a modest acceleration—artillery shells experience accelerations of the order of $10,000\,g$, which would give circular velocity in 20 metres! However, power and constructional problems would be more easily met if values of not more than $100\,g$ were utilised.

To give a mass of 1 tonne a velocity of 2 km./sec. would require the expenditure of 2×10^{16} ergs, or 2×10^9 joules—an average power, over 2 seconds, of 1,000,000 kW. With the use of a uniform acceleration, the power required would rise linearly from zero to 2,000,000 kW at the end of the 2 seconds. (Fig. 1.) It must be realised, however, that there would be no need to build electric generators with a continuous rating of anything like this value. All the energy required for a "shot" would be stored up—perhaps over several hours—by bringing large flywheels up to speed and then coupling them to generators designed to deliver high currents for very short periods, and hence capable of withstanding enormous overloads. (This was the technique used by Kapitza at the Mond Laboratory to obtain very intense magnetic fields for his experiments in low-temperature physics.)

Since the use of a constant acceleration necessarily implies a continuously increasing power, it would be more realistic to assume that the amount of power available was fixed, and to calculate the resulting acceleration, velocity, and distance, relations. If the power available per unit mass accelerated is c, the mass is m, and the total power is P, then with the usual symbols f, v, s, and t, we have these relations:—

$$P = mfv$$
$$\therefore c = fv \quad \dots\dots\dots\dots\dots\dots\dots\text{(i)}$$

Hence
$$f\frac{dv}{dt} + v\frac{df}{dt} = 0$$

or from (i),
$$\frac{df}{f^3} = -\frac{dt}{c}$$

$$\therefore f = \sqrt{\frac{c}{2t}} \quad \dots\dots\dots\dots\dots\dots\text{(ii)}$$

(since $v = 0$ when $t = 0$).

Also
$$v = c/f = \sqrt{(2ct)} \quad \dots\dots\dots\dots\dots\text{(iii)}$$

and
$$s = \int v\,dt = \frac{2}{3}\sqrt{(2c)}t^{3/2} \quad \dots\dots\dots\dots\text{(iv)}$$

Taking the case $P = 10^6$ kW, $m = 1$ tonne, we find that a launching track 2·67 km. long would be required, while the time to reach 2 km./sec. would be 2 seconds, as before. The acceleration would begin at a very high value (in theory, infinity) and would fall to 50 g at the end of the 2 seconds. (Fig. 1.)

In practice, of course, the power would not start suddenly at the full 10^6 kW value, but would rise from zero, and the acceleration would start at some limited initial value. The power would also be expected to drop during the shot, as the kinetic energy stored in the flywheel was absorbed, and for these reasons the length of the launching track might have to be increased to about 3 km. Alternatively, a second "booster" generator could be brought into operation near the end of the shot. It is worth noting that the 2×10^{16} ergs necessary per launch equals the energy of a 50 tonne flywheel, radius of gyration 2·2 m. revolving at 1,200 r.p.m.

This paper is not primarily concerned with the engineering details of such a system, but it is interesting to note that a similar device, known as an "Electropult," has been developed in the United States by the Westinghouse Corporation.[3] This consists essentially of a large induction "motor" laid out flat into a 1,400 ft. long track, with a small shuttle, carrying the aircraft, which acts as a "rotor." The power supply comes from a 750 kW d.c. motor, driving an alternator with a 24-ton flywheel working at 1,300 r.p.m. The power transmitted during take-off is 12,000 kW and a fighter can be given a speed of over 100 m.p.h. in 4 seconds, after a run of only 340 ft. It will be seen that in many respects this system is a miniature replica of the one discussed above.

It is, of course, quite possible that other methods of launching than electric might be preferred, since such a machine could not be built until the lunar colony had established engineering plants on the largest scale. The use of chemical energy (as in the V.1 launching track) might be a simpler solution, but the electrical method would have the advantage of better control and much lower running costs, if the use of solar or atomic generators is assumed.

Operating Features

It has already been mentioned that though such a launcher could shoot a body completely away from the Moon, it could not project anything into a *closed* orbit of the type desired for refuelling. It, therefore, remains to be seen how much additional rocket power would be needed for this.

We will assume that the launcher is horizontal, with no obstacles in the line of flight. The orbit of a projectile fired at 2 km./sec. is shown in Fig. 2. It would reach a maximum distance from the Moon's centre at B of 4,760 km. and would return to its starting point after $2\frac{1}{2}$ hours. The velocity at B would be 0·78 km./sec., and circular velocity at this point is 1·00 km./sec. Hence an additional velocity of 0·22 km./sec. must be given to the missile at B for it to remain in a circular orbit. If we assume that the projectile carries a small rocket motor with an exhaust velocity of 4 km./sec., it would, therefore, be necessary for it to eject about 60 kg. of propellant per tonne of initial mass. This 6 per cent. penalty is trivial. Rather more serious would be the weight of

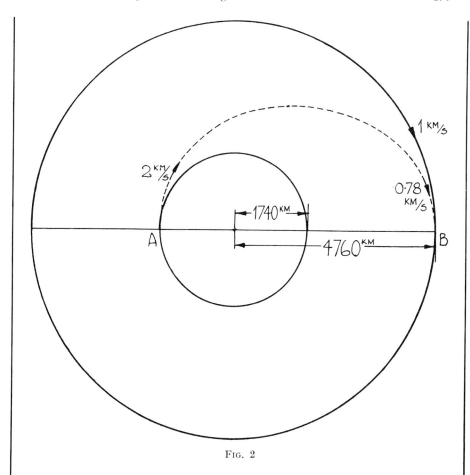

Fig. 2

the motor and the resulting complexity of control circuits, etc. to ensure that the impulse was provided at the correct moment.

This difficulty might be avoided if somewhat greater launching velocities were used and the missile was sent away from the Moon on a very elongated orbit with a period of several days. At extreme range it would then be moving very slowly and there would be plenty of time for fuel transfer operations. It would not matter if the (relatively light) empty containers then crashed on the Moon when they had completed their orbit.

In principle, therefore, if we assume that in due course it is possible to set up a self-supporting lunar colony, and that all the normal minerals can be found on the Moon, it would appear possible to establish large fuel reserves in space almost entirely by means of electrical energy. One could imagine the setting up of an orbital satellite, at a height of a few thousand kilometres, whose task it would be to collect the fuel carriers as they were propelled upwards into its orbit. (It might be equipped with a number of small tanker rockets whose duty it was to make the transfer, thus obviating the need for any propulsive mechanism in the carriers.) It is hardly necessary to point out that some care would be needed to avoid "shooting-up" the space-station! The high degree of control possible with an electric launcher would help to avoid such unfortunate accidents.

The possibilities opened up by a moon-based launcher are by no means exhausted here. Dynamical considerations indicate that to project a body from the Moon into an orbit *round the Earth* requires only about 20 per cent. more initial velocity than to project it into a path around the Moon. Hence spaceships after take-off from the Earth could be refuelled more economically from lunar sources than from the planet only a few hundred kilometres below. This would certainly involve severe problems in missile control, but little expenditure of rocket power. If this technique becomes feasible, then the problem of Earth-Moon travel is enormously simplified. No spaceship need ever be designed for any mission more difficult than the entry of a circular orbit round the Earth, since refuelling would be possible both in circum-terrestrial and circum-lunar orbits. The total amount of propellant required would be reduced to a small fraction of that needed if rocket power was used exclusively, for if sub-orbital techniques were employed as normally envisaged, colossal quantities of propellant would still be required to get small amounts of fuel into position.

Looking further afield, it should be noted that initial velocities of only 4 km./sec. would project material from the Moon to Mars or Venus under the most favourable conditions. Until such time as refuelling operations can be carried out on these planets, the Moon-based launcher might well provide the key to interplanetary as well as lunar travel.

Still further in the future, it is interesting to speculate on the use of launching systems which are themselves in space, either as adjuncts to space-stations or as independent structures. One of the chief problems to be overcome in this case would be that of momentum change and the preservation of the launcher's orbit despite its ejection of material. Whether such engineering feats ever become necessary only time will tell. Since there seems no physical limit either to the lengths or accelerations which might be utilised in this case (if sufficient power were available) such projectors may conceivably play a part in the development of interstellar flight.

Ignoring these remote speculations, the lunar launching system is of importance since it could, in theory, make interplanetary travel practicable with propellants of a much lower exhaust velocity than any assumed hitherto. Even chemical fuels might then be adequate for the task. Of course, there is still the tremendous initial problem of establishing the lunar colony and building up its industrial potential—but this is a problem which has to be solved in any case. We are rather in the position of trying to run a trans-Atlantic airline when there is no possibility of refuelling on the other side until we have drilled our own oil-wells and set up our own refineries!

It is quite possible that other technical developments, such as the successful harnessing of atomic energy for rocket propulsion, may make such schemes quite unnecessary. But if not, it is as well to keep the Moon-based electro-magnetic launcher in reserve as a solution of the long-term problems of space-flight.

REFERENCES

(1) "Akkas Pseudoman" (Dr. E. F. Northrup), *Zero to Eighty* (1937).
(2) H. E. Ross, "Orbital Bases," *J.B.I.S.*, Jan., 1949; K. W. Gatland, "Rockets in Circular Orbits," *J.B.I.S.*, March, 1949.
(3) *The Engineer*, **182**, 379–80, 25th Oct., 1946; *Westinghouse Engineer*, **6**, 160–1, Sept., 1946.

IX | *The Space Elevator—and Beyond*

21 The Space Elevator: 'Thought Experiment', or Key to the Universe?

During the late sixties I heard for the first time, with some incredulity, of an extraordinary idea for reaching space without rockets. This differed from the usual run of crank antigravity and "space drive" schemes because it was based on sound scientific principles.

The "space elevator," to give it one of its many names, stuck in the back of my mind for almost a decade; it fascinated me, not only as a possible future reality but as a wonderful idea for science fiction. However, I did nothing about it because I felt sure that half a dozen of my fellow writers must already be busily at work on the theme.

Eventually, I got fed up with waiting, and in 1976 started to write *The Fountains of Paradise*. I had almost left it too late; a few months after my novel appeared in 1979, Charles Sheffield quite independently came out with *The Web Between the Worlds*. There were such striking—yet inevitable—similarities between the two books that anyone not knowing how engineering concepts are developed might suspect plagiarism. To forestall such charges, I was happy to write an introduction to Charles' book—and I'm sure he would have done the same for me had *I* been second over the finishing line.

While writing *The Fountains of Paradise* (which, I assured everyone, would definitely be my last novel), I accumulated a great deal of technical material, and in 1979 organised it into an address which I delivered at the Thirtieth Congress of the International Astronautical Federation, Munich, 1979.

Three years after publication of *The Fountains of Paradise*, I had the great pleasure of meeting the shy and charming inventor of the concept, Yuri Artsutanov, in his Leningrad home. (An account of that meeting, and other Russian encounters, appears in *1984: Spring*.) He and other engineers have now taken the idea much further, and it seems more and more likely that one day we will be able to get away from Earth without using rockets. But no one has yet discovered a substitute for them in their true medium—deep space.

THE SPACE ELEVATOR: 'THOUGHT EXPERIMENT', OR KEY TO THE UNIVERSE?*

Abstract—The space elevator (*alias* Sky Hook, Heavenly Ladder, Orbital Tower, or Cosmic Funicular) is a structure linking a point on the equator to a satellite in the geostationary orbit directly above it. By providing a 'vertical railroad' it would permit orders-of-magnitude reduction in the cost of space operations. The net energy requirements would be almost zero, as in principle all the energy of returning payloads could be recaptured; indeed, by continuing the structure beyond the geostationary point (necessary in any event for reasons of stability) payloads could be given escape velocity merely by utilising the 'sling' effect of the Earth's rotation.

The concept was first developed in detail by a Leningrad engineer, Yuri Artsutanov, in 1960 and later by several American engineers quite unaware of Artsutanov's work. All studies indicate that the idea, outrageous though it appears at first sight, is theoretically feasible and that its practical realisation could follow from the mass-production of high-strength materials now known as laboratory curiosities.

This paper is a semi-technical survey of the rapidly expanding literature of the subject, with some speculations about ultimate developments. Whether or not the 'space elevator' can be actually built, it is of great interest as the *only* known device which could replace the rocket as a means of escaping from the earth. If it is ever developed, it could make mass space travel no more expensive than any other mode of transportation.

INTRODUCTION

WHAT I want to talk about today is a space transportation system so outrageous that many of you may consider it not even science-fiction, but pure fantasy. Perhaps it is; only the future will tell. Yet even if it is regarded as no more than a 'thought-experiment', it is one of the most fascinating—and stimulating—ideas in the history of astronautics.

This paper is essentially a survey; in the unlikely event that it contains anything original, it's probably wrong. Your complaints should be addressed to Director-General Roy Gibson, who is responsible for getting me here.

What's in a name?

First of all, we have a severe problem in nomenclature. It is very difficult to talk about something, until people have agreed on its name. In this case, we have an embarrassingly wide choice.

The Russian inventor used the charming 'heavenly funicular'. American writers have contributed 'orbital tower', 'anchored satellite', 'beanstalk', 'Jacob's Ladder'—and, of course, 'Skyhook'. I prefer 'space elevator'; it is euphonious (at least in English) and exactly describes the subject.

Historical

As usual, it all began with Tsiolkovski—specifically, with his 1895 paper 'Day-Dreams of Heaven and Earth' [1]. During his discussion of possible ways of escaping from the earth, he considered the building of a high tower, and described what would happen as one ascended it. I quote:

'On the tower, as one climbed higher and higher up it, gravity would decrease gradually; and if it were constructed on the Earth's equator and, therefore, rapidly rotated together with the earth, the gravitation would disappear not only because of the distance from the centre of the planet, but also from the centrifugal force that is increasing proportionately to that distance. The gravitational force drops . . . but the centrifugal force operating in the reverse direction increases. On the earth the gravity is finally eliminated at the top of the tower, at an elevation of 5.5 radii of the earth (36 000 km).

'As one went up such a tower, gravity would decrease steadily, without changing direction; at a distance of 36 000 km, it would be completely annihilated; and then it would be again detected . . . but its direction would be reversed, so that a person would have his head turned towards the earth. . . .'

Tsiolkovski then calculates the height of similar towers on the Sun and planets, but his comments—at least as I read the translation ('it would be excessive to discuss how possible these towers would be on the planets')—suggest that he does not regard the concept as a serious practical proposition. And of course he is quite right: it would be impossible, if I dare use such a risky word, to construct *free-standing* towers tens of thousands of kilometres high. If Tsiolkovski failed to mention the alternative solution, it may be because he was concerned only with the first steps away from earth. And the space-elevator is completely useless in the pioneering days of astronautics, unless you are lucky (?) enough to live on a very small, rapidly spinning planet.

Nevertheless, it is interesting to find how high a tower we could build, if we really tried. In early 1962

[Published in *Advances in Earth Orientated Applications of Space Technology*, Vol. I, no. 1, 1981, pp. 39–48] the Convair Division of General Dynamics carried out a feasibility study, to see if very high towers would be of value for astronomy, high altitude research, communications and rocket launching platforms [2]. It turns out that steel towers could be built up to 6 km high, aluminium ones up to almost 10. Nature can do just as well; it would be cheaper to use Mount Everest.

However, we now have much better materials than steel and aluminium in the form of composites, which give both high strength *and* low density. Calculations show that a tower built of graphite composite struts could reach the very respectable height of 40 km, tapering from a 6 km-wide base. I dare not ask what it would cost; but it's startling to realise that, even with today's technology, we could build a structure *100 times* as high as the world's tallest building.

But the geostationary orbit is a thousand times higher still, so we can forget about building up towards it. If we hope to establish a physical link between Earth and space, we have to proceed in the opposite direction—from orbit, *down*-wards.

That it might be useful to hang a long cable from a satellite must have occurred to a great many people. I myself toyed with the idea in 1963 while preparing an essay on comstats for UNESCO, published next year in *Astronautics* [3]. At that thime, there was still considerable uncertainty about the effects of the time-delay in satellite telephone circuits; some thought that it might have proved intolerable in ordinary conversation.

Although we should be duly grateful to Nature for giving us the geostationary orbit, one can't help wishing, for INTELSAT'S sake, that it was a good deal closer. So I wondered if it would be possible to suspend a satellite repeater 10000 or more kilometres below the 36000 km altitude that the law of gravity, and the Earth's rotational speed, has dictated.

Some desultory calculations soon convinced me that it couldn't be done with existing materials, but as I wanted to leave the option open I wrote cautiously: 'As a much longer-term possibility, it might be mentioned that there are a number of theoretical ways of achieving a *low-altitude, twenty-four hour satellite*; but they depend upon technical developments unlikely to occur in this century. I leave their contemplation as "an exercise for the student"!' In 1969, 6 years later, Collar and Flower came to exactly the same conclusion in a *J.B.I.S.* paper 'A (relatively) low altitude 24-h satellite' [4]. To quote their summary:

'The scheme for launching a twin-satellite system into a 24-h orbit with the inner satellite relatively close to the earth's surface is theoretically possible, although with the materials currently available no operational advantage would result. New materials now being developed, however, if used to the limit of their strength, could result in a system that considerably improved a communication efficiency. Even with materials that are strong enough and light enough many problems exist. Static and dynamic stability investigations would need to be made, and temperature effects allowed for. In the design of the system, means of deployment and of minimising meteorite damage would in particular need careful consideration.

'The final conclusion is that while theoretically possible, the twin satellite system is impracticable at the present time, but will show ever increasing promise as new, strong, light materials are developed.'

Incidentally, Collar and Flower did mention that it would be possible for the cable to reach *all the way down to the Earth's surface*, though they did not elaborate on this point, and were apparently unaware of earlier work in this field. For it now appears that at least half a dozen people invented the space elevator, quite independently of each other, and doubtless more pioneers will emerge from time to time.

In the West, the group that got there first consisted of John Isaacs, Allyn Vine, Hugh Bradner and George Bachus, from the Scripps Institute of Oceanography and the Woods Hole Oceanographic Institute. It is, perhaps, hardly surprising that oceanographers should get involved in such a scheme, since they are about the only people who concern themselves with very long hanging cables. Very long, that is, by ordinary standards; but in their 1966 letter to *Science* [5] Isaacs *et al.* discussed a cable over *three thousand* times longer than one to the bottom of the Marianas Trench, a mere 11 km down.

Their brief but very comprehensive paper made the following points:

The cable would have to be tapered, and would have to be spun out in both directions simultaneously—that is, towards the Earth and away from it, so that the structure was always balanced around the geostationary point. One would start with the smallest possible cable—perhaps with a minimum diameter of only a few thousandths of a centimetre—and the lower end would have to be guided down to earth by some kind of reaction device. Once the initial cable had been established between stationary orbit and the point on the equator immediately below it, it could be used to establish a stronger cable, until one of the required carrying capacity was attained. In principle, it would then be possible to hoist payloads from earth into space by purely mechanical means.

Now, you will recall that, as one ascends Tsiolkovski's hypothetical space tower, gravity decreases to zero at stationary orbit—*and its direction then reverses itself.* In other words, though one would have to do work to get the payload up to the geostationary position, once it had passed that point it would continue to travel on outwards, at an increasing acceleration—falling upwards, in fact. Not only would it require no energy to move it away from earth—it could *generate* energy, which could be used to lift other payloads! Of course, this energy comes from the rotation of the earth, which would be slowed down in the process. I have not attempted to calculate how much mass one could shoot off into space before the astronomers complained that their atomic clocks were running fast. It would certainly be a long time before anyone else could notice the difference....

Isaacs *et al.* go on to say:

'In addition to their use for launching materials into space, such installations could support laboratories for observation of conditions in space at high altitudes; they could resupply energy or materials to satellites or spacecraft, collect energy or materials from space and the high atmosphere, support very tall structures on the earth's surface, and others. There is no immediate limit to the total mass that could be retained near the 1-day orbit by such a cable.'

Isaacs *et al.*, discussed only briefly the obviously vital question of possible materials, listing amongst others quartz, graphite and beryllium. The *total* mass, with the best material, of a cable strong enough to withstand 200 km h^{-1} wind forces, turns out to be surprisingly low—only half a ton! Needless to say, its diameter at the earth and would be extremely small—one five-hundredth of a centimetre. And before anyone starts to spin this particular thread, I should point out that the material proposed is quite expensive. I don't know what the market quotation would be for half a ton of—*diamond*.

The first reaction to the Isaacs paper came some three months later [6] when an unlucky American scientist fell into a neat dynamical trap. He was not the only one to do so, apparently; but James Shea was unfortunate enough to have his letter published. The objection he raised was ingenious and so apparently convincing that he stated flatly: 'The system is inefficient as well as mechanically unsound and *theoretically* impossible.' (My italics.)

Shea's paradox can best be appreciated as follows: Consider the payload to be sent up the cable, when it is resting on the equator at the beginning of its journey. Obviously, because of the Earth's spin, it's actually moving eastwards at about 1700 km h^{-1}.

Now it is sent up the cable—*how* is, for the moment, unimportant—until it reaches the geostationary orbit, 36000 km above the Earth. It is still exactly above the point from which it started, but almost six times further from the centre of the Earth. So to stay here, it must obviously move six times faster—about 11000 km h^{-1}. How does it acquire all this extra tangential velocity?

There's no problem when you consider the analogous case of a fly crawling from the hub out along the spoke of a spinning wheel. The wheel is a rigid structure, and automatically transmits its rotational velocity to the fly. But how can a flexible cable extending out into space perform the same feat?

The explanation may be found by looking at one of mankind's simplest, oldest and most cost-effective weapons—the sling. I wonder if Goliath's technical advisers told him not to worry about that kid with the ridiculous loop of cloth—it couldn't possibly transfer any kinetic energy to a pebble. If so, they forgot that the system contained a rigid component—David's strong right arm. So also with the space elevator. Its lower end is attached to the 6000 km radius of the Earth—quite a lever.

Having easily refuted this criticism, Isaacs & Co. were now in for a shock. More than a year after their letter had appeared, *Science* printed a lengthy note [7] from Vladimir Lvov, Moscow correspondent of the Novosti Press Agency, pointing out that they had been anticipated by a half a decade. A Leningrad engineer, Yuri N. Artsutanov, had already published an article in *Pravda* which not only laid down *all* the

* Artsutanov's own translation is: 'Into space with the help of an electric locomotive' (see Acknowledgements).

basic concepts of the space elevator, but developed them in far greater detail.

This 1960 paper, which may turn out to be one of the most seminal in the history of astronautics, has the unassuming title 'Into the Cosmos by electric vehicle'.* Unfortunately, it has never been translated into English, nor have the extensive calculations upon which it is obviously based yet been published. The summary that follows is therefore based on Lvov's letter.

Artsutanov's initial minimum cable, constructed from materials which already exist but which have so far only been produced in microscopic quantities, would be able to lift two tons, would have a diameter of about one millimetre at the earth's surface, and would have a total mass of about 900 tons. It would extend to a height of 50000 km—that is, 14000 km beyond geostationary altitude, the extra length providing the additional mass needed to keep the whole system under tension. (The weight, as it were, on the end of the sling.)

But this is just a beginning. Artsutanov proposed to use the initial cable to multiply itself, in a sort of boot-strap operation, until it was strengthened a thousandfold. Then, he calculated, it would be able to handle 500 tons *an hour* or 12000 tons a day. When you consider that this is roughly equivalent to one Shuttle flight every *minute*, you will appreciate that Comrade Artsutanov is not thinking on quite the same scale as NASA. Yet if one extrapolates from Lindbergh to the state of transatlantic air traffic 50 yr later, dare we say that he is over-optimistic? It is doubtless a pure coincidence, but the system Artsutanov envisages could just about cope with the current daily increase in the world population, allowing the usual 22 kg of baggage per emigrant....

Lvov uses two names to describe Artsutanov's invention: a 'cosmic lift', and a 'heavenly funicular'. But a funicular, strictly speaking, is a device operated by a rope or cable—and we may be sure that the space elevator will not hoist its payloads with the aid of moving cables tens of thousands of kilometres long.

One would have thought that this correspondence, in one of the world's leading scientific journals, would have triggered a large scale discussion. Not a bit of it; to the best of my knowledge, there was no reaction at all. This may be because the Apollo project was then moving towards its climax—the first moon landing was less than two years away—and everyone was hypnotised by big rockets, as well they might be.

But the idea must have been quietly circulating in the U.S.S.R. because it is illustrated in the handsome volume of paintings by Leonov and Sokolov *The Stars and Awaiting Us* (1967). On p. 25 there is a painting entitled 'Space Elevator', showing an assembly of spheres—hovering, I am pleased to see, over Sri Lanka—from which a cable stretches down to the earth. Part of the descriptive text reads as follows:

'If a cable is lowered from the (24 h) satellite to the earth you will have a ready cable-road. An "Earth-Sputnik-Earth" elevator for freight and passengers can then be built, and it will operate without any rocket propulsion.'

Rather surprisingly, there is no reference to the inventor. Sokolov's original painting, incidentally, has been acquired by my insatiably acquisitive friend Fred Durant for the National Air and Space Museum, which by now must surely have the world's finest collection of space art (and space hardware).

The next major development was not for another *eight* years. Then Jerome Pearson of the Flight Dynamics Laboratory, Wright-Patterson Air Force Base, invented the idea all over again and published the most comprehensive study yet in *Acta Astronautica* [8]. His computer search of the literature had failed to turn up any prior references, and in view of the indexing problem I'm not surprised. How would you look up such a subject? Pearson called it an 'orbital tower', and presumably never thought of telling his computer to hunt for 'sky-hook', which might have located the *Science* correspondence.

I speak with some feeling on this, because for 2 years I was solely responsible for indexing *Physics Abstracts*, and you'll find some very strange entries round 1950. But the problem is insoluble, unless you can do retrospective re-indexing. When a new phenomenon is discovered, you may not even know how to *classify* it, let alone what to call it (after all, we're still stuck with X-rays, after almost a century...).

Pearson's 1975 paper was the most thorough study of the project yet published, and emphasised one of the space elevator's most important characteristics. Like a terrestrial elevator, it *could be used in both directions*. Returning payloads could be brought back to Earth without the use of heat-shields and atmospheric braking. Not only would this reduce environmental damage; it would mean that virtually all the energy of re-entry could be recovered, and not wasted as is the case today.

This characteristic makes the space elevator unique—at least, until someone invents anti-gravity. *It is a conservative system.* If, as would probably be the case, electrical energy is used to lift payloads up the elevator, and the mass flow is the same in both directions, incoming traffic could provide all the energy needed to power outgoing traffic. In practice, of course, there could be the inevitable conversion and transmission losses, but they could be quite small.

In this and subsequent papers [9] Pearson was the first to go into the dynamics of the system, discussing the vibration modes of the structure due to launch loads, gravity, tides etc. He decided that none of these, though important, would cause any insuperable problems. Indeed, I have suggested elsewhere that they could even be used to advantage [10].

Pearson has also located at least three other independent originators of the concept [11], though none prior to Artsutanov's 1960 paper. From now on, at least, further re-invention is unnecessary; however, as we shall see later, novel and often surprising extensions of the basic system are still appearing.

THE PROBLEM OF MATERIALS

The very minimum requirement for a space elevator is, obviously, a cable strong enough to support its own weight when hanging from geostationary

---

* My brief apologies to purists for invoking this fictitious entity.

orbit down to earth, 36 000 km below. That is a very formidable challenge; luckily, things are not quite as bad as they look because only the lowest portion of the cable has to withstand one full gee.

As we go upwards, gravity falls off according to Newton's inverse square law. But the *effective* weight of the cable diminishes even more rapidly, owing to the centrifugal force* on the rotating system. At geostationary altitude the two balance and the net weight is zero; beyond that, weight appears to increase again—but *away* from the Earth.

So our cable has no need to be strong enough to hang 36 000 km under *sea-level* gravity; allowing for the effects just mentioned, the figure turns out to be only one-seventh of this. In other words, if we could manufacture a cable with sufficient strength to support 5000 km (actually, 4960) of its own length at one gee, it would be strong enough to span the gap from geostationary orbit to Equator. Mathematically—though not physically—Jacob's ladder need be only 5000 km long to reach Heaven.... This figure of 5000 km I would like to call 'escape length', for reasons which will soon be obvious.

How close are we to achieving this with known materials? Not very. The best steel wire could manage only a miserable 50 km or so of vertical suspension before it snapped under its own weight. The trouble with metals is that, though they are strong, they are also heavy; we want something that is both strong and *light*. This suggests that we should look at the modern synthetic and composite materials. Kevlar (Tm) 29, for example [12] could sustain a vertical length of 200 km before snapping—impressive, but still totally inadequate compared with the 5000 needed.

This 'breaking length', also known as 'rupture length' or 'characteristic length', is the quantity which enables one to judge whether any particular material is adequate for the job. However, it may come as a surprise to learn that a cable can hang vertically for a distance many times greater than its breaking length!

This can be appreciated by a simple 'thought experiment'. Consider a cable which is just strong enough to hang vertically for a hundred kilometres. One more centimetre, and it will snap....

Now cut it in two. Obviously, the upper 50 km can support a length of 50 km—the identical lower half. So if we put the two sections side by side, they can support a *total* length of 100 km. Therefore, we can now span a vertical distance of 150 km, using material with only 100 km breaking length.

Clearly, we can repeat the process indefinitely, bundling more and more cables together as we go upwards. I'm sure that by now you've recognised an old friend—the 'step' principle, but in reverse. Step *rockets* get smaller as we go higher; step cables get bigger.

I apologise if, for many of you, I'm labouring the obvious, but the point is of fundamental importance and the rocket analogy so intriguing that I'd like to take it a little further.

We fossils from the pre-space age—the Early Paleoastronautic Era—must all remember the depressing calculations we used to make, comparing rocket exhaust velocities with the 11.2 km S' of Earth escape velocity. The best propellents we knew then—

and they are *still* the best today!—could provide exhaust velocities only a quarter of escape velocity. From this, some foolish critics argued that leaving the Earth by chemical rocket was impossible *even in theory* [13].

The answer, of course, was the step or multi-stage rocket—but even this didn't convince some sceptics. Willy Ley [14] records a debate between Oberth and a leading German engineer, who simply wouldn't believe that rockers could be built with a mass-ratio of twenty. For Saturn V, incidentally, the figure is about five hundred.

We escaped from earth using propellants whose exhaust velocity was only a fraction of escape velocity, by paying the heavy price demanded by multi-stage rockets. An enormous initial mass was required for a small final payload.

In the same way, we can achieve the 5000 km 'escape length', even with materials whose breaking length is a fraction of this, by steadily thickening the cable as we go upwards. Ideally, this should be done not in discrete steps, but by a continuous taper. The cable should flare outwards with increasing altitude, its cross-section at any level being just adequate to support the weight hanging below.

With a stepped, or tapered, cable it would be theoretically possible to construct the space elevator from *any* material, however weak. You could build it of chewing gum, though the total mass required would probably be larger than that of the entire universe. For the scheme to be practical we need materials with a breaking length a very substantial fraction of escape length. Even Kevlar 29's 200 km is a mere 25th of the 5000 km goal; to use that would be like fuelling the Apollo mission with damp gunpowder, and would require the same sort of astronomical ratio.

So, just as we were once always seeking exotic propellents, we must now search for super-strength materials. And, oddly enough, we will find them in the same place on the periodic table.

Carbon crystals have now been produced in the laboratory with breaking lengths of up to 3000 km—that is, more than *half* of escape length. How happy the rocket engineers would be, if they had a propellent whose exhaust products emerged with 60% of escape velocity!

Whether this material can ever be produced in the megaton quantities needed is a question that only future technologies can answer; Pearson [8] has made the interesting suggestion that the zero gravity and vacuum conditions of an orbiting factory may assist their manufacture, while Sheffield [15] and I [10] have pointed out that essentially unlimited quantities of carbon are available on many of the asteroids. Thus when space mining is in full swing, it will not be necessary to use super-shuttles to lift vast quantities of building material up to geostationary orbit—a mission which, surprisingly, is somewhat more difficult than escaping from Earth.

It is theoretically possible that materials stronger—indeed, vastly stronger—than graphite crystals can exist. Sheffield [15] has made the point that only the outer electrons of the atoms contribute, through their chemical bonds, to the strength of a solid. The nucleus provides almost all the mass, but nothing else; and in this case, mass is just what we *don't* need.

So if we want high-strength materials, we should look at elements with low atomic weights—which is why carbon (A.W.12) is good and iron (A.W.56) isn't. It follows, therefore, that the best material for building space elevators is—solid hydrogen! In fact, Sheffield calculates that the breaking length of a solid hydrogen crystal is 9118 km—almost twice 'escape length'.

By a curious coincidence, I have just received a press release from the National Science Foundation headed 'New form of hydrogen created as Scientists edge closer to creating metallic hydrogen' [16]. It reports that, at a pressure of half a million atmospheres, hydrogen has been converted into a *dense crystalline solid at room temperature*. The scientists concerned go on to speculate that, with further research—and I quote—'hydrogen solids can be maintained for long periods without containment'.

This is heady stuff, but I wonder what they mean by 'long periods'. The report adds casually that 'solid hydrogen is 25 to 35 times more explosive than TNT'. So even if we *could* make structures from solid hydrogen, they might add a new dimension to the phrase 'catastrophic failure'.

However, if you think that crystalline hydrogen is a tricky building material, consider the next item on Dr Sheffield's shopping list. The ultimate in theoretical strength could be obtained by getting rid of the useless dead mass of the nucleus, and keeping only the bonding electrons. Such a material has indeed been created in the laboratory; it's 'positronium'—the atom, for want of a better word, consisting of electron-positron pairs. Sheffield calculates that the breaking length of a positronium cable would be a fantastic 16 700 000 km! Even in the enormous gravity field of Jupiter, a space elevator need have no appreciable taper.

Positronium occurs in two varieties, both unfortunately rather unstable. Para-positronium decays into radiation in one-tenth of a nanosecond—but ortho-positronium lasts a thousand times longer, a whole tenth of a microsecond. So when you go shopping for positronium, make sure that you buy the brand marked 'Ortho'.

Sheffield wonders wistfully if we could stabilise positronium, and some even more exotic speculations are made by Moravec [17]. He suggests the possible existence of 'monopole' matter, and hybrid 'electric/magnetic' matter, which would give not only enormous strength but superconductivity and other useful properties.

Coming back to earth—or at least to this century—it seems fair to conclude that a small cable could certainly be established from geostationary orbit down to sea level, using materials that may be available in the near future. But that, of course would be only the first part of the problem—a mere demonstration of principle. To get from a simple cable to a working elevator system might be even more difficult. I would now like to glance at some of the obstacles, and suggest a few solutions; perhaps the following remarks may stimulate others better qualified to tackle them.

DEPLOYING THE CABLE

The space elevator may be regarded as a kind of

bridge, and many bridges begin with the establishment of a light initial cable—sometimes, indeed, no more than a string towed across a canyon by a kite. It seems likely that the space elevator will start in the same way with the laying of a cable between geostationary orbit and the point on the equator immediately below.

This operation is not as simple as it sounds, because of the varying forces and velocities involved, not to mention the matter of air resistance after atmospheric entry. But there are two existing technologies which may provide a few answers, or at least hints at them.

The first is that of submarine cable laying, now considerably more than a century old. Perhaps one day we may see in space something analogous to the triumphs and disasters of the *Great Eastern*, which laid the first successful transatlantic telegraph cable— the Apollo Project of its age.

But a much closer parallel, both in time and sophistication, lies in the development of wire-guided missiles. These lethal insects can spin out their metallic gossamer at several hundred kilometres an hour. They may provide the prototype of the vehicle that lays a thread from stationary orbit down to earth.

Imagine a spool, or bobbin, carrying some 40 000 km of filament, a few tenths of a millimetre thick at the outer layers, and tapering down to a tenth of this at the core—the end that finally reaches Earth. Its mass would be a few tons, and the problem would be to play it out evenly at an average velocity of a kilometre a second along the desired trajectory. Moreover, an equivalent mass has to be sent outwards at the same time, to ensure that the system remains in balance at the stationary orbit.

My friend Professor Ruppe has investigated [12] the dynamics of the mission, and concludes that it can be achieved with modest mass-ratios. But the mechanical difficulties would obviously be formidable, and it may well turn out that material of such tensile strength is too stiff to be wound on to a spool of reasonable radius.

Sheffield [18] has suggested an alternative method of installation which I find—to say the least—hair-raisingly implausible. He proposes constructing the entire space elevator system in orbit, and then launching it towards the earth, grabbing the lower end when it reaches the equator! The atmospheric entry of a few megatons dead weight, which must impact within metres of the aiming point, seems likely to generate a lot of opposition from the environmentalists. I call it 'harpooning the Earth', and would prefer to be near one of the Poles if it's ever tried out.

THE MASS ANCHOR

In order to balance the weight of the lower portion, and to compensate for the reaction produced by ascending payloads, the space elevator has to extend far beyond geostationary orbit. The upper portion may be regarded as the mass which keeps the cosmic sling taut, as it whirls round the Earth every 24 h.

This mass could be provided by another tapered cable, extending out into space, but it has to be very much longer than the lower portion to produce equi-

librium. Indeed, calculations show that it must reach the enormous height of 144 000 km. I do not think that a cosmic flail extending a third of the way to the moon will make the Earth a nice place to visit.

The alternative is to have a large mass anchored at a much lower altitude, not far above the geostationary orbit. The closer it is, the larger the mass required; it might be many megatons, or even gigatons. Both Sheffield and I have suggested that captured asteroids could be used for this purpose, and as many of them now appear to be largely carbonaceous they could also supply much of the material of the elevator, the remaining *debris* providing the anchor.

CATASTROPHES

A structure extending right through the atmosphere and on into space for at least 50 000 km would be a considerable navigational hazard, both to aircraft and spacecraft. Very elaborate anti-collision measures would have to be taken and all air traffic would have to be diverted from the equatorial danger zone. Probably the structure would be strong enough to survive impacts at atmospheric velocities; *cosmic* speeds would be another matter.

The problem here is aggravated by the fact that, over a long enough period of time, *all* satellites with perigees below geostationary altitude would eventually collide with the space elevator, as their orbits precess around the earth. So before the elevator is built, there would have to be a thorough job of garbage collection, and thereafter all remaining satellites would have to be closely watched. Whenever they approached too near the elevator, they would have to be nudged into a safer orbit. The impulses required would be trivial, and need be applied only very infrequently.

Meteorites present a more difficult problem, since they would not be predictable. But the impact of a large one would be a very rare occurrence indeed, and the elevator would have to be designed with enough redundancy to withstand any reasonable danger. Thus if it was in the form of an open framework—like a box girder—a meteorite should be able to pass through it in any direction without causing a structural failure.

But what if the elevator *is* severed?

Well, if the elevator is cut through at the Earth's surface, it would de exactly the opposite of a terrestrial building. It wouldn't fall down—but would rise up into the sky! In theory, the loose end might be secured and fastened down again; but that would be, to say the least, a tricky operation. It might even be easier to build a new system....

If the break occurred at any altitude up to about 25 000 km, the lower portion of the elevator would descend to Earth and drape itself along the equator, while the now unbalanced upper portion would rise to a higher orbit.

Hopefully, such major catastrophes can be avoided by good design; after all, it is very rare indeed for a modern bridge to collapse. (Though it *has* happened!) Much more likely—indeed, inevitable—is that objects would accidentally fall off the elevator. Their subsequent fate would depend upon their initial altitude.

The situation here is totally different from that encountered in orbital flight. If you step outside a spacecraft, you stay with it. But if you step off the elevator, it's rather like jumping out the window on the thousandth—or ten thousandth—floor of a rather tall skyscraper. Even so, you might still be quite safe—because you wouldn't fall vertically. You would share the structure's horizontal velocity as it whirls round with the spinning Earth; in other words, you would be injected into an elliptical orbit.

If your initial height is less than 23000 km, too bad. Your orbit will intersect the atmosphere in a few hours—or even minutes—and you'll burn up on the other side of the planet. Above this critical altitude, you would be in a stable orbit, skimming the atmosphere and coming back, after one revolution, to the place you started from. Of course, by then the elevator would be somewhere else, but with luck your friends might be waiting for you with a net and some well-chosen words of advice. Of if not on *this* revolution, on a subsequent one....

If you stepped off at the geostationary altitude itself, here, and only here, you would remain with the elevator, just as in conventional orbital flight. At higher altitudes, you would be injected into orbits of increasing eccentricity, with periods of one day and upwards.

That is, until you reached *another* critical altitude—47000 km. At this point, you'd be slung off into space at more than the local escape velocity, and would never return. You would become an independent planet of the Sun, and it might not be possible, owing to budgetary considerations, to rescue you and bring you back to Earth.

The analogy with a sling is now complete. Payloads released anywhere above the 47000 km altitude would escape from the Earth's gravitational field, and by going to greater and greater altitudes any desired launch speed could be attained. Pearson [9] has shown that *all* the planets can be reached by this technique, without the use of any other propulsion. The energy comes, of course, from the rotation of the Earth.

BEYOND THE EARTH

The lower the gravitational field of a planet, and the quicker its speed of rotation, the easier it is to build a space elevator. On a small asteroid the feat would be absurdly simple, and could even be achieved by a free-standing tower. There would be no need for suspended cables made of exotic materials.

Pearson [9] has pointed out the advantages of *lunar* space elevators—in this case, linking the Moon's equator with the well-known Lagrangian points in the line joining Earth and Moon. He calls them 'anchored lunar satellites', and they could be constructed of materials already available. Working in conjunction with the earth-based elevator, they would permit two-way traffic between Earth and Moon with almost zero use of rocket propellents.

The planet which seems ideally suited for the space elevator is Mars, with only one third of Earth's grav-

ity. What is more, the outer satellite Deimos is only slightly above stationary orbit—in just the right position to provide a mass anchor! Moreover, it appears to be largely carbonaceous, so could supply the required construction material.

But there is one big problem—about ten million-million tons—in connection with the Mars elevator, and that's the inner moon, Phobos. Moving almost exactly in the equatorial plane, it would slice through the elevator at very frequent intervals. Phobos is much too big to tow away, and blowing it up would only make matters worse. I refer you to *The Fountains of Paradise* for one solution....

DYNAMIC SYSTEMS

A daring extension of the space elevator principle has been put forward by Hans Moravec of Stanford University [17]. He imagines a 'skyhook' which is at a very low altitude, and is therefore not stationary with respect to the earth, but orbiting around it.*

Consider a very elongated satellite in a two hour orbit, rotating like a propeller blade (remember them?) as it rolls around the equator. The blades are just long enough to touch the earth, and if everything is properly synchronised, the tips would always touch the *same* spots on the equator at regular intervals.

From the point of view of the earth it would be, as Dr Robert Forward has put it, 'a Jacob's Ladder coming down out of the sky, pausing for a moment, then lifting off again at 1.4 *g*'. One could grab hold of the end, and get a free lift into space—and of course come back the same way.

It's a delightful concept, but the presence of the atmosphere, not to mention the fact that the equator isn't a perfect circle, and a few other practical details, make it rather unlikely. However, something similar may be possible in space, because very large rotation systems might serve as 'velocity banks' an idea discussed by Pearson and Sheffield [9, 15].

If you could hook on to the edge of a spinning disc—or an asteroid with a long extension from its equator—you could let go again at the appropriate point and so obtain a major velocity change without using any propellent. However, we would need such an enormous number of these 'cosmic carousels' scattered round the solar system that the idea is not really practical, except perhaps for very special applications.

I'd like to conclude this section on 'dynamic systems' by mentioning, even more briefly, an idea that has just emerged from Japan [19]—the 'Space *Escalator*'.

Imagine two satellites in circular orbits above the equator, one a few hundred kilometres above the other. Each carries a launching mechanism and a catching mechanism, which could be something as simple as a hook and elastic cord. By means of this mechanism, payloads could be transferred in either direction without the use of propellent. With a whole series of satellites—about a hundred—you could hop, or leap-frog, all the way up to the stationary orbit. But it would be a computational and operational nightmare, keeping track of all the constantly changing orbits, and launching and catching payloads at

---

* Once again, Artsutanov got there first! (See Acknowledgements.)

the right time. It think I'll stick to the elevator, rather than take the escalator.

POWER AND PROPULSION

The physics laboratories of British schools once boasted—and probably still do—an instructive device known as Atwood's Machine. I don't know what it's called elsewhere, and in any case Galileo was first with something very similar. It's an almost frictionless pulley over which runs a light cord, with equal weights suspended on either side. In this state nothing happens, of course, but even a small additional weight on one side sets the system in motion, at a very low acceleration.

This device may be regarded as the mechanical analogue of the Space Elevator. I don't suggest for a moment that we would actually use moving cables to lower and raise our payloads, but it demonstrates the basic principles involved. Such a system is inherently *conservative*—if it's properly balanced, it requires *no* energy to run it, except the very small amount lost by friction. In principle, arbitrary large masses can be raised or lowered through any distance. Unlike the rocket, which wastes precisely 100% of its available energy on a round trip, Atwood's machine wastes only a few per cent. And it's a lot quieter.

In practice, the space elevator would almost certainly be electrically powered, and the energy generated by the returning payloads during the braking and descent would be pumped back into the system—as happens with electric railroads in mountainous country. But there is also another reason why electric propulsion would be mandatory.

Though inanimate payloads might be in no hurry to reach the geostationary orbit, 36000 km up, human passengers are easily bored and have to be fed, entertained or at least tranquillised by alcohol and inflight movies. By the time the space elevator is likely to be operating, no journey on Earth will last more than a couple of hours. I don't think that the average space tourist will tolerate a great deal of time in what will be little more than a glorified elevator cage, though one with a magnificent view.

So we will require operating speeds of several thousand kilometres an hour, which can be provided only by some kind of electric propulsion system with *no mechanical contact*—a linear motor, for example.

I am not competent to discuss the problems involved in switching huge amounts of electric power over distances a hundred times greater than those encountered in terrestrial systems. Presumably superconductors will be available by the time the elevator is built, but the weight penalty of the associated cooling systems may make them quite impracticable. It would be marvellous, of course, if our superstrength material was *also* a superconductor—and at room temperature (or higher)! But to expect not merely one but *three* miracles simultaneously is a little greedy.

Perhaps we can avoid enormously long transmission lines by using microwave or laser beams to get the power where it is wanted. And if it ever proves possible to build *small* nuclear generators, then perhaps we can hang the power stations at strategic points along the elevator.

However, this suggests an even more attractive possibility. There is no *theoretical* reason why small fusion—or even fission—generators cannot be built. If they prove to be practicable, then we could forget electrical transmission systems altogether and put the power plants in the vehicles. This would not be a retrograde step, because the weight of the 'fuel' would be essentially zero.

The space elevator could even make possible a far more efficient *chemically* fuelled transport system. In this case, the Earth–orbit structure would merely provide physical support—the railbed, as it were, for the equivalent of a self-contained diesel locomotive, not a centrally-powered electric one. Unlike a rocket, the space-train would not have to use much of its fuel merely to *maintain* altitude; it could do that simply by putting on the brakes. On the other hand, it would be at a disadvantage over the rocket as it would have to lift some of its propellents all the way to the stationary orbit. I have not calculated at what particular specific impulse the chemical *elevator* will be more efficient than the chemical rocket.

SUBSIDIARY PROBLEMS

As is well known, satellites in the geostationary orbit will not normally stay above the same point on the equator, but drift in longitude owing to the fact that the Earth's gravitational field is not symmetrical. However, there are two points of maximum stability—one in the Pacific over the Galapagos, and the other above the Maldive Islands, seven hundred kilometres to the south west of Sri Lanka. The latter point is the more stable; by an odd coincidence, it is directly above the small island of Gan, which in the 1960s was one of the staging posts for the Blue Streak rocket when it was being ferried from the United Kingdom to the Woomera launching site. If orbital stability is important, Gan—abandoned by the Royal Air Force several years ago, to the great distress of its inhabitants, though not of the central Maldivian government—may one day be the most important piece of real estate on Earth.

Other orbital perturbations—including ones in the north–south direction—are caused by the Sun and Moon. Probably all of these are only important to free satellites, and will be insignificant in a structure which is tethered to the ground. In any case, the upper section of the elevator could—and probably would—sway through an arc many thousands of kilometres across without causing operational problems.

The effect of hurricanes on the lower portion of the structure has worried some writers; although high winds are rare on the equator itself, they *can* occur, and if they did nothing else they could generate the severe torsional vibrations which our revered colleague Dr von Kármán studied in connection with the ill-fated Tacoma Narrows Bridge. So it might be worthwhile siting the structure on a very high mountain to reduce aerodynamic loads; unfortunately, there aren't any high mountains near the stable points.

A RING AROUND THE WORLD

There are now scores of satellites in the geostationary orbit, and the problem of collision and interference—which not long ago would have seemed an absurd fantasy—is already of practical importance. What is more, some equatorial countries are attempting to establish jurisdiction over this large but still restricted narrow ring around our planet. This has provoked the appalling pun, which perhaps fortunately cannot be translated from English, that there should be another U.N. Committee—on the Useful Pieces of Outer Space.

In 1977, while working on the final chapters of *The Foundains of Paradise*, I had one of those sudden glimpses of the perfectly obvious out of which I have cunningly fashioned my reputation as a prophet. One way of preventing geostationary satellites colliding or drifting around the equator would be to link them together with cables. As the forces involved would be extremely small, for the most purposes nothing much stronger than a nylon fishing line would be adequate, and the total mass needed to tie together all the satellites in the stationary orbit would be negligible.

But why stop there? The next step would be to build a continuous, habitable structure—a 'Ring City'—right around the Earth. All the legions of geostationary satellites could be attached to it, and reached for servicing by an internal circular railroad. And it could serve as a launch platform for almost all missions, manned or unmanned, into deep space.

It would be reached, of course, by space elevators, which would take the form of several spokes linking the ring city with the equator. The Earth would, in fact, now be the hub of a gigantic wheel, 85000 km in diameter. Passengers could move up and down the spokes, or around the rim, just as freely as they now move around the surface of the Earth. The distinction between Earth and space would be abolished, though the advantages of either could still be retained.

A Russian engineer, G. Polyakov had the same idea almost simultaneously, and published a paper with the title 'A space necklace about the Earth' [20]. However, as I might have guessed, we were both anticipated by Professor Buckminster Fuller. To quote from the notes he wrote for the sleeve of my *Fountains of Paradise* recording (Caedmon TC 1606):

'In 1951, I designed a free floating tensegrity ringbridge to be installed way out from and around the Earth's equator. Within this halo bridge, the Earth could continue its spinning while the circular bridge would revolve at its own rate. I foresaw Earthian traffic vertically ascending to the bridge, revolving and descending at preferred Earth loci.'

All that Bucky's vision needs to make it reality is the space elevator.

And when will we have that? I wouldn't like to hazard a guess, so I'll adapt the reply that Arthur Kantrowitz gave, when someone asked a similar question about his laser propulsion system.

The Space Elevator will be built about 50 years after everyone stops laughing.

Acknowledgements—My first thanks must go to the late A. V. Cleaver, F.B.I.S., F.R.Ae.S., with whom I discussed the subject of this paper for several years. It is a great sorrow to many, besides myself, that he never lived to see the final outcome of our deliberations.

I would also like to thank Professor Harry O. Ruppe, Dr Charles Sheffield, Dr Robert Forward, Dr Alan Bond, Frederick C. Durant, and Jerome Pearson for much material and helpful correspondence.

Finally, I am especially grateful to Mr Vladimir Lvov for giving me biographical material on Yuri Artsutanov (Born 1929, Leningrad) and for putting me in touch with him. Indeed, while this paper was in its final draft I was delighted to receive a letter from Mr Artsutanov (dated April 1979) of such interest and importance that it demands quoting at length:

'It may be interesting for you to know how the idea of the space elevator (s.e.) originated. At the beginning of 1957 a friend of mine, who like myself graduated at the Leningrad Technological Institute... told me about a material which could hold its weight at the length of 400 km. I thought that at such a height the gravitating force is less and consequently the length could be enlarged. Then it became interesting for me to calculate the strength of the material to prolong the vertical rod made of it to infinity.... Immediately the thought came that this rod should have a changeable section and it was easy to derive the equation... which showed that the rod could be done out of any material and its mass did not become absurdly large....

'At first I told some of my friends about this idea. Some months later the cosmic theme became very popular. In Summer 1960 I was in Moscow on business and visited the editor of *Komsomolskaya Pravda* with a proposal to publish my article without any equations... to my mind, they could be derived by any student who understood the idea. A week later the article was published under the title "Into space with the help of an electric locomotive...."

'In 1969 the magazine *Knowledge is Force* (*Znanije-Sila*) No. 7, p. 25 published my article developing the idea of the s.e. It was proposed to sink the rods not from a synchronous satellite but from an ordinary one, for example 1000 km, height. In this case the contact with Earth and the passing of denser layers of the atmosphere would take place at a comparative low speed. The rods would be like spokes of a wheel rolling along the equator.... Having attached itself to the end of such a rod during a half-turn of this wheel the cosmic ship will gain the speed of 14 km/s. Similarly the ship returning from the cosmic space will lose the speed and land during another halfturn....'

It will be seen that this proposal is virtually the same as that put forward by Moravec 8 years later [17].

Until now, Yuri Artsutanov's work has only been published in simplified form for the benefit of the lay public. Let us hope that it will soon appear in its original version, so that his peers can fully appreciate the full genius of this remarkable Leningrad engineer.

REFERENCES

[1] K. E. Tsiolkovski, *Grezi o zemle i nebe*, p. 35. U.S.S.R. Academy of Sciences edition (1959).

[2] Personal communication, Edward J. Hujsak to Fred C. Durant, January 6 (1978).

[3] Arthur C. Clarke, The world of the communications satellite, *Astronautics*, February (1964). Now in *Voices From the Sky*. Harper & Row, N.Y. (1965); Gollancz, London (1966).

[4] A. R. Collar and J. W. Flower, A (relatively) low altitude 24 hour satellite, *J.B.I.S.* **22**, 442–457, 1969.

[5] John D. Isaacs, Allyn C. Vine, Hugh Bradner and George E. Bachus, Satellite elongation into a true "Sky-Hook", *Science* **151**, 682–683 (1966).

[6] James H. Shea, Sky-Hook. Reply by Isaacs *et al.*, *Science* **152**, 800 (1966).

[7] Vladimir Lvov, Sky-Hook: old idea, *Science* **158**, 946–947 (1967).

[8] J. Pearson, The orbital tower; a spacecraft launcher using the Earth's rotational energy. *Acta Astronautica* **2**, 785–799 (1975).

[9] J. Pearson, Using the orbital tower to launch Earth-escape payloads daily. AIAA Paper 76–123, 27th IAF Congress (1976); Anchored lunar satellites for cislunar transportation and communication. *J. Astronaut. Sci.* **XXVII**, No. 1, 39–62 (1979). "Lunar Anchored Satellite Test": AIAA/AAS Astrodynamics Conference, Palo Alto, 7–9 August, 1978.

[10] Arthur C. Clarke, *The Fountains of Paradise*. Harcourt Brace Jovanovich, N.Y.; Gollancz, London (1979).

[11] These include G. C. Weiffenbach, G. Colombo, E. M. Gaposchkin and M. D. Grossi, who arrived at the concept as a result of their work on tethered satellites, and T. Logsdon and R. Africano [see T. Logsdon, *The Rush to the Stars*, Franklin (1970)].

[12] Professor Harry O. Ruppe, Hyperfilament's First Strand. 15 February (1979) (Personal Communication).

[13] For a classic example, see my *Profiles of the Future*, Chapt. 1. Harper & Row, N.Y. (1973); Gollancz, London (1974).

[14] Willy Ley, *Rockets, Missiles and Men In Space*, Chap. 5. Viking (1968).

[15] Charles Sheffield, How to Build a Beanstalk, in press.

[16] NSF Press Release PR 79–15, 2 March, (1979).

[17] Hans Moravec, A non-synchronous orbital skyhook. *J. Astronaut. Sci.* **XXV**, No. 4, 307–322 (1977).

[18] Charles Sheffield, *The Web Between the Worlds*. ACE (1979).

[19] Space escalator, a quasi permanent engine in space. Tsuotomu Iwata, National Space Development Agency of Japan. Application to the XXX IAC, 8 March (1979).

[20] G. Polyakov, A space 'Necklace' about the earth (Kosmicheskoye ozherel'ye zemli). *Teknika Molodezhi*, No. 4 41–43 (1977). (NASA TM-75174).

22 | *An Optimum Strategy for Interstellar Robot Probes*

While working on *The Fountains of Paradise*, I had an idea slightly more conventional than the space elevator, which after working into the novel I summarised in a letter to the *Journal of the British Interplanetary Society*. I still think it makes good sense, and perhaps in a few hundred years we may be doing the same sort of thing ourselves.

An Optimum Strategy for Interstellar Robot Probes

The concept of 'gravity assistance' whereby a spacecraft makes a close encounter with another celestial body in order to change its trajectory to some preferred direction was apparently first discussed in detail by Derek F. Lawden [1]. Its actual employment in the Mariner, Pioneer and Voyager missions is now well-known and has been highly successful.

This technique has a much wider application which suggests an 'optimum strategy' for interstellar searches by robot space-probes. Once a civilisation has reached the level where it can build probes with mean-times-to-failure measured in thousands of years (a not impossible goal with solid state electronics, multiple redundancy and self-repairing systems) it might then proceed as follows:-

A probe is launched towards the nearest promising star with enough energy to reach it with a modest excess above escape velocity. It makes a survey of the star and any associated planets while passing through the system, then carries out a perturbation maneouvre at periastron which aims it at the next target sun. As no propellent is required (except for a very small amount for course correction — and even this might be eliminated by skillful 'solar sailing') the operation could be repeated indefinitely.

A few very rough figures will give some idea of the time scales involved. In theory, a close approach can produce a change in orbital direction of almost 180 degrees; but this would require zero hyperbolic (i.e. interstellar cruise) velocity. When cruise velocity equals the velocity of escape at periastron, the probe rounds the star at $\sqrt{2}$ local escape velocity and its orbit is deflected through 45 degrees [2]. This would appear ample to give a good selection of target stars for the next rendezvous. Higher cruise speeds, while shortening flight times, would limit the choice of targets.

Since the escape velocity of likely suns, at the point of closest safe approach, would be of the order of 500 km/sec., this might be the maximum useful cruise speed for a passive probe. At an average star separation of five light years, transit times would thus be 3,000 years. Such a probe would take a year to cross our Solar System, and would be within Earth's orbit for a week. This would give plenty of time for a survey, the results of which could be relayed back to base at a low bit rate during the millenia before the next port of call.

Such a probe could explore many stars, and its lifetime would be limited only by internal breakdowns or cosmic accidents. The electrical energy needed for housekeeping during the cruise mode would be trivial, and all that required for survey operations and later data transmission could be obtained just when it was needed — during the periastron passage — by tapping the star's radiation field.

This argument suggests that there may be an optimum velocity for robot probes, of about 0.02c, with corresponding transit times between stars of a few thousand years. Even if it was technically possible to build probes with cruise velocities of 0.5c, and thus transit times of a decade, such vehicles could investigate only a single star system, and for a very short (one day) period of time. They would be travelling far too fast to be deflected towards another system within reasonable range.

Clearly there are some interesting trade-offs here, and a long-lived civilisation might consider slow probes, capable of investigating many stars, a better investment than quick one-shot missions. A detailed numerical analysis, using actual parameters for various parts of the Galaxy, may be worthwhile. Meanwhile, I have explored some consequences of this idea in a work of fiction [3].

ARTHUR C. CLARKE,
Sri Lanka.

REFERENCES

1. Lawden, Derek F., 'Perturbation Manoeuvres', *JBIS* **13**, 329-334, 1954
2. Hunter, Maxwell W., *'Thrust into Space'*, p. 97, Holt, 1966
3. Clarke, Arthur C., *'The Fountains of Paradise'*, Harcourt Brace, Jovanovich; New York, Gollancz; London, 1979

[Published in the *Journal of the British Interplanetary Society*, November 1978, Vol. 33, no. 11, p. 438]

X | *Mathematical Recreations*

23 | HELP! I Am a Pentomino Addict!

I cannot remember a time when I was *not* interested in mathematics, but I can quite vividly remember the moment when I first became aware of its power to astonish the mind by revealing unexpected beauties.

The occasion was one of the rather rare lectures by our Headmaster at Huish's, Arnold Goodliffe. He was a large, imposing figure in the great tradition of English pedagogues; we all regarded him with awe and respect, but not with fear (unless there was good reason; in those far-off days corporal punishment was still permitted, and the Old Man knew how to apply it). His duties as Head must have left him little time for taking classes, but he must have been an inspiring teacher or he would not have made such an impact on my mind.

The lesson was one in elementary algebra. We all knew the simple formula for the sum of the first n integers:

$$n(n + 1)/2$$

and Arnold Goodliffe posed the question, which had probably never occurred to any of us: Is there a formula that gives the sum of the *squares* of the first n integers? He then proceeded to derive it by the process of induction, and I was at once struck by the power and elegance of the method. It impressed me enormously; but I had a bigger surprise in store.

When Dr. Goodliffe had written down the plausible but not very exciting solution

$$n(2n + 1)(n + 1)/6$$

he went on to the obvious next step—the sum of the *cubes* of the first *n* integers. The technique was exactly the same, though a little more cumbersome; clearly, with time and patience this ingenious method of "proof by induction" could be extended indefinitely.

But this time, the result was—to me, at least—a stunning surprise. It turned out that the sum of the cubes of the first *n* integers was exactly the same as the square of their sums! Who would have dreamed that

$$1^3 + 2^3 + 3^3 + 4^3 + \cdots + n^3$$

was equal to

$$(1 + 2 + 3 + 4 + \cdots + n)^2$$

What a beautiful and astonishing fact: and what on earth did it *mean*?

Of course, mathematics is full of such surprises; this particular one is trivial, but some are not only beautiful but of such profundity that they contain universes. Much later, I experienced the same *frisson* of pure intellectual delight when I encountered Euler's Equation:

$$e^{i\pi} + 1 = 0$$

This still seems to me the most amazing relationship in the whole of mathematics (well, that 0.01% with which I am familiar). At the same time, I have always found it aesthetically rather disturbing: it looks a little lopsided. Perhaps this is an example of Bacon's "there is no excellent beauty that hath not some strangeness in the proportion."

Forty years after Dr. Arnold Goodliffe started me thinking about the powers of the integers, I returned to the subject with the aid of some scientific hardware that would certainly have amazed my old headmaster. In the meantime, my mathematical odyssey had taken many detours besides those described in this volume.

Taking my degree in Pure and Applied Mathematics at King's College had convinced me that, much as I loved the subject, I would never be really good at it; at the best, I might make a competent instructor. For the rest of my life, it would be no more than an occasional clumsy tool, a fascinating hobby—and a recreation, in the best sense of the word. Mathematical puzzles would always intrigue me, though I would usually be too impatient to work them out.

Naturally, I became an avid reader of Martin Gardner's famous *Scientific American* feature "Mathematical Games," (inherited by Douglas Hofstadter), and it was through Martin that I discovered the fascinating world of Polyominoes. . . .

HELP! I Am a Pentomino Addict!

I have never been particularly interested in intellectual games and puzzles, partly because I regard them as a waste of time, but more probably because I can't be sure of winning. I have stubbornly refused even to learn the rules of chess, feeling that if I did so there might be real danger of addiction. This was fortunate, because Stanley Kubrick establishes psychological oneupmanship over his colleagues by clobbering them at chess.

Yet it was through Stanley that I got hooked on 12 small pieces of plastic which, starting as a geometrical problem understandable by any child, can rather rapidly escalate – if you have that sort of mind – into a way of life. It all started because in the first version of *2001* David Bowman was going to match his wits against the computer HAL, not at chess, but a game which is both simpler and more complicated which Dr Solomon Golumb (of whom more anon) patented under the name Pentominoes.

At this point, gentle reader (and how long is it since you were last called that?), you have a choice. You can turn this page. Or you can get pencil and paper (preferably squared – a centimetre grid will do nicely). Later you may want scissors and stiff card; by that time there is no known cure.

For various legal reasons the game of Pentominoes was never used in *2001*; HAL played chess instead. But I had become intrigued, and during the last half of the Sixties must have spent hundreds of hours playing with a beautiful plastic set of Pentominoes which I stole from a small niece, who found it in a London toyshop. Ten years later they formed a key element in my novel *Imperial Earth* and are now the basis of the rug I designed for my office.

You are doubtless wondering what the wretched things are. When I tell you, you will snort impatiently, "Is *that* all?" So I beg you – don't get overconfident. I, too, once thought I could take them or leave them. . . .

Pentominoes are nothing more complicated than the various shapes made by placing *five* equal squares in contact, edge to edge (this is where the squared paper and pencil will be helpful). The simplest arrangement is to have them all in line; this gives the bar-shaped or I-Pentomino. Or you can have four in line and the fifth offset at the end, giving a letter L. Or you can have one in the middle and the other four around it; this is the X-Pentomino.

By now you will have got the idea, and will appreciate that there are only a relatively few possibilities. Actually, there are just 12, and it will take you only a few minutes of doodling to find them all. The complete sequence gives figures closely resembling the letters P, I, L, F, N, T, U, V, W, X, Y, Z, which give a convenient means of identification. If you like to torture your friends by offering a prize of a thousand (or a million) pounds for a 13th Pentomino, go right ahead. You are perfectly safe.

Now, since each of these 12 distinct figures is made up of five equal squares, the complete set covers 60 squares – and this is where the fun begins. For 60 is a nice round number that splits up into lots of factors – 6×10, 5×12, 4×15, 3×20, 2×30. The problem then arises: can the 12 Pentominoes be dovetailed together, like pieces in a jigsaw, to make perfect rectangles with all these proportions? I can tell you at once that the complete answer to this

[Published under the title "Could you solve Pentominoes?" in the *Sunday Telegraph Magazine*, September 14, 1975]

apparently trivial question is something that no one would ever guess, and which I can still hardly believe.

We can eliminate the long, thin 2×30 rectangle right away; several of the Pentominoes – the X, for example – are obviously too fat to go into it. But this still leaves four other possibilities, starting with the 6×10 rectangle, which is the one with the most aesthetically satisfying shape.

At this point you may still have a chance of escaping; all you have to do is to stop reading and forget the whole business. But if you are still confident of your selfcontrol – or, alas, are already hooked – you will now have to beg, borrow, buy, steal or make the complete set of 12 Pentominoes.

They are all too easily made – it is only necessary to draw the shapes on squared paper and cut them out of fairly stiff card. However, the home-grown variety gets quickly frayed round the edges, and the plastic sets sold as puzzles in well-stocked toy-shops are much more satisfactory. I have a very compact set which fits nicely in the palm of the hand; it is made under the trademark Peter Pan.

My set, which I am liable to produce at the drop of a hat – or much less – snuggles neatly inside a flat box 6×10 units on a side – proving that *this* solution, at any rate, is possible. But once the pieces are tipped out of the box, it is diabolically difficult to put them back in again. That a jigsaw puzzle consisting of only 12 pieces cannot be quickly solved seems incredible, and no one will believe it until he has tried. It is not too difficult to get *11* of the 12 pieces back into the box – but the 12th is the wrong shape to fit into the remaining hole. I am slightly ashamed to confess that it took me a full month of occasional juggling before I was able to arrange the Pentominoes in a 6×10 rectangle; however, on one brilliant day I managed to find *three* separate solutions to the puzzle. For there are, in fact, more ways than one of putting the 12 pieces back into the box – and this is a rather spectacular understatement.

After you have struggled with the puzzle for a few hours without being able to complete the 6×10 rectangle even once, you may admit grudgingly that two or three different solutions could exist. But would you believe ten? Probably not. A hundred – ridiculous; completely out of the question!

Well, the unbelievable fact is that there are more than 2,000 different ways of put-

ting the 12 pieces back into a 6×10 box; one could spend a lifetime looking for them all. No human being has ever completed this task, and it is only thanks (?) to a computer that we know just how enormous it is.

There are also many ways – how many, I do not know, but I suspect there are hundreds – in which the 12 Pentominoes can be fitted together to give rectangles of 5×12 and 4×15 units on a side. The most interesting case, however, is that of the long, thin rectangle only 3 units wide and 20 long.

In his book *Mathematical Puzzles and Recreations*, the *Scientific American*'s Martin Gardner reveals that just *two* solutions exist to this problem, but sadistically leaves them "for the interested reader to construct".

This interested reader devoted so many hours to the problem that, without Martin Gardner's categorical assurance, he would have been prepared to bet that *no* solution existed. Eventually, to avoid wasting any more time, I announced a grand prize of ten rupees to anyone who could find the answer. To my delighted astonishment, one of my Sinhalese friends quickly secured the bonanza. As a public service, here is the order in which the Pentominoes must be arranged to give a 3×20 rectangle:

U X P I L N F T W Y Z V.

The only other solution is obtained by leaving the L N F T W Y Z section untouched and exchanging the two ends.

This apparently easy example, where all the pieces are laid in one line with a minimum of overlapping, also shows why only a computer can deal with the general problem. If you attempted to solve this by brute force, trying every possible arrangement, you would have 12 choices for the first letter, 11 for the second, 10 for the third, and so on, giving a total of $12 \times 11 \times 10 \times 9 \times 8 \times 7 \times 6 \times 5 \times 4 \times 3 \times 2$ permutations. This comes to the impressive number 479,001,600 – but the real number is *very* much higher still, for most of the letters can assume at least four positions – and some can be flipped over to make their own mirror images, giving *eight* distinct cases. (Only the completely symmetrical X looks exactly the same whichever way, and whichever side, you put it down.)

This little complication increases the possibilities by another 2^{27} or 134,217,728 arrangements, giving a grand total of more than sixty thousand million *million*. If you tried every possible way of placing the 12 Pentominoes in line, putting down one piece a second, it would take over 20 billion years, or the currently accepted age of the universe, to examine them all . . . and only 24 seconds out of that time would give the two correct answers. I do not feel so bad now about not finding them, and consider that my ten rupees was well spent.

But we have nowhere near exhausted the ramifications of these 12 apparently innocent figures, and they have other aspects to which many lifetimes could be devoted (I will not say profitably). For example, can we construct perfect, but smaller, rectangles, if we leave out one or more polyominoes?

It turns out that every theoretical possibility can exist, except for the rectangle of area 10 units. (The simplest solution – what the mathematicians call a trivial one – is the 1-Pentomino itself, which gives an area of five units.) There are no less than seven ways in which three Pentominoes can be arranged to make a little rectangle of area 15 units; they are all easy to find.

After that, the numbers escalate rapidly; I have found a dozen solutions for area 20 (four Pentominoes) and there may be many more. Perhaps the prettiest is the perfect square that can be constructed from five Pentominoes; there are at least six ways of doing this, but I have not attempted to make an exhaustive search.

I used to find it extremely relaxing, after a hard day's work, to set myself the goal of finding various solutions, not always knowing whether they were possible or not. It was a great surprise, and gave me a feeling of considerable triumph, when I found that one could omit the 1-Pentomino and *still* construct a rectangle of area 5 × 11 or 55 units from the remaining 11 pieces, a fact which somehow seemed intuitively unlikely. But as we have seen with the 2,000 solutions for the 6 × 10 case, intuition is a treacherous guide here. There is one case (probably unique) where the 12 Pentominoes can be divided into two sets of six, *each* of which will make a 6 × 5 rectangle. If you think it's easy to construct these, go right ahead. The two sets are F, N, P, U, V, X and I, L, T, W, Y, Z. Good luck.

Let us raise our sights a little higher. Obviously, it is not possible to construct a square out of the complete set of 12 Pentominoes, since they cover an area of 60 units. But if we allow a blank, or hole, of four units, giving a total area of 64, then we do have a number which is a perfect square. You may not be surprised to learn that an 8 × 8 square can be constructed on this basis, and in a great many different ways.

There are 65 solutions with the four-unit hole exactly in the centre of the larger square, and there may be a thousand (nobody really knows) other solutions, with the empty square off centre or split into four separate unit holes.

If you have survived this far, you will now be in a position to appreciate the game of Pentominoes, which I mentioned as my own introduction to the subject. It is played on a checkerboard and each of the two (or more) players has his own set of the 12 Pentominoes, distinctively coloured.

The rules could hardly be simpler, but the game is extremely subtle and its full theory still defies mathematical analysis. The players take turns putting their pieces on the board; the last player to be able to place one of his men is the winner. Obviously, the trick is to divide the board up into territories into which you can fit your own remaining men, while leaving your opponent no suitably shaped holes for his. Simple though it sounds, this game has more openings than chess; perhaps fortunately, a draw is impossible and no contest can go beyond 12 moves.

If you think this exhausts the subject of Pentominoes, you are sadly mistaken; the time has now come to take a wider view. One of the seductive fascinations of mathematics is that every subject turns out, in the long run, to be merely a small part of something else; thus at an early age we are shocked to discover that arithmetic is just a minor province of algebra, and later on *that* becomes a part of symbolic logic. So it is with Pentominoes; they are merely the fifth class in the endless series of *n*-ominoes, or polyominoes.

The lower orders (to use a phrase redolent of Victorian novels) can be quickly dismissed as of little interest. There is only one "monomino"; a simple square. Ditto for the 2-omino, which is the familiar domino; for two squares can only be joined together in just one way, to give a 1 × 2 rectangle. And it is easy to see that there are two "trominoes" and five "tetrominoes" – not enough to allow of any interesting possibilities. It is not until we get to the pentomino, with its 12 variants, that the really fascinating complexities start to unfold.

But what about the *next* step – the hexominoes, or shapes made by arranging *six* squares in every possible way? You are now peering into an abyss of infinite depth and width but if you insist on pressing on, let us conclude with a brief glimpse of the ultimate geometrical nightmare at the end of the polyomino trail.

So far, we have mentioned only *flat* figures, made from squares lying in one plane. But suppose we started not with squares, but with cubes – like children's building blocks – and began glueing them together in all possible ways, to make the sets of solids that could be constructed from 2, 3, 4, 5 and so on cubes. Obviously, we could have three-dimensional equivalents of all the problems mentioned above.

And not only three-dimensional ones; we could go on to the fourth, fifth . . . and *m*th dimension. Such figures could not actually be constructed, of course, but they could be analysed and enumerated theoretically. Yet I rather doubt if, no matter how long the human race exists, anyone will be able to work out the possible number of ways of assembling the set of *m*-dimensional *n*-polyominoes, where *n* and *m* are fair-sized numbers (larger than five, perhaps).

I suspect that any survivors of this obstacle course had better be put in touch with a connection, before withdrawal symptoms become acute.

I have already mentioned Martin Gardner, the mathematical Torquemada of the *Scientific American*, who occasionally discusses the subject in his monthly column. But the chief pusher in the U.S. is Dr Solomon Golumb, author of a book called (surprise!) *Polyominoes*, published by Scribners in 1965. Dr Golumb is Professor of Electrical Engineering and Mathematics at the University of Southern California, and therefore has many helpless victims in his power.

Meanwhile, I am glad to report, the writing of this report has almost cured my own addiction. For the first time in a year I feel that I have the urge under control. Dominoes, anyone?

24 | *HAL Jr. versus the Integers*

My fascination with Pentominoes lasted for several years, and provided an important element in the novel *Imperial Earth*. Even today I carry a neat little 6×10 plastic set with me on my rare travels, but it is many years since I have attempted to find any new solutions, for a simple psychological reason. In the November 1979 issue of *Byte*, Douglas A. Macdonald and Yekta Gursel, of Caltech's Theoretical Astrophysics Department, gave a computer programme which had churned out all the 2,339 6×10 configurations (it took two days on a Commodore PET). Later, they very kindly sent me their printout of *all* the possible rectangular tilings. There are just 2 3×20 solutions, as already mentioned; then there are 368 4×15's, 1,010 5×12's, and 2,339 6×10's—altogether, 3,719.

And in 1980 Kadon Enterprises (1227 Lorene Drive, Pasadena, Md. 21122—did you know that there was a Pasadena in Maryland?) sent me one of their beautiful 3-D sets, trademarked "Quintillions." These are cut from extremely hard wood by a laser, so precisely that they fit together almost like machined metal blocks.

Just a year later, of course, Erno Rubik—but let us ignore that global saga of strained thumbs and blistered fingers, and return to the ethereal realm of pure mathematics.

I got back to summing the powers of the integers by a rather devious route. In a way, it began with my arrival in London in 1936 to work in the civil service. For a few months, I rented a minute room near Paddington Station and commuted to Whitehall every day on the Underground. (Not long ago I drove past that little hotel—21, Norfolk Square—and as far as I could see, it was completely unchanged. I wondered who was now occupying my bed-sitting room.)

During weekends, it was pleasant to walk across Kensington Gardens to the Science Museum, and that soon became one of my favourite haunts. In particular, I was fascinated by the section devoted to mathematical machines; I don't believe I knew of their existence until I encountered them in their intricate and gleaming beauty. Kelvin's Tide Predictor—complicated multiarmed balances with sliding weights which somehow solved simultaneous equations—analysers for extracting Fourier coefficients—they stretched my mind and made my fingers itch. But the star of the show was the uncompleted fragment of the Babbage Machine. Today, of course, it is famous as the premature herald of the Computer Age; but in 1936 only a few specialists had ever heard of it. And I certainly never imagined that, forty years later, the BBC would be filming me beside it, talking about HAL. . . .

Yet though mechanical calculators were not uncommon, even in the late thirties, I don't recall meeting one in my entire civil service career—not in the Exchequer and Audit Department, the Treasury or the Post Office (though there must have been some tucked away in the P.O. Engineering Department). Nor did I feel the need for one in my official duties. The beauty of being an auditor is that you don't have to get the answer *exactly* right—that's the job of the humble accountant. An accuracy of one percent always seemed to me perfectly adequate for spotting errors, though I don't remember ever making this policy clear to my superiors. And with the fastest slide rule in Whitehall, I could do my day's work in a couple of hours, leaving the rest of the time available for more important business (e.g., the British Interplanetary Society).

Even when I entered Number 9 Radio School, Yatesbury, and so came into contact with advanced technology, I don't recall meeting as much as a hand-operated calculator. Yet sometime around 1941, I began to fantasise about what *could* be done with electronic techniques, and I pictured a machine rather like a typwriter, but with a cathode-ray tube on which the curves for any mathematical function could be displayed. I never made any attempt to work out the details; it was "obvious" to me that such a machine would be possible one day, and that was all that mattered. If I ever did brood over the circuitry, my thinking would have been on analogue lines; I knew nothing of digital systems, though of course their basic elements were in the radar sets all around me.

Now cut to twenty-seven years in the future—1969, the year of the first Moon landing. Electronic computers are now commonplace, but most of them occupy small—or large—rooms. I am browsing through an issue of *Science* when I suddenly encounter one that doesn't, and recognise it at once. True, its CRT only has three lines of numerical readout, but that's a lot more useful than curve-tracing (which can be provided on an additional plug-in plotting table, anyway). It's even more beautiful than the machine of my dreams, and I fall in love with it at once, despite the fact that I haven't the slightest practical use for it; my old college slide rule is perfectly adequate for the few calculations I have to perform. . . .

From time to time, in the scientific journals, I continue to come across this advertisement, and to salivate briefly before turning the page. But I give no serious thought to the matter until, around the middle of 1969, I receive a postcard which the editor of the American Airlines inflight magazine has sent out to various celebrities (or notorieties), obviously intending to provide material for a topical feature at the end of the year. It asks the simple question: "What present would you like this Christmas?"

Having no ideas on the subject and many better things to do than fill in questionnaires, I throw the card away. But half an hour later, on a sudden obscure impulse, I fish it out of the wastepaper basket and write on the dotted line "HEWLETT-PACKARD 9000." Then I mail the postcard and forget it completely—until a few months later when I receive a letter from Dr. Bernard Oliver, H/P Vice President in Charge of Research, beginning: "Yes, Arthur—there *is* a Santa Claus. . . ."

You can guess the rest—though not such details as obtaining Cabinet approval for such an unusual import, and the unprecedented feat of clearing the package through the Ceylon Customs *on a Saturday morning*. For more than a dozen years, HAL Jr. has been sitting in my office, bearing the inscription "Presented to Arthur C. Clarke by his many admirers at Hewlett-Packard, Christmas 1969." A few years later, I was able to thank those friends personally at Palo Alto—especially Bill Hewlett himself, and Barney Oliver, now well-known as an advocate of SETI (Search for Extra-Terrestrial Intelligence) and director of the CYCLOPS study.

As soon as HAL Jr. arrived, I took a week off and learned the elements of programming for the first time. Eventually I was able to arrange some quite amusing visual displays—dances of 0's and 1's—on the CRT; not only was that fun, but it taught me a lot about the machine's abilities. And, a few years later, I was able to put it to good use doing the calculations involved in the novel *Rendezvous with Rama*.

The H/P 9000 was the forerunner of today's pocket

calculators, many of which now far surpass it in power and memory, at a fraction of the price. To me, this is perhaps the most astonishing—and totally unexpected—development in the whole of technology. No one could ever have dreamed, no one would have believed that within less than a decade that very symbol of the engineer-scientist's trade, the essential slide rule, would no longer even be manufactured. And with it were swept away whole libraries of tables of logarithms and trigonometrical functions; overnight, it became far quicker to calculate them, than to look them up.

I can vividly recall some of the calculations—modest though they were—which I had to make while working on space-travel theory (Section VII). At one time I decided to tabulate and plot some of the functions encountered in astronautics, such as $\theta + \sin\theta\cos\theta$. It looks simple enough; but you might see how long you take to calculate just one value, even to a mere four figures, if you have to look up the logs of the trig functions, add them, look up the antilog, etc. Today you can write down the values just as quickly as you can press a button—or even get them printed out before your eyes.

No post-1970 student can truly appreciate the transformation caused by pocket calculators, for those born to power can never know the intoxicating excitement of acquiring it. To borrow an analogy from another field, it is as if we went from bullock carts to rockets overnight—*and the rockets were cheaper*.

From time to time I would be tempted to have a serious dialogue with HAL Jr., and once I set him running all night to check the integers for the property which Douglas Hofstadter, with his usual flair for horrid puns, has called "wondrousness" (see Chapter XII of *Godel, Escher, Bach*).

I do not know exactly what impulse started me thinking again about Dr. Goodliffe's lesson in induction, forty or so years in the past. In any event, I asked myself a question which surely must have been answered in many higher algebra books—though none I've been able to find here in Colombo. If the "sum of the cubes" equals the "square of the sum," do any similar relationships exist among the higher powers? And going beyond this, is there any general formula for the sum of the pth powers of n integers?

I quickly discovered that to take the matter beyond $p = 3$ involved the solving of simultaneous equations with larger and larger coefficients. To give an example, I've just found in my notes:

$$15552a + 2592b + 432c + 72d + 12e + 2f = 4067$$

In principle, solving sets of equations like this could be

done with pencil and paper—but not by me. In any calculation of more than ten steps, I would make one mistake—and a different one when I did the checking.

But HAL Jr., I discovered, could cheerfully perform the hundreds of longwinded calculations involved; I only had to feed in the coefficients and let him crunch them up. After a few days' work, the two of us had got as far as $p = 8$, but, alas, there was no sign of any general law emerging. Though some regularities emerged, the formulae as a whole became nastier and nastier, and I decided it was not worth going any further. But because it recalls happy days with HAL Jr., here is my farewell to Higher Algebra.

It really looks as if Kronecker was right.

God made the integers; all else is the work of man.

$$\Sigma_1^n \, n^p$$

$p = 1$ $\Sigma = \dfrac{n}{2}(n + 1)$

$p = 2$ $\Sigma = \dfrac{n}{1 \cdot 2 \cdot 3}(n + 1)(2n + 1)$

$p = 3$ $\Sigma = \dfrac{n \cdot n}{1 \cdot 2 \cdot 2}(n + 1)(n + 1)$ $= [\Sigma n]^2$

$p = 4$ $\Sigma = \dfrac{n}{1 \cdot 2 \cdot 3 \cdot 5}(n + 1)(2n + 1)(3n^2 + 3n - 1)$

$p = 5$ $\Sigma = \dfrac{n \cdot n}{1 \cdot 2 \cdot 2 \cdot 3}(n + 1)(n + 1)(2n^2 + 2n - 1)$

$p = 6$ $\Sigma = \dfrac{n}{1 \cdot 2 \cdot 3 \cdot 7}(n + 1)(2n + 1)(3n^4 + 6n^3 - 3n + 1)$

$p = 7$ $\Sigma = \dfrac{n \cdot n}{1 \cdot 2 \cdot 2 \cdot 3}(n + 1)(n + 1)(3n^4 + 6n^3 - n^2 - 4n + 2)$

$p = 8$ $\Sigma = \dfrac{n(n + 1)(2n + 1)}{1 \cdot 2 \cdot 3 \cdot 3 \cdot 5}[5n^3(n^3 + 3n^2 + n - 3) - n^2 + 9n - 3]$

XI | *Beyond the Global Village*

25 *Beyond the Global Village*

1983 was declared World Telecommunications Year, and on May 17 (World Telecommunications Day) I was invited to give the keynote address at the United Nations headquarters. It was a great privilege to stand in the shadow of history and speak from the podium of the General Assembly Chamber itself; the experience was made somewhat unreal by seeing so many of my friends sitting at desks still bearing the names of the UN's 150+ disputatious members. The proceedings were filmed by David Kennard (Senior Producer of *Cosmos*, as well as coproducer of *The Ascent of Man*) for a forthcoming TV series, *The Messengers*, some of which we had already shot in Sri Lanka.

"Beyond the Global Village," though nontechnical, nevertheless makes an entirely appropriate conclusion to this volume. I have also included it, together with selected essays on space, marine exploration, problems of war and peace, communications, literature and other matters in the Del Rey book *1984: Spring*. (Don't blame me for that title: I wanted to call it something completely different: *Spring of '84. . . .*)

There is always something new to be learned from the past, and I would like to open with two anecdotes from the early days of the telephone. They illustrate perfectly how difficult—if not impossible—it is to anticipate the social impact of a truly revolutionary invention.

Though the first story is now rather famous—and I must apologise to those who've heard it before—I hope it's unfamiliar to most of you.

When news of Alexander Graham Bell's invention reached the United Kingdom, the Chief Engineer of the British Post Office failed to be impressed. "The Americans," he said loftily, "have need of the telephone—but we do not. We have plenty of messenger boys. . . ."

The second story I heard only quite recently, and in some ways it's even more instructive. In contrast to the British engineer, the mayor of a certain American city was wildly enthusiastic. He thought that the telephone was a marvellous device, and ventured this stunning prediction: "I can see the time," he said solemnly, *"when every city will have one."*

If, during the course of this talk, you think that I am getting a little too fanciful, please remember that mayor . . .

We have now reached the stage when virtually anything we want to do in the field of communications is possible: The constraints are no longer technical, but economic, legal or political. Thus if you want to transmit the *Encyclopaedia Britannica* around the world in one second, you can do so. But it may be a lot cheaper if you're prepared to wait a whole minute—and you must check with the *Britannica's* lawyers first.

Yet while recognising and applauding all these marvels, I am only too well aware of present realities. In Sri Lanka, for example, a major problem is that the village postmaster may not even have the stamps he needs—to put on the telegrams that must be *mailed*, because copper thieves have stolen the overhead wires. And Sri Lanka, compared to some countries, is rich. It has already imported over 100,000 TV sets and thousands of videotape recorders. That would have been unthinkable only a few years ago—but human beings need information and entertainment almost as much as they need food, and when an invention arrives which can provide both in unprecedented quantities, sooner or later everyone manages to find the money for it.

This is particularly true when the cost of the hardware drops tenfold every decade—look at the example of pocket calculators! So please don't dismiss my future because no one can afford it. The human race can afford anything it really needs—and improvements in communications often pay for themselves more swiftly than improvements in transportation. A developing country may sometimes be better advised to build telephone links than roads to its outlying provinces, if it has to make the choice.

Let me now focus on the only aspect of the communications revolution which I am at all competent to discuss, and which has profoundly affected my own lifestyle—not to mention that of millions of other people.

Until 1976, making an international telephone call from my home in Sri Lanka was an exercise in frustration that might last several days. Now, thanks to the Indian Ocean satellite, I can get through to London or New York in slightly less time than it takes to dial the 13-digit number. As a result, I can now live exactly where I please, and have cut my travelling to a fraction of its former value.

Comsats have created a world without distance, and have already had a profound effect on international business, news-gathering and tourism—one of the most important industries of many developing countries. Yet their real impact has scarcely begun: Before the end of this century—only seventeen years ahead!—they will have transformed the planet, sweeping away much that is evil and, unfortunately, not a few things that are good.

The slogan "A telephone in every village" should remind you of that American mayor, so don't laugh. I believe it is a realistic and (equally important!) desirable goal by the year 2000. It can be achieved now that millions of kilometres of increasingly scarce copper wire can be replaced by a handful of satellites in stationary orbit. And on the ground we need a simple, rugged handset and solar-powered transceiver plus antenna, which could be mass-produced for tens rather than hundreds of dollars.

At this point I would like to borrow an expression from the military: "force multipliers." A force multiplier is a device which increases, often by a very large factor, the effectiveness of an existing system. For example, it may take fifty old-fashioned bombs to knock out a bridge. But if you give them TV guidance, you will need only one or two, though the explosive power per bomb remains exactly the same.

I suggest that the "Telephone in the Village" would be one of the most effective "force multipliers" in history, because of its implications for health, animal husbandry, weather forecasts, market advice, social integration and human welfare. Each installation would probably pay for itself, in hard cash, within a few months. I would like to see a cost-effectiveness study of rural satellite telephone systems for Africa, Asia and South America. But the financial benefits, important though they undoubtedly would be, might yet be insignificant compared with the social ones. Unlike its military equivalent, *this* force multiplier would increase the health, wealth and happiness of mankind.

However, long before the global network of *fixed* telephones is established, there will be a parallel development which will eventually bypass it completely—though perhaps not until well into the next century. It is starting now, with cellular networks, portable radio-phones and paging devices, and will lead ultimately to our old science-fiction friend, the wristwatch telephone.

Before we reach that, there will be an intermediate stage.

During the coming decade, more and more businessmen, well-heeled tourists and virtually *all* news-persons will be carrying attache case-sized units that will permit direct two-way communication with their homes or offices, via the most convenient satellite. These will provide voice, telex and video facilities (still photos and, for those who need it, live TV coverage). As these units become cheaper, smaller and more universal, they will make travellers totally independent of national communications systems.

The implications of this are profound—and not only to media news-gatherers who will no longer be at the mercy of censors or inefficient (sometimes nonexistent) postal and telegraph services. It means the end of closed societies and will lead ultimately—to repeat a phrase I heard Arnold Toynbee use forty years ago—to the Unification of the World.

You may think this is a naive prediction because many countries wouldn't let such subversive machines across their borders. But they would have no choice; the alternative would be economic suicide because very soon they would get no tourists and no businessmen offering foreign currency. They'd get only spies, who would have no trouble at all concealing the powerful new tools of their ancient trade.

What I am saying, in fact, is that the debate about the Free Flow of Information which has been going on for so many years will soon be settled—by engineers, not politicians. (Just as physicists, not generals, have now determined the nature of war.)

Consider what this means. No government will be able to conceal, at least for very long, evidence of crimes or atrocities—even from its own people. The very existence of the myriads of new information channels, operating in real-time and across all frontiers, will be a powerful influence for civilised behaviour. If you are arranging a massacre, it will be useless to shoot the cameraman who has so inconveniently appeared on the scene. His pictures will already be safe in the studio five thousand kilometres away; and his final image may hang you.

Many governments will not be at all happy about this, but in the long run everyone will benefit. Exposures of scandals or political abuses—especially by visiting TV teams who go home and make rude documentaries—can be painful, but also very valuable. Many a ruler might still be in power today, or even alive, had he known what was really happening in his own country. A wise statesman once said: "A free press can give you hell; but it can save your skin." That is even more true of TV reporting—which, thanks to satellites, will soon be instantaneous and ubiquitous. Let us hope that it will also be responsible. Considering what has often happened in the past, optimism here may well be tempered with concern.

A quarter of a century ago, the transistor radio began to sweep across the world, starting a communications revolution in all countries, developed and undeveloped. It is a continuing revolution—a steady explosion, if I may be permitted the paradox—and it is nowhere near completed. Indeed, it will accelerate when the cheap solar-powered radio eliminates dependence on batteries, so expensive and difficult to obtain in remote places.

The transistor radio has already brought news, information and entertainment to millions who would otherwise have been almost totally deprived of so much that we take for granted. But TV is a far more powerful medium, and thanks to the new generation of satellites, its time has now arrived.

I hesitate to add to the megawords—if not gigawords—written about educational TV and direct broadcast satellites. But despite all this verbiage, there still seem to be a number of points that are not generally understood, perhaps because of the human dislike for facing awkward truths.

Attempts have been made, in some quarters, to regulate or even prohibit direct broadcasting from space. But radio waves do not recognise frontiers, and it is totally impossible to prevent spillover. Even if country A did its best to keep its programmes from reaching its neighbour B, it could not always succeed. During the 1976 Satellite Instructional Television Experiment (SITE), the beam from the ATS 6 satellite was deliberately slanted toward India to give maximum signal strength there. Yet good images were still received in England, a quarter of the way around the globe!

Those who would promulgate what might be called "permission to receive" laws remind me of the fabled American state legislature, which, back in the last century, ruled that the value of pi is exactly 3, as given in the Old Testament. (Alas, this delightful story isn't true; but it can be matched by similar absurdities at this very moment.)

In any event, technology has once again superseded politics. All over the United States, the Caribbean and South America, small "receive only" dishes are sprouting like mushrooms, tuning in to the hundreds of satellite channels now available—and there's little that anyone can do about it, without spending a lot of money on scramblers and encrypting devices which may sometimes defeat their own purpose.

In Sri Lanka, radio amateurs with quite simple equipment have been receiving excellent pictures from the Soviet Union's powerful EKRAN satellites; thanks to these, we were able to enjoy the Moscow Olympics. I would like to express my gratitude to the Russian engineers for their continuing large-scale demonstration, over the whole of Asia, that the politicians are not only talking technical nonsense, but are ignoring their own proclamations.

They are not the only ones guilty of hypocrisy, as my good friend Dr. Yash Pal pointed out in these words several years ago:

> In the drawing rooms of large cities you meet many people who are concerned with the damage that one is going to cause to the integrity of rural India by exposing her to the world outside. After they have lectured you about the dangers of corrupting this innocent, beautiful mass of humanity, they usually turn round and add: "Well, now that we have a satellite, when are we going to see some American programmes?" Of course, they themselves are immune to cultural domination or foreign influences. . . .

When I quoted this at the 1981 UNESCO IPDC meeting in Paris, I added these words:

> I am afraid that cocktail party intellectuals are the same everywhere. Because we frequently suffer from the scourge of information pollution, we find it hard to imagine its even deadlier opposite—information starvation. I get very annoyed when I hear arguments, usually from those who have been educated beyond their intelligence, about the virtues of keeping happy, backward peoples in ignorance. Such an attitude seems like that of a fat man preaching the benefits of fasting to a starving beggar.

And I am not impressed by the attacks on television because of the truly dreadful programmes it often carries. Every TV programme has some educational content; the cathode tube is a window on the world—indeed, on many worlds. Often it is a very murky window, but I have slowly come to the conclusion that, on balance, even bad TV is better than no TV at all.

Many will disagree with this—and I sympathise with them. Electronic cultural imperialism will sweep away much that is good, as well as much that is bad. Yet it will only accelerate changes which were in any case inevitable; and on the credit side, the new media will preserve for future generations the customs, performing arts and ceremonies of our time, in a way that was never possible in any earlier age.

Of course, there are a great many of our present customs which should *not* be preserved, except as warnings to future generations. Slavery, torture, racial and religious persecution, treatment of women as chattels, mutilation of children because of ancient superstitions, cruelty to animals—the list is endless, and no country can proclaim total innocence. But looming monstrously above all these evils is the ever-present threat of nuclear war.

I wish I could claim that improved communications would lead to peace, but the matter is not as simple as that. Excellent communications—even a common language!—have not brought peace to Northern Ireland, to give but one of many possible examples. Nevertheless, good communications of every type, and at all levels, are essential if we are ever to establish peace on this planet. As the mathematicians would say, they are necessary, but not sufficient.

Perhaps an additional necessity may be the International Monitoring Satellite system proposed by the French government in 1978, and now the subject of a UN report which is being reissued this month (May 1983) at the request of the General Assembly. I refer you to this 123-page document (E.83.IX.3—*The Implications of Establishing an International Satellite Monitoring Agency*) for details; all I need say here is that it considers the potential benefits to mankind if *all* nations had access to the orbital reconnaissance information now available only to the United States and the Soviet Union. Roughly speaking, these powers now have the ability to observe any piece of military equipment larger than a rifle, in clear weather during daylight; and to track surface vessels at *any* time.

You will not be surprised to know that both the U.S. and the U.S.S.R. agree in opposing any scheme that will break their joint monopoly on strategic information, and one of their main criticisms of the Monitoring Satellite System is all too valid. Even if it were established, could it *really* work during a period of international crisis—if more than a hundred nations each had a finger on the ERASE button of the computer that stored the disputed information?

I have a modest proposal. The French, who suggested the IMS in the first place, are about to launch an Earth Resources Satellite (SPOT) whose capabilities in some respects approach those of military reconnaissance satellites. Its images will be available, on a purely commercial basis, to anyone who wants to buy them, at the rate of about 30 cents per square kilometre.

Suppose a small consortium of traditionally neutral countries set up an image-processing and intelligence-evaluating organisation. (Sweden, with its Stockholm International Peace Research Institute, is an obvious choice; one could add Switzerland and the Netherlands— perhaps that would be enough!) It would contract with the SPOT image company for satellite information, and analyse it for any country which considered itself threatened—on condition that the results were made available to the whole world.

This would only be a beginning, of course; the next step would be to purchase a SUPERSPOT with much higher resolution. I leave others to work out the details, but none of the problems seems insuperable. And with all respect to the distinguished organisation in whose premises we are assembled, three or four nations could have the system running smoothly—*years* before 155 could even agree on its desirability.

Such an institute could well adopt, without irony, the ambiguous slogan of the U.S. Strategic Air Command: "Peace is our profession." And though I wish I could offer the facilities of the Centre for Modern Technologies which we hope to set up in Sri Lanka, I fear that it will be quite a while before it would possess the necessary skills and equipment. Yet nothing would be more appropriate, for here in this very building I once heard Prime Minister Sirimavo Bandaranaike make her proposal for an Indian Ocean Zone of Peace. We might take at least one small step toward that goal, if everything moving on the face of the Indian Ocean was clearly labelled for all the world to see.

I would like to end this survey of our telecommunications future with one of the most remarkable predictions ever made. In the closing decade of the nineteenth century, an electrical engineer, W.E. Ayrton, was lecturing at London's Imperial Institute about the most modern of communications devices, the submarine telegraph cable. He ended with what must, to all his listeners, have seemed the wildest fantasy:

There is no doubt that the day will come, maybe when you and I are forgotten, when copper wires, gutta-percha coverings and iron sheathings will be relegated to the Museum of Antiquities. Then, when a person wants to telegraph to a friend, he knows not where, he will call in an electromagnetic voice, which will be heard loud by him who has the electromagnetic ear, but will be silent to everyone else. He will call, "Where are you?" and the reply will come, "I am at the bottom of the coal mine" or "Crossing the Andes" or "In the middle of the Pacific"; or perhaps no reply will come at all, and he may then conclude that his friend is dead.

This truly astonishing prophecy was made in 1897, long before anyone could imagine how it might be fulfilled. A century later, by 1997, it will be on the verge of achievement, because the wristwatch telephone will be coming into general use. And if you still believe that such a device is unlikely, ask yourself this question: Who could have imagined the personal watch, back in the Middle Ages—when the only clocks were clanking, room-sized mechanisms, the pride and joy of a few cathedrals?

For that matter, many of you carry on your wrists miracles of electronics that would have been beyond belief even twenty years ago. The symbols that flicker across those digital displays now merely give time and date. When the zeroes flash up at the end of the century, they will do far more than that. They will give you direct access to most of the human race, through the invisible networks girdling our planet.

The long-heralded Global Village is almost upon us, but it will last for only a flickering moment in the history of Mankind. Before we even realise that it has come, it will be superseded—by the Global Family.

Postscript

Sometime in the spring of 1984, the Tenth Marconi Fellowship ceremony is planned to take place at the White House. I will then have to follow up my address at The Hague with a longer report, in which I have the moral obligation of accounting for the $35,000 then presented to me.

As it happens, that particular problem has been neatly solved. In 1982 the Sri Lanka academic and cultural authorities decided to set up a center for Communications, Computers, Energy, Space Technologies and Robotics at the University of Moratuwa, and to name it after me—an honor which I deeply appreciate even though it makes me feel slightly posthumous. (President Jayawardene appointed me Chancellor of this technologically orientated university, twenty kilometres south of Colombo, in 1979. My first five Convocation addresses will be found in *1984: Spring*.)

At this very moment, after much massaging in my word-processor, the Act setting up the Arthur C. Clarke Centre is being translated into Sinhala and Tamil. The first buildings should be ready by November 1983, just in time to receive a U.S. delegation led by Robert Cooper, publisher of the monthly *Coop's Satellite Digest*. He is bringing with him, as a very generous gift of the manufacturers, three 15-25 foot TVRO (Receive-Only) earth stations, one of which will be set up on the roof of my Colombo house, while the other two will be installed at the university and ACC.

"Coop," incidentally, has been a principal activist in the campaign to affix my name to the geostationary orbit. This recently provoked a letter in the British Inter-

223

planetary Society's *Spaceflight* (Vol. 24, 11, November 1982) from Duncan Lunan, pointing out that as the 24-hour orbit had been mentioned by Tsiolkovski at the beginning of the century "should we not, for accuracy, refer to 'Clarke satellites in Tsiolkovski orbit'?"

I replied in the same issue as follows:

> . . . The International Astronomical Union has the right idea; you have to be safely dead before you can be immortalised on the Moon or planets (though exceptions have been made for astronauts and cosmonauts).
>
> . . . Nevertheless, I don't consider (this prior reference) justifies labelling it with Tsiolkovski's name. In the first place, the idea of a 24-hour satellite is so trivial that it would have been obvious to any astronomer from the time of Kepler onwards. I don't know when it first appeared in print (when the moons of Mars were discovered?) and suggest this as an interesting research project.
>
> Secondly, if every idea that Tsiolkovski mentioned had his name attached to it, there's very little in the whole field of astronautics that would be excluded!
>
> A much better case would be made for the man who first worked out detailed engineering plans for a space station—and then placed it in synchronous orbit. I refer, of course, to the Austrian Captain Potočnik whose book, *Das Problem der Befahrung des Weltraums*, was published under the name Hermann Noordung in 1928. Though I have never seen Potočnik's book, I knew of its basic ideas and it is the only astronautical reference in both my *Wireless World* paper and the earlier (25 May 1945) BIS Memorandum.
>
> Even the proposed name "Clarke satellite" for a space relay could be challenged; in various forms, the idea was fairly common in the science fiction of the 1930–45 period. (See especially George O. Smith's "Venus Equilateral" series.) What I did was to take two already existing elements, combine them synergistically, and point out the implications of the result.
>
> Incidentally, I consider the lunar launcher . . . a much more original idea, since to the best of my knowledge there are no precedents (though of course the idea of an Earth-based launcher is an old one). In the long run it may be even more important than the communications satellite.
>
> However, nomenclature is decided not by logic or justice but by accident and convenience. History will settle these matters, as it always does.

Meanwhile, as the foundations of the ACC are being laid in Moratuwa, *another* Foundation has been established in Washington to support it, as was announced in a press release issued at the White House on June 23, 1983. The Board of Directors of the "U.S. Foundation for the Arthur Clarke Centre for Modern Technologies" includes Representative George E. Brown (California), the

Presidents of Ford Aerospace and Hughes Space Division and the Vice-President of COMSAT. I hope to meet all these gentlemen, and many other friends—especially Gioia Marconi Braga—when the cherry blossoms are once again blooming in Washington.

It may very well be my last visit to that beautiful city, though not through any intimations of mortality, (I come of a long-lived family; the great-grandfather whose first name I bear was still riding horseback at the age *I* shall be in 2010.) But I find travelling—except by ship or Concorde—more and more intolerable; and despite recent tragic racial violence here, I resent anything that takes me away from the country that now holds almost everything I love.

And, thanks to the comsat revolution, there is no longer any need for me to leave home. The technology I have been writing about for almost forty years has well and truly caught up with me: Indeed, it has transformed my life. I can call my friends instantly, wherever they may be. Though that is no substitute for an actual meeting, it can still provide a precious link.

Now, with somewhat mixed feelings, I am learning to cope with the latest electronic marvel in the Spaghetti Junction that my office has become. Having rashly announced that the World Premiere of *Odyssey Two* will be at Christmas 1984, MGM/UA has sent me a Kaypro II computer plus modem so that director Peter Hyams can transmit scripts, via the Indian Ocean satellite, while I am sleeping. In the morning, I'll find them waiting for me on the floppy disk, and can send back my comments a few hours later. In this way, we can collaborate despite the fact that Los Angeles and Colombo are almost exactly twelve hours apart, and we are seldom awake at the same time. (When we are, we can have a real-time conversation via our keyboards, but there seems little point in this as (1) we're both lousy typists, and (2) it's much easier and quicker—not to mention cheaper—to talk. However, any typed conversation is permanently stored for future reference, which has its advantages . . . and disadvantages.)

This power over time and space still seems a marvel to me, even though I have been preaching its advent for decades. But the next generation will take it completely for granted, and will wonder how we ever managed to run the world without it.

Which, of course, we never did.

May these new tools help them to succeed, where we failed so badly.

Colombo, Sri Lanka
September 18, 1983

Added 20 January

I am very happy to say that the friendly American invasion went very well, despite transportation and other problems. Often working though the night, the enthusiastic visitors set up their three earth stations, which are a priceless asset to the technology of the country. I would like to express my gratitude to the principal donors: Dave Johnson *(Paradigm Manufacturing, Inc.)*, Bob Behar *(Hero Communications)*; and James Gowen *(Antenna Development and Manufacturing, Inc.)* and, of course, the indefatigable Bob Cooper—who organised the whole thing, and reported on it engagingly in the January 1984 issue of his digest.